SACRED
SPACE

SACRED SPACE

The Prayer Book 2022

from the website www.sacredspace.ie
Prayer from the Irish Jesuits

LOYOLA PRESS.
A JESUIT MINISTRY
Chicago

LOYOLA PRESS.
A JESUIT MINISTRY
www.loyolapress.com

Loyola Press in Chicago thanks the Irish Jesuits and Messenger Press for preparing this book for publication.

Cover art credit: Shutterstock/pluie_r.

ISBN-13: 978-0-8294-5097-2

Printed in the United States of America.
20 21 22 23 24 25 26 27 28 29 Versa 10 9 8 7 6 5 4 3 2 1

Contents

Sacred Space Prayer

Bless all who worship you, almighty God,
from the rising of the sun to its setting:
from your goodness enrich us,
by your love inspire us,
by your Spirit guide us,
by your power protect us,
in your mercy receive us,
now and always.

Preface

In 1999 an Irish Jesuit named Alan McGuckian had the simple – but at the time radical – idea of bringing daily prayer to the Internet. No one imagined that his experimental project would grow into a global community with volunteers translating the prayer experience into seventeen different languages.

Millions of people, from numerous Christian traditions, visit www.sacredspace.ie each year, and what they find is an invitation to step away from their busy routines for a few minutes a day to concentrate on what is really important in their lives. Sacred Space offers its visitors the opportunity to grow in prayerful awareness of their friendship with God.

Besides the daily prayer experience, Sacred Space also offers Living Space, with commentaries on the Scripture readings for each day's Catholic Mass. The Chapel of Intentions allows people to add their own prayers, while Pray with the Pope joins the community to the international Apostleship of Prayer. In addition, Sacred Space provides Lenten and Advent retreats, often in partnership with Pray as You Go, an audio prayer service from the British Jesuits.

Despite the increased use of *Sacred Space* on mobile devices, many people want a book they can hold and carry, and this book has proven especially helpful for prayer groups.

I am delighted to bring you the Sacred Space book, and I pray that your prayer life will flourish with its help.

Yours in Christ
Paul Campbell SJ

Introduction to *Sacred Space: The Prayer Book 2022*

One of the things that can be hard for Christians to accept is that we have been created by God and that God continues to seek constant communication with us. It is a wondrous thing that God could be so close and interested in us that it should transform the way we pray and live. Often, however, we get discouraged and doubt ourselves and God.

The Ignatian or Jesuit contribution to a life of faith and prayer is that God communicates with us directly but we have to do our part, by disposing or preparing ourselves for this communication. This is not as easy as it sounds as all sorts of things get in the way of this relationship: false ideas about God, the tendency to get distracted or to fall into 'addictive' preoccupations (e.g. daydreaming).

Saint Ignatius, who initially knew life as a soldier and courtier, offers us some helpful tips from his Spiritual Exercises that help us to understand our humanity and make it work for our advantage in prayer. With his understanding of the role of desire, emotion and imagination, Ignatius is often called the first psychologist. He outlined a process for preparing and disposing ourselves to God, aware of our humanity's foibles and using them creatively in our favour.

The first step is coming into the presence of God, making a prayer or petition of what is my deepest desire: to connect with this loving God who holds me in being. The amazing thing about this prayer is that, even if we don't feel it, it taps into our deepest desire for God and orients us to what will really satisfy us. There is something profound about when I align my often weak and feeble desire with the great and constant desire that God has for me. It is a small thing but it has an extraordinary effect on prayer; it points us in the right direction and opens up possibility.

The second step is freedom, acknowledging that often we are not free; we have many addictions and dependencies that keep us in chains and away from God. Ignatius knew this reality personally, the problem of vanity and egoism that is so much a part of being human and which we need to work with if we are to move beyond ourselves. Again, the

Ignatian approach is to name it and to ask for God's help in overcoming it. Making a prayer of it helps us to be more free, to loosen the shackles a little bit every time and come closer to God.

The third step is consciousness, reminding ourselves of how God has worked with us in the past. We are part of an ongoing story or relationship that is developing and moving. By remembering the past, I can affirm how God works for our good, and trust that the future will also be good.

The fourth step is the Word; direct contact with the Word of God from the Scriptures, which reminds us how God has worked in the lives of those faithful in history. This is especially evident in the person of Jesus, how God is compassionately present in the Gospels. This is the clearest sense of how God in Jesus relates to our humanity, person to person. Ignatius recommends using our human faculty of imagination to make the scenes come alive. He recommends we place ourselves in the presence of Jesus and recreate the dialogue and the interaction. The Word comes alive for us to transform our experience.

The fifth step is conversation; inviting Jesus to have a two-way conversation with us. We can speak of our lives and reality, and have conversation and dialogue about it. This is about bringing it all back home, realising God's great love and desire for me personally, to have that much needed 'live' conversation that we so want. Sweeping away all the distractions and distance, this is the prayer of the heart, speaking heart to heart with the beloved.

The really good news is that God will meet us more than halfway; our loving God is waiting to be generous to us.

Brendan McManus SJ

How to Use This Book

During each week of the liturgical year, begin by reading the section entitled 'Something to think and pray about each day this week'. Then proceed through 'The Presence of God', 'Freedom' and 'Consciousness' steps to prepare yourself to hear the word of God in your heart. In the next step, 'The Word', turn to the Scripture reading for each day of the week. Inspiration points are provided in case you need them. Then return to the 'Conversation' and 'Conclusion' steps. Use this process every day of the year.

The First Week of Advent
28 November–4 December 2021

Something to think and pray about each day this week:

For us, in this Advent season, we are being called to realise that the tidy soul, like the tidy house, has to be worked at. It doesn't just happen. If we truly want the Lord to come and stay a while, we have to prepare the way. It's about putting the house in order – the soul in order. Somewhere and somehow we need to hear the centurion's words again and realise his words are ours too: 'Lord, I am not worthy to have you under my roof'.

For that, we need a plan of action, a road map of sorts, to guide us on the journey.

The Sacrament of Reconciliation supplies some of that road map. Its coordinates are already there for us, and the initial movement might be found in 'Bless me Father, for I have sinned'.

Vincent Sherlock,
Let Advent be Advent

The Presence of God
'Be still, and know that I am God!' Lord, your words lead us to the calmness and greatness of your presence.

Freedom
God is not foreign to my freedom. The Spirit breathes life into my most intimate desires, gently nudging me towards all that is good. I ask for the grace to let myself be enfolded by the Spirit.

Consciousness
Where do I sense hope, encouragement and growth in my life? By looking back over the past few months, I may be able to see which activities and occasions have produced rich fruit. If I do notice such areas, I will determine to give those areas both time and space in the future.

The Word
The word of God comes down to us through the Scriptures. May the Holy Spirit enlighten my mind and my heart to respond to the Gospel teachings.

(Please turn to the Scripture on the following pages. Inspiration points are there, should you need them. When you are ready, return here to continue.)

Conversation
What is stirring in me as I pray? Am I consoled, troubled, left cold? I imagine Jesus standing or sitting at my side, and I share my feelings with him.

Conclusion
Glory be to the Father, and to the Son and to the Holy Spirit,
As it was in the beginning, is now and ever shall be,
World without end. Amen.

Sunday 28 November
First Sunday of Advent
Luke 21:25–28.34–36

There will be signs in the sun, the moon, and the stars, and on the earth distress among nations confused by the roaring of the sea and the waves. People will faint from fear and foreboding of what is coming upon the world, for the powers of the heavens will be shaken. Then they will see 'the Son of Man coming in a cloud' with power and great glory. Now when these things begin to take place, stand up and raise your heads, because your redemption is drawing near. . . .

Be on guard so that your hearts are not weighed down with dissipation and drunkenness and the worries of this life, and that day does not catch you unexpectedly, like a trap. For it will come upon all who live on the face of the whole earth. Be alert at all times, praying that you may have the strength to escape all these things that will take place, and to stand before the Son of Man.

- Advent is a season of hope and expectation. We are invited to prepare joyfully for the coming of Christ. He comes in history (his conception and birth), in mystery (through the sacraments, and especially the Eucharist) and in majesty (at the Last Day). In the first weeks of Advent the stress is on this third coming in majesty. Hence today's Gospel, which we have already prayed with in recent days. The old liturgical year has ended, and the new one has begun, with our calling to mind the Lord's final coming at the end of time. We look forward to it with happy anticipation, not with fear.

Monday 29 November
Matthew 8:5–11

When he entered Capernaum, a centurion came to him, appealing to him and saying, 'Lord, my servant is lying at home paralysed, in terrible distress.' And he said to him, 'I will come and cure him.' The centurion answered, 'Lord, I am not worthy to have you come under my roof; but only speak the word, and my servant will be healed. For I also am a man under authority, with soldiers under me; and I say to one, "Go", and he goes, and to another, "Come", and he comes, and to my slave, "Do this", and the slave does it.' When Jesus heard him, he was amazed and said to those who followed him, 'Truly I tell you, in no one in Israel have I found such faith. I tell you, many will come from east and west and will eat with Abraham and Isaac and Jacob in the kingdom of heaven.'

- Not many people could amaze Jesus, but this man does: he believes that Jesus can speak a word of healing, and that will be enough to cure his servant. Like the centurion, I may be used to giving and receiving instructions. Do I ever amaze Jesus with my faith?

- 'I will come and cure him.' Jesus reveals God's compassion and shows that the reign of God knows no boundaries. Not only Jews, but Gentiles from east and west, are welcomed by God into the kingdom. I pray to share God's breadth of vision.

Tuesday 30 November
Saint Andrew, Apostle
Matthew 4:18–22

As he walked by the Sea of Galilee, he saw two brothers, Simon, who is called Peter, and Andrew his brother, casting a net into the lake – for they were fishermen. And he said to them, 'Follow me, and I will make you fish for people.' Immediately they left their nets and followed him. As he went from there, he saw two other brothers, James son of Zebedee and his brother John, in the boat with their father Zebedee, mending their nets, and he called them. Immediately they left the boat and their father, and followed him.

- Andrew, together with his more famous brother Peter, is the first to be called by Jesus to follow him. This humble fisherman must have seen something very special in this man to make him immediately leave his nets, his livelihood, and follow him. What is Jesus' call to me in this period of my life? I pray for the grace not to be deaf to his call but prompt and generous in my response to it.

- Andrew was a member of that small yet amazing group of men who were ready to trust Jesus fully and obey his incredible command to take the Gospel to all nations. It is thanks to Andrew and his companions that we, and hundreds of millions like us, believe in Jesus. I stand in awe and thanksgiving before this man and his Master.

Wednesday 1 December
Matthew 15:29–37

After Jesus had left that place, he passed along the Sea of Galilee, and he went up the mountain, where he sat down. Great crowds came to him, bringing with them the lame, the maimed, the blind, the mute, and many others. They put them at his feet, and he cured them, so that the crowd was amazed when they saw the mute speaking, the maimed whole, the lame walking, and the blind seeing. And they praised the God of Israel.

Then Jesus called his disciples to him and said, 'I have compassion for the crowd, because they have been with me now for three days and have nothing to eat; and I do not want to send them away hungry, for they might faint on the way.' The disciples said to him, 'Where are we to get enough bread in the desert to feed so great a crowd?' Jesus asked them, 'How many loaves have you?' They said, 'Seven, and a few small fish.' Then, ordering the crowd to sit down on the ground, he took the seven loaves and the fish; and after giving thanks he broke them and gave them to the disciples, and the disciples gave them to the crowds. And all of them ate and were filled; and they took up the broken pieces left over, seven baskets full.

- The people who came to Jesus were broken people. It was true then and is still true today. It is why I am here, listening to him. Where is my life broken? Where do I need his healing power? It is important to get in touch with that place in my life in order to get closer to him.

Thursday 2 December
Matthew 7:21.24–27

'Not everyone who says to me, "Lord, Lord", will enter the kingdom of heaven, but only one who does the will of my Father in heaven. . . .

'Everyone then who hears these words of mine and acts on them will be like a wise man who built his house on rock. The rain fell, the floods came, and the winds blew and beat on that house, but it did not fall, because it had been founded on rock. And everyone who hears these words of mine and does not act on them will be like a foolish man who built his house on sand. The rain fell, and the floods came, and the winds blew and beat against that house, and it fell – and great was its fall!'

- We all know that actions speak louder than words. We are told here that our eternal life depends upon our ability to act according to God's will. It is a stark message, but it is reassuring to know that our true efforts will reap their own rewards.

- I am challenged by Jesus to take time daily to reflect and discern the Father's will. Otherwise I will live a shallow existence that will not survive the floods and storms of life.

Friday 3 December
Matthew 9:27–31

As Jesus went on from there, two blind men followed him, crying loudly, 'Have mercy on us, Son of David!' When he entered the house, the blind men came to him; and Jesus said to them, 'Do you believe that I am able to do this?' They said to him, 'Yes, Lord.' Then he touched their eyes and said, 'According to your faith let it be done to you.' And their eyes were opened. Then Jesus sternly ordered them, 'See that no one knows of this.' But they went away and spread the news about him throughout that district.

- Desire is important. Knowing what I want – and having energy to pursue it – guides me. The Lord has desires for me, too. These desires can meet, as happened for the blind men. Their faith and their need brought them to Jesus. I am invited to do the same, recognising that Jesus can transform my desires to bring them into harmony with his own.

- What are my deepest desires and how influential are they in my living as a follower of Jesus? I pray to be in touch with Jesus' desire for me, knowing that my blindness can get in the way.

Saturday 4 December
Matthew 9:35–10:1.5–8

Then Jesus went about all the cities and villages, teaching in their synagogues, and proclaiming the good news of the kingdom, and curing every disease and every sickness. When he saw the crowds, he had compassion for them, because they were harassed and helpless, like sheep without a shepherd. Then he said to his disciples, 'The harvest is plentiful, but the labourers are few; therefore ask the Lord of the harvest to send out labourers into his harvest.' . . .

Then Jesus summoned his twelve disciples and gave them authority over unclean spirits, to cast them out, and to cure every disease and every sickness. . . .

These twelve Jesus sent out with the following instructions: 'Go nowhere among the Gentiles, and enter no town of the Samaritans, but go rather to the lost sheep of the house of Israel. As you go, proclaim the good news, "The kingdom of heaven has come near." Cure the sick, raise the dead, cleanse the lepers, cast out demons. You received without payment; give without payment.'

- I travel in imagination with Jesus as he makes his journeys. I ask him what gives him so much energy to serve the sick, many of whom must have been frightening to look at and touch. He talks with me about compassion, and I ask that my small heart grow to be as compassionate as his. I sense his compassion towards me, and it comforts me.

- Jesus has a mission for me. Who are the 'lost sheep' today whom he may want me to help? Am I generous enough to do what he asks of me?

The Second Week of Advent
5–11 December 2021

Something to think and pray about each day this week:

Christmas can bring out the best in us to care for the needy. We are surrounded by charities looking for aid. We know that Jesus hears the cries of the poor, and he joins every carol singing group trying to help.

Christmas also asks us to consider our honesty and integrity, for we know that many are poor, at home and abroad, because of the greed of others. Christmas is a reminder and a challenge that all can live with the dignity we have come to regard as a human right – with education, safety, shelter, food, water, employment, freedom. The Christ child, who was born poor, represents all the poor of the world, especially children. As he was born ordinary, he represents the God who meets, greets and helps us in the ordinary aspects of life.

The one who is to come is the one who will live and love according to these truths of human dignity and equality.

Donal Neary SJ,
Gospel Reflections for Sundays of Year C: Luke

The Presence of God

As I sit here, the beating of my heart,
the ebb and flow of my breathing, the movements of my mind
are all signs of God's ongoing creation of me.
I pause for a moment and become aware
of this presence of God within me.

Freedom

I will ask God's help
to be free from my own preoccupations,
to be open to God in this time of prayer,
to come to know, love and serve God more.

Consciousness

At this moment, Lord, I turn my thoughts to you.
I will leave aside my chores and preoccupations.
I will take rest and refreshment in your presence.

The Word

Now I turn to the Scripture set out for me this day. I read slowly over the
words and see if any sentence or sentiment appeals to me.
*(Please turn to the Scripture on the following pages. Inspiration points are there,
should you need them. When you are ready, return here to continue.)*

Conversation

Begin to talk to Jesus about the Scripture you have just read. What part
of it strikes a chord in you? Perhaps the words of a friend – or some story
you have heard recently – will slowly rise to the surface of your consciousness. If so, does the story throw light on what the Scripture passage may
be saying to you?

Conclusion

Glory be to the Father, and to the Son and to the Holy Spirit,
As it was in the beginning, is now and ever shall be,
World without end. Amen.

Sunday 5 December
Second Sunday of Advent
Luke 3:1–6

In the fifteenth year of the reign of Emperor Tiberius, when Pontius Pilate was governor of Judea, and Herod was ruler of Galilee, and his brother Philip ruler of the region of Ituraea and Trachonitis, and Lysanias ruler of Abilene, during the high-priesthood of Annas and Caiaphas, the word of God came to John son of Zechariah in the wilderness. He went into all the region around the Jordan, proclaiming a baptism of repentance for the forgiveness of sins, as it is written in the book of the words of the prophet Isaiah,

'The voice of one crying out in the wilderness:
"Prepare the way of the Lord,
make his paths straight.
Every valley shall be filled,
and every mountain and hill shall be made low,
and the crooked shall be made straight,
and the rough ways made smooth;
and all flesh shall see the salvation of God."'

- Passage through the wilderness was an integral part of John's mission, as it was for Abraham, Moses, Elijah and Jesus. Where, in all the hurly-burly of modern life, do we find a holy place where we can be apart and encounter God daily? Might it be here and now, on our desktop, laptop or mobile device, as we pray with Sacred Space?

- Do I believe that if I have the courage to place myself in the hands of my maker, I will feel the heavens open and grace rain down upon me, transforming my desert, making the crooked straight, the rough places smooth, until – at last – I will see the salvation of God?

Monday 6 December
Luke 5:17–26

One day, while he was teaching, Pharisees and teachers of the law were sitting nearby (they had come from every village of Galilee and Judea and from Jerusalem); and the power of the Lord was with him to heal. Just then some men came, carrying a paralysed man on a bed. They were trying to bring him in and lay him before Jesus; but finding no way to bring him in because of the crowd, they went up on the roof and let him down with his bed through the tiles into the middle of the crowd in front of Jesus. When he saw their faith, he said, 'Friend, your sins are forgiven you.' Then the scribes and the Pharisees began to question, 'Who is this who is speaking blasphemies? Who can forgive sins but God alone?' When Jesus perceived their questionings, he answered them, 'Why do you raise such questions in your hearts? Which is easier, to say, "Your sins are forgiven you", or to say, "Stand up and walk"? But so that you may know that the Son of Man has authority on earth to forgive sins' – he said to the one who was paralysed – 'I say to you, stand up and take your bed and go to your home.' Immediately he stood up before them, took what he had been lying on, and went to his home, glorifying God. Amazement seized all of them, and they glorified God and were filled with awe, saying, 'We have seen strange things today.'

- Sometimes we need to be helped to ask for healing, or we need to help others do so. It was the faith of his friends and not the paralysed man's own faith to which Jesus responded, 'And when Jesus saw their faith, he said to the paralytic, "My friend, your sins are forgiven." ' When we forgive, and when we are forgiven, a crippling burden is lifted from our shoulders. We can then, like the man in this episode, rise and walk.

Tuesday 7 December
Matthew 18:12–14

What do you think? If a shepherd has a hundred sheep, and one of them has gone astray, does he not leave the ninety-nine on the mountains and go in search of the one that went astray? And if he finds it, truly I tell you, he rejoices over it more than over the ninety-nine that never went astray. So it is not the will of your Father in heaven that one of these little ones should be lost.

- Let us never grow accustomed to this parable. It is the most astonishing suggestion you could imagine. Modern business would focus on the ninety-nine well-behaved and conformist sheep. Jesus turns our eyes to that bit of ourselves that wants to do our own thing, go our own way, even when it is self-destructive. As parents have learned with heartbreak, it is only love that will save the lost sheep.

- I cling to that last assurance: 'It is not the will of your Father that one of these little ones should be lost.'

Wednesday 8 December
The Immaculate Conception of the Blessed Virgin Mary
Luke 1:26–38

In the sixth month the angel Gabriel was sent by God to a town in Galilee called Nazareth, to a virgin engaged to a man whose name was Joseph, of the house of David. The virgin's name was Mary. And he came to her and said, 'Greetings, favoured one! The Lord is with you.' But she was much perplexed by his words and pondered what sort of greeting this might be. The angel said to her, 'Do not be afraid, Mary, for you have found favour with God. And now, you will conceive in your womb and bear a son, and you will name him Jesus. He will be great, and will be called the Son of the Most High, and the Lord God will give to him the throne of his ancestor David. He will reign over the house of Jacob for ever, and of his kingdom there will be no end.' Mary said to the angel, 'How can this be, since I am a virgin?' The angel said to her, 'The Holy Spirit will come upon you, and the power of the Most High will overshadow you; therefore the child to be born will be holy; he will be called Son of God. And now, your relative Elizabeth in her old age has also conceived a son; and this is the sixth month for her who was said to be barren. For nothing will be impossible with God.' Then Mary said, 'Here am I, the servant of the Lord; let it be with me according to your word.' Then the angel departed from her.

- Repeating a phrase in prayer may make it go deep within us. It's like a favourite piece of music that we can hum over and over again. It is part of us. 'I am the servant of the Lord' was such a phrase for Mary, spoken first at one of the biggest moments in her life. In dry times of prayer, a sentence like that can occupy mind and heart and raise us close to God.

Thursday 9 December

Matthew 11:11–15

Truly I tell you, among those born of women no one has arisen greater than John the Baptist; yet the least in the kingdom of heaven is greater than he. From the days of John the Baptist until now the kingdom of heaven has suffered violence, and the violent take it by force. For all the prophets and the law prophesied until John came; and if you are willing to accept it, he is Elijah who is to come. Let anyone with ears listen!

- God does not force himself upon us. We must ourselves seize the kingdom. In his book, *Heaven Taken by Storm*, seventeenth-century Puritan pastor Thomas Watson asks: 'Do we use violence in prayer? Is the wind of the Spirit filling our sails? Do we pray in the morning as if we were to die at night? Do we thirst for the living God? Is our desire constant? Is this spiritual pulse always beating?'

- 'Let anyone with ears listen!' What is Jesus saying to me in this time of meditation?

Friday 10 December

Matthew 11:16–19

'But to what will I compare this generation? It is like children sitting in the market-places and calling to one another,
"We played the flute for you, and you did not dance;
we wailed, and you did not mourn."
'For John came neither eating nor drinking, and they say, "He has a demon"; the Son of Man came eating and drinking, and they say, "Look, a glutton and a drunkard, a friend of tax-collectors and sinners!" Yet wisdom is vindicated by her deeds.'

- Jesus notices those who sit back and do nothing except judge others. John is too strange, while Jesus is too normal for such people. Am I occasionally cynical and critical? Do I disparage the humble efforts of others when they do their best?

- Do I bear faithful witness to Jesus by good deeds? Such deeds may be costly, but the ultimate course of events will reveal that they were wise decisions.

Saturday 11 December
Matthew 17:9a.10–13

As they were coming down the mountain, Jesus ordered them, 'Tell no one about the vision until after the Son of Man has been raised from the dead.' And the disciples asked him, 'Why, then, do the scribes say that Elijah must come first?' He replied, 'Elijah is indeed coming and will restore all things; but I tell you that Elijah has already come, and they did not recognise him, but they did to him whatever they pleased. So also the Son of Man is about to suffer at their hands.' Then the disciples understood that he was speaking to them about John the Baptist.

- Shortly before this scene, Jesus' disciples had a vision of Jesus transfigured in glory and flanked by Moses and Elijah, so obviously the latter was still on their minds. They ask Jesus for confirmation regarding the role of Elijah as forerunner of the End Time.

- Jesus' reply was unexpected in more ways than one: the real forerunner is John the Baptist, he has been badly treated, and this will also be the fate of Jesus himself.

- By our prayer this Christmas, we can ensure that the newly born Jesus is welcome in our lives – even if his message turns some of our values on their heads.

12–18 December 2021

Something to think and pray about each day this week:

She got off at the same stop as me.The busyness of the bus was drowned out by her cry: 'My bags ... they're gone!' Someone had taken her last-minute shopping. Presents from Santa, gifts for under the Christmas tree, kindly items for neighbours, clothes for the day and the necessary ingredients to enhance the dinner ... all gone.

What upset her most was trying to think of what she was going to say to some of the people she'd bought gifts for, especially her children. She could see their disappointed faces and she was stumped as how she could begin to explain what had happened. Christmas Eve – the season of good will drained away before her eyes.

There is no doubt that the world can challenge our efforts at good will. At times it might appear to us that trying to make the world a better place is akin to pushing a rock up a steep hill, but the Christian cannot give in to despair.The God we believe in would never have joined us on our dusty roads if he didn't believe in the triumph of the good. If despair was king, hope would never have been born among us in human flesh.

Alan Hilliard,
Dipping Into Advent

The Presence of God

At any time of the day or night we can call on Jesus.
He is always waiting, listening for our call. What a wonderful blessing.
No phone needed, no e-mails, just a whisper.

Freedom

If God were trying to tell me something, would I know?
If God were reassuring me or challenging me, would I notice?
I ask for the grace to be free of my own preoccupations
and open to what God may be saying to me.

Consciousness

Help me, Lord, become more conscious of your presence. Teach me to recognise your presence in others. Fill my heart with gratitude for the times your love has been shown to me through the care of others.

The Word

In this expectant state of mind, please turn to the text for the day with confidence. Believe that the Holy Spirit is present and may reveal whatever the passage has to say to you. Read reflectively, listening with a third ear to what may be going on in your heart.

(Please turn to the Scripture on the following pages. Inspiration points are there, should you need them. When you are ready, return here to continue.)

Conversation

As I talk to Jesus, may I also learn to pause and listen.
I picture the gentleness in his eyes and the love in his smile.
I can be totally honest with Jesus as I tell him my worries and cares.
I will open my heart to Jesus as I tell him my fears and doubts.
I will ask him to help me place myself fully in his care, knowing that he always desires good for me.

Conclusion

I thank God for these moments we have spent together and for any insights I have been given concerning the text.

Sunday 12 December
Third Sunday of Advent
Luke 3:10–18

And the crowds asked him, 'What then should we do?' In reply he said to them, 'Whoever has two coats must share with anyone who has none; and whoever has food must do likewise.' Even tax-collectors came to be baptised, and they asked him, 'Teacher, what should we do?' He said to them, 'Collect no more than the amount prescribed for you.' Soldiers also asked him, 'And we, what should we do?' He said to them, 'Do not extort money from anyone by threats or false accusation, and be satisfied with your wages.'

As the people were filled with expectation, and all were questioning in their hearts concerning John, whether he might be the Messiah, John answered all of them by saying, 'I baptise you with water; but one who is more powerful than I is coming; I am not worthy to untie the thong of his sandals. He will baptise you with the Holy Spirit and fire. His winnowing-fork is in his hand, to clear his threshing-floor and to gather the wheat into his granary; but the chaff he will burn with unquenchable fire.'

So, with many other exhortations, he proclaimed the good news to the people.

• John doesn't ask tax-collectors to stop collecting, or tell soldiers to desert. His message is simple: social justice. Share what you have, be honest, do not oppress people. He does not call for heroics. But sometimes heroics seem easier than living daily life well. How can I bring the divine into my ordinary actions and make my faith a living thing?

• What must I do to prepare to meet the Messiah?

Monday 13 December
Matthew 21:23–27

When he entered the temple, the chief priests and the elders of the people came to him as he was teaching, and said, 'By what authority are you doing these things, and who gave you this authority?' Jesus said to them, 'I will also ask you one question; if you tell me the answer, then I will also tell you by what authority I do these things. Did the baptism of John come from heaven, or was it of human origin?' And they argued with one another, 'If we say, "From heaven", he will say to us, "Why then did you not believe him?" But if we say, "Of human origin", we are afraid of the crowd; for all regard John as a prophet.' So they answered Jesus, 'We do not know.' And he said to them, 'Neither will I tell you by what authority I am doing these things.'

- What authority does Jesus have? If he turned up today, would we want to see his qualifications before allowing him to preach? Or would his attitudes, words and deeds resonate deeply within us, so that we would say, 'All that he says and does, and the way he does it, are just right'?

- God's wisdom is not confined to the worldly wise. God's grace is not confined to those of whom the world approves. I consider how I might be open to revelation from unusual sources, unlikely people and in unexpected places.

Tuesday 14 December
Matthew 21:28–32

'What do you think? A man had two sons; he went to the first and said, "Son, go and work in the vineyard today." He answered, "I will not"; but later he changed his mind and went. The father went to the second and said the same; and he answered, "I go, sir"; but he did not go. Which of the two did the will of his father?' They said, 'The first.' Jesus said to them, 'Truly I tell you, the tax-collectors and the prostitutes are going into the kingdom of God ahead of you. For John came to you in the way of righteousness and you did not believe him, but the tax-collectors and the prostitutes believed him; and even after you saw it, you did not change your minds and believe him.

- In this parable, the tax collectors and prostitutes – those most despised and rejected by society – are ahead of the self-righteous ones. They were the ones who were open to the word of God and to change.

- Lord, you continually invite me to fullness of life. I pray that through Sacred Space my faith in you may grow ever deeper and that it may be expressed by my desire to serve others.

Wednesday 15 December
Luke 7:18b–23

The disciples of John reported all these things to him. So John summoned two of his disciples and sent them to the Lord to ask, 'Are you the one who is to come, or are we to wait for another?' When the men had come to him, they said, 'John the Baptist has sent us to you to ask, "Are you the one who is to come, or are we to wait for another?"' Jesus had just then cured many people of diseases, plagues, and evil spirits, and had given sight to many who were blind. And he answered them, 'Go and tell John what you have seen and heard: the blind receive their sight, the lame walk, the lepers are cleansed, the deaf hear, the dead are raised, the poor have good news brought to them. And blessed is anyone who takes no offence at me.'

• The readings before Christmas search my heart profoundly. Am I longing for Jesus to come more deeply into my life this Advent? Or am I waiting for God to come in some other form? Would I prefer a different kind of 'good news' than the Gospel about Jesus?

• The Jews wanted a political Messiah who would dramatically terminate their oppression by the Romans. But Jesus only has good news for the blind, the lame, the lepers, the deaf, the dead and the poor. I ask him that I may not get lost in political issues but share my love with those who are marginalised and unwanted by the world.

Thursday 16 December
Luke 7:24–30

When John's messengers had gone, Jesus began to speak to the crowds about John: 'What did you go out into the wilderness to look at? A reed shaken by the wind? What then did you go out to see? Someone dressed in soft robes? Look, those who put on fine clothing and live in luxury are in royal palaces. What then did you go out to see? A prophet? Yes, I tell you, and more than a prophet. This is the one about whom it is written,

"See, I am sending my messenger ahead of you,
    who will prepare your way before you."

I tell you, among those born of women no one is greater than John; yet the least in the kingdom of God is greater than he.' (And all the people who heard this, including the tax-collectors, acknowledged the justice of God, because they had been baptised with John's baptism. But by refusing to be baptised by him, the Pharisees and the lawyers rejected God's purpose for themselves.)

- What do I go out to see? What are my true values? What impresses me? Jesus was impressed by John because he expressed God's values and chose simplicity of life. I ask him if he is impressed by me, and I listen in my heart to what he says to me.

Friday 17 December
Matthew 1:1–17

An account of the genealogy of Jesus the Messiah, the son of David, the son of Abraham.

Abraham was the father of Isaac, and Isaac the father of Jacob, and Jacob the father of Judah and his brothers, and Judah the father of Perez and Zerah by Tamar, and Perez the father of Hezron, and Hezron the father of Aram, and Aram the father of Aminadab, and Aminadab the father of Nahshon, and Nahshon the father of Salmon, and Salmon the father of Boaz by Rahab, and Boaz the father of Obed by Ruth, and Obed the father of Jesse, and Jesse the father of King David.

And David was the father of Solomon by the wife of Uriah, and Solomon the father of Rehoboam, and Rehoboam the father of Abijah, and Abijah the father of Asaph, and Asaph the father of Jehoshaphat, and Jehoshaphat the father of Joram, and Joram the father of Uzziah, and Uzziah the father of Jotham, and Jotham the father of Ahaz, and Ahaz the father of Hezekiah, and Hezekiah the father of Manasseh, and Manasseh the father of Amos, and Amos the father of Josiah, and Josiah the father of Jechoniah and his brothers, at the time of the deportation to Babylon.

And after the deportation to Babylon: Jechoniah was the father of Salathiel, and Salathiel the father of Zerubbabel, and Zerubbabel the father of Abiud, and Abiud the father of Eliakim, and Eliakim the father of Azor, and Azor the father of Zadok, and Zadok the father of Achim, and Achim the father of Eliud, and Eliud the father of Eleazar, and Eleazar the father of Matthan, and Matthan the father of Jacob, and Jacob the father of Joseph the husband of Mary, of whom Jesus was born, who is called the Messiah.

So all the generations from Abraham to David are fourteen generations; and from David to the deportation to Babylon, fourteen generations; and from the deportation to Babylon to the Messiah, fourteen generations.

- This Gospel weaves the threads of the long history that eventually brings us to Jesus. His family tree is a mix of holy and unholy figures, public sinners and outcasts. Yet each played an important role and no one's life was insignificant in God's plan. Jesus does own his family story. He does not airbrush out any of his ancestors. Do I?

- Lord, I thank you for all who have been carriers of your grace to me. Let not my limitations and inadequacy impede me from believing that I am important. Let me play my part in being a carrier of your love to the world.

Saturday 18 December
Matthew 1:18–25

Now the birth of Jesus the Messiah took place in this way. When his mother Mary had been engaged to Joseph, but before they lived together, she was found to be with child from the Holy Spirit. Her husband Joseph, being a righteous man and unwilling to expose her to public disgrace, planned to dismiss her quietly. But just when he had resolved to do this, an angel of the Lord appeared to him in a dream and said, 'Joseph, son of David, do not be afraid to take Mary as your wife, for the child conceived in her is from the Holy Spirit. She will bear a son, and you are to name him Jesus, for he will save his people from their sins.' All this took place to fulfil what had been spoken by the Lord through the prophet:

'Look, the virgin shall conceive and bear a son,
and they shall name him Emmanuel',

which means, 'God is with us.' When Joseph awoke from sleep, he did as the angel of the Lord commanded him; he took her as his wife, but had no marital relations with her until she had borne a son; and he named him Jesus.

- In a mysterious, miraculous way, known only in faith, the Spirit's action brings the gift to the world of the God-person, the human in the divine and the divine in the human in a totally physical and spiritual way. In the humanity of Mary, Jesus is growing from embryo to child. In the faith of Joseph, the call first came to all of us to believe the mystery. In prayer we might picture Mary and Joseph talking together about all that has happened and picture the Holy Spirit in the love and in the atmosphere around them. Bring that presence of the Spirit into your day today.

The Fourth Week of Advent/Christmas
19–25 December 2021

Something to think and pray about each day this week:

God has visited his people in and through the person of his Son, Jesus. This visitation reveals the tender mercy of God. Jesus' coming is spoken of as the rising Sun from on high bringing light to those who live in darkness and in the shadow of death. The sun is the source of light and life. In an even more fundamental sense, Jesus is the source of light and life. In revealing God's tender mercy, Jesus brings the light of God's merciful love into the darkness of our lives and he also offers us a sharing in God's own life, thereby scattering the shadow that death casts over us. The true meaning of Christmas is to be found here. In celebrating the birth of Jesus, we are celebrating the coming of God's light and life, a light that no darkness can overcome and a life that is stronger than all forms of death. Christmas is the feast of Jesus, the light of life. It is a truly hopeful feast because it proclaims that we need no longer remain in darkness or in the shadow of death.

Martin Hogan,
The Word of God is Living and Active

The Presence of God

Dear Jesus, as I call on you today, I realise that often I come asking for favours. Today I'd like just to be in your presence.

Freedom

It is so easy to get caught up with the trappings of wealth in this life.
Grant, O Lord, that I may be free from greed and selfishness.
Remind me that the best things in life are free:
Love, laughter, caring and sharing.

Consciousness

How am I really feeling? Lighthearted? Heavyhearted? I may be very much at peace, happy to be here.
Equally, I may be frustrated, worried or angry.
I acknowledge how I really am. It is the real me whom the Lord loves.

The Word

Lord Jesus, you became human to communicate with me.
You walked and worked on this earth.
You endured the heat and struggled with the cold.
All your time on this earth was spent in caring for humanity.
You healed the sick, you raised the dead.
Most important of all, you saved me from death.
(Please turn to the Scripture on the following pages. Inspiration points are there, should you need them. When you are ready, return here to continue.)

Conversation

Do I notice myself reacting as I pray with the word of God? Do I feel challenged, comforted, angry? Imagining Jesus sitting or standing by me, I speak out my feelings, as one trusted friend to another.

Conclusion

Glory be to the Father, and to the Son, and to the Holy Spirit,
As it was in the beginning, is now and ever shall be,
World without end. Amen.

Sunday 19 December
Fourth Sunday of Advent
Luke 1:39–45

In those days Mary set out and went with haste to a Judean town in the hill country, where she entered the house of Zechariah and greeted Elizabeth. When Elizabeth heard Mary's greeting, the child leapt in her womb. And Elizabeth was filled with the Holy Spirit and exclaimed with a loud cry, 'Blessed are you among women, and blessed is the fruit of your womb. And why has this happened to me, that the mother of my Lord comes to me? For as soon as I heard the sound of your greeting, the child in my womb leapt for joy. And blessed is she who believed that there would be a fulfilment of what was spoken to her by the Lord.'

- Lord, as Christmas draws ever closer, free me from being self-absorbed and self-centred. Instead fill me with eagerness and generosity of heart. Like Mary, may I too go out in loving service of others and experience your Love leaping up in me and in those with whom I come in contact.

Monday 20 December
Luke 1:26–38

In the sixth month the angel Gabriel was sent by God to a town in Galilee called Nazareth, to a virgin engaged to a man whose name was Joseph, of the house of David. The virgin's name was Mary. And he came to her and said, 'Greetings, favoured one! The Lord is with you.' But she was much perplexed by his words and pondered what sort of greeting this might be. The angel said to her, 'Do not be afraid, Mary, for you have found favour with God. And now, you will conceive in your womb and bear a son, and you will name him Jesus. He will be great, and will be called the Son of the Most High, and the Lord God will give to him the throne of his ancestor David. He will reign over the house of Jacob for ever, and of his kingdom there will be no end.' Mary said to the angel, 'How can this be, since I am a virgin?' The angel said to her, 'The Holy Spirit will come upon you, and the power of the Most High will overshadow you; therefore the child to be born will be holy; he will be called Son of God. And now, your relative Elizabeth in her old age has also conceived a son; and this is the sixth month for her who was said to be barren. For nothing will be impossible with God.' Then Mary said, 'Here am I, the servant of the Lord; let it be with me according to your word.' Then the angel departed from her.

- In our lives there are turning points where we may experience an invitation to embrace something difficult rather than discard it; something that wrecks our dreams for ourselves or for our loved ones. There's a need to discern the spirits.

- If it is disconcerting that does not mean that it is bad. What response would your better self give?

Tuesday 21 December
Luke 1:39–45

In those days Mary set out and went with haste to a Judean town in the hill country, where she entered the house of Zechariah and greeted Elizabeth. When Elizabeth heard Mary's greeting, the child leapt in her womb. And Elizabeth was filled with the Holy Spirit and exclaimed with a loud cry, 'Blessed are you among women, and blessed is the fruit of your womb. And why has this happened to me, that the mother of my Lord comes to me? For as soon as I heard the sound of your greeting, the child in my womb leapt for joy. And blessed is she who believed that there would be a fulfilment of what was spoken to her by the Lord.'

- The journey from Nazareth to Ein Karim was long and uncomfortable. Mary, who carries the secret – she is the womb of God. This visitation was a Eucharistic moment. The light of Christ comes to Elizabeth through Mary. Both women rejoice! Mary's one desire is to go out in loving service to help her pregnant cousin.

Wednesday 22 December
Luke 1:46–56

And Mary said,

> 'My soul magnifies the Lord,
> and my spirit rejoices in God my Saviour,
> for he has looked with favour on the lowliness of his servant.
> Surely, from now on all generations will call me blessed;
> for the Mighty One has done great things for me,
> and holy is his name.
> His mercy is for those who fear him

from generation to generation.
He has shown strength with his arm;
he has scattered the proud in the thoughts of their hearts.
He has brought down the powerful from their thrones,
and lifted up the lowly;
he has filled the hungry with good things,
and sent the rich away empty.
He has helped his servant Israel,
in remembrance of his mercy,
according to the promise he made to our ancestors,
to Abraham and to his descendants for ever.'

And Mary remained with her for about three months and then returned to her home.

- I imagine that am invited to stay with Elizabeth and Mary for the three months they spent together. I observe what they say and do, and how quietly happy they both are, as they each carry the mystery of God in their wombs.

- Mary praises the God who turns human history upside down. God scatters the proud, pulls down the mighty and dismisses the rich. In their place he exalts the unimportant ones and feeds the starving. Do I value the despised and downtrodden of this world above the famous and the wealthy? I talk to Mary about this.

Thursday 23 December
Luke 1:57–66

Now the time came for Elizabeth to give birth, and she bore a son. Her neighbours and relatives heard that the Lord had shown his great mercy to her, and they rejoiced with her.

On the eighth day they came to circumcise the child, and they were going to name him Zechariah after his father. But his mother said, 'No; he is to be called John.' They said to her, 'None of your relatives has this name.' Then they began motioning to his father to find out what name he wanted to give him. He asked for a writing-tablet and wrote, 'His name is John.' And all of them were amazed. Immediately his mouth was opened and his tongue freed, and he began to speak, praising God. Fear came over all their neighbours, and all these things were talked about throughout the entire hill country of Judea. All who heard them pondered them and said, 'What then will this child become?' For, indeed, the hand of the Lord was with him.

- I join in the excitement around the birth of Elizabeth's baby. I become aware that God is fulfilling his plans through human beings who collaborate. So too God wants the child to be called John, and this is what happens. In Luke's understanding of salvation, what God decides will eventually be fulfilled. I ask for faith to believe this and to be free of anxiety.

Friday 24 December
Luke 1:67–79

Then his father Zechariah was filled with the Holy Spirit and spoke this prophecy:

> 'Blessed be the Lord God of Israel,
> for he has looked favourably on his people and redeemed them.
> He has raised up a mighty saviour for us
> in the house of his servant David,
> as he spoke through the mouth of his holy prophets from of old,
> that we would be saved from our enemies and from the hand of all
>   who hate us.
> Thus he has shown the mercy promised to our ancestors,
> and has remembered his holy covenant,
> the oath that he swore to our ancestor Abraham,
> to grant us that we, being rescued from the hands of our enemies,
> might serve him without fear, in holiness and righteousness
> before him all our days.
> And you, child, will be called the prophet of the Most High;
> for you will go before the Lord to prepare his ways,
> to give knowledge of salvation to his people
> by the forgiveness of their sins.
> By the tender mercy of our God,
> the dawn from on high will break upon us,
> to give light to those who sit in darkness and in the shadow of
>   death,
> to guide our feet into the way of peace.'

- The Benedictus is a prayer of prophecy about the coming of the Saviour. This 'Most High' that Zechariah mentions comes not in a cloud of glory, but as a vulnerable child, with an ordinary family, in a cold stable. That is the kind of God we have.

Saturday 25 December
The Nativity of the Lord
John 1:1–18

In the beginning was the Word, and the Word was with God, and the Word was God. He was in the beginning with God. All things came into being through him, and without him not one thing came into being. What has come into being in him was life, and the life was the light of all people. The light shines in the darkness, and the darkness did not overcome it.

There was a man sent from God, whose name was John. He came as a witness to testify to the light, so that all might believe through him. He himself was not the light, but he came to testify to the light. The true light, which enlightens everyone, was coming into the world.

He was in the world, and the world came into being through him; yet the world did not know him. He came to what was his own, and his own people did not accept him. But to all who received him, who believed in his name, he gave power to become children of God, who were born, not of blood or of the will of the flesh or of the will of man, but of God.

And the Word became flesh and lived among us, and we have seen his glory, the glory as of a father's only son, full of grace and truth. (John testified to him and cried out, 'This was he of whom I said, "He who comes after me ranks ahead of me because he was before me."') From his fullness we have all received, grace upon grace. The law indeed was given through Moses; grace and truth came through Jesus Christ. No one has ever seen God. It is God the only Son, who is close to the Father's heart, who has made him known.

- It has been an eventful year that leaves lasting memories. We have the fidelity of God to sustain us in the many challenges of life. We need light in the darkness and hope in the uncertainty that is around us. God has given us the Eternal Word and the living word of scripture to guide us. We pray to welcome and appreciate those words more fully, asking that our words may be in harmony with them. What word does the Lord desire me to take with me as I enter the New Year?

The First Week of Christmas
26 December 2021–1 January 2022

Something to think and pray about each day this week:

Faith, prayer, Mass and the Church can bring us through a lot in bad days.

Prayer can be a valued part of family life. In all the different stresses today of family life, if we teach by word and example the value and place of prayer in their lives we have given a lot. The example of love and care, even in stressful times, can never be underestimated.

Some pray at night or in the morning, before a meal or leaving the house; Mass and the inclusion of prayer at high points of family life are ways of including prayer in family life. Family is the school of faith and the place of God in the ordinary, everyday world.

Donal Neary SJ,
Gospel Reflections for Sundays of Year C: Luke

The Presence of God

Dear Jesus, I come to you today longing for your presence. I desire to love you as you love me. May nothing ever separate me from you.

Freedom

Lord, grant me the grace to have freedom of the Spirit. Cleanse my heart and soul so that I may live joyously in your love.

Consciousness

Where am I with God? With others?
Do I have something to be grateful for? Then I give thanks.
Is there something I am sorry for? Then I ask forgiveness.

The Word

The word of God comes down to us through the Scriptures. May the Holy Spirit enlighten my mind and my heart to respond to the Gospel teachings.

(Please turn to the Scripture on the following pages. Inspiration points are there, should you need them. When you are ready, return here to continue.)

Conversation

How has God's word moved me? Has it left me cold?
Has it consoled me or moved me to act in a new way?
I imagine Jesus standing or sitting beside me;
I turn and share my feelings with him.

Conclusion

I thank God for these moments we have spent together and for any insights I have been given concerning the text.

Sunday 26 December
The Holy Family of Jesus, Mary and Joseph
Luke 2:41–52

Now every year his parents went to Jerusalem for the festival of the Passover. And when he was twelve years old, they went up as usual for the festival. When the festival was ended and they started to return, the boy Jesus stayed behind in Jerusalem, but his parents did not know it. Assuming that he was in the group of travellers, they went a day's journey. Then they started to look for him among their relatives and friends. When they did not find him, they returned to Jerusalem to search for him. After three days they found him in the temple, sitting among the teachers, listening to them and asking them questions. And all who heard him were amazed at his understanding and his answers. When his parents saw him they were astonished; and his mother said to him, 'Child, why have you treated us like this? Look, your father and I have been searching for you in great anxiety.' He said to them, 'Why were you searching for me? Did you not know that I must be in my Father's house?' But they did not understand what he said to them. Then he went down with them and came to Nazareth, and was obedient to them. His mother treasured all these things in her heart.

And Jesus increased in wisdom and in years, and in divine and human favour.

- Lord, you have tasted human uncertainties and the difficulties of survival. Your mother, so blissfully happy when she prayed the Magnificat, had to adjust rapidly to homelessness and the life of an asylum-seeker. Let me be equally unsurprisable when plans go awry and you ask me to taste uncertainties.

Monday 27 December
Saint John, Apostle
John 20:1a. 2–8

Early on the first day of the week, while it was still dark, Mary Magdalene came to the tomb and saw that the stone had been removed from the tomb. So she ran and went to Simon Peter and the other disciple, the one whom Jesus loved, and said to them, 'They have taken the Lord out of the tomb, and we do not know where they have laid him.' Then Peter and the other disciple set out and went towards the tomb. The two were running together, but the other disciple outran Peter and reached the tomb first. He bent down to look in and saw the linen wrappings lying there, but he did not go in. Then Simon Peter came, following him, and went into the tomb. He saw the linen wrappings lying there, and the cloth that had been on Jesus' head, not lying with the linen wrappings but rolled up in a place by itself. Then the other disciple, who reached the tomb first, also went in, and he saw and believed.

• It is sometimes tempting to cling to the glow of Christmas. While I value the gift of this season, this Easter scene reminds me that faith calls me to move on, to seek the Risen Lord.

• When Mary Magdalene did not find Jesus where she expected, she went first to her community. As questions arise for me, I bring them to God and to others whom I trust.

Tuesday 28 December
Matthew 2:13–18

Now after they had left, an angel of the Lord appeared to Joseph in a dream and said, 'Get up, take the child and his mother, and flee to Egypt, and remain there until I tell you; for Herod is about to search for the child, to destroy him.' Then Joseph got up, took the child and his mother by night, and went to Egypt, and remained there until the death of Herod. This was to fulfil what had been spoken by the Lord through the prophet, 'Out of Egypt I have called my son.'

When Herod saw that he had been tricked by the wise men, he was infuriated, and he sent and killed all the children in and around Bethlehem who were two years old or under, according to the time that he had learned from the wise men. Then was fulfilled what had been spoken through the prophet Jeremiah:

'A voice was heard in Ramah,
wailing and loud lamentation,
Rachel weeping for her children;
she refused to be consoled, because they are no more.'

• Starting with the scene of the Holy Family forced to flee into Egypt, we reflect in our prayer on the whole Jewish people finding themselves in captivity in Egypt (and on their eventual release being withheld by Pharaoh, until first the blood of a child flowed in every house of his own population).

• The road to the fullness of freedom for the Jewish people in the Promised Land had tragic turns. The same was true of the road Jesus himself walked, and the same is true, one way or another, of the road each of us walks.

Wednesday 29 December
Luke 2:22–35

When the time came for their purification according to the law of Moses, they brought him up to Jerusalem to present him to the Lord (as it is written in the law of the Lord, 'Every firstborn male shall be designated as holy to the Lord'), and they offered a sacrifice according to what is stated in the law of the Lord, 'a pair of turtle-doves or two young pigeons.'

Now there was a man in Jerusalem whose name was Simeon; this man was righteous and devout, looking forward to the consolation of Israel, and the Holy Spirit rested on him. It had been revealed to him by the Holy Spirit that he would not see death before he had seen the Lord's Messiah. Guided by the Spirit, Simeon came into the temple; and when the parents brought in the child Jesus, to do for him what was customary under the law, Simeon took him in his arms and praised God, saying,

'Master, now you are dismissing your servant in peace,
according to your word;
for my eyes have seen your salvation,
which you have prepared in the presence of all peoples,
a light for revelation to the Gentiles
and for glory to your people Israel.'

And the child's father and mother were amazed at what was being said about him. Then Simeon blessed them and said to his mother Mary, 'This child is destined for the falling and the rising of many in Israel, and to be a sign that will be opposed so that the inner thoughts of many will be revealed – and a sword will pierce your own soul too.'

• Lord, in Simeon I see hope triumphant, hope richly rewarded. The years of waiting – the centuries before he himself was born and the long years that he had lived – did not blunt the edge of his faith. His hope and yearning left him alive to the prompting of God, ready to hear it when it came. Grant that I may learn from him.

Thursday 30 December
Luke 2:36–40

There was also a prophet, Anna the daughter of Phanuel, of the tribe of Asher. She was of a great age, having lived with her husband for seven years after her marriage, then as a widow to the age of eighty-four. She never left the temple but worshipped there with fasting and prayer night and day. At that moment she came, and began to praise God and to speak about the child to all who were looking for the redemption of Jerusalem.

When they had finished everything required by the law of the Lord, they returned to Galilee, to their own town of Nazareth. The child grew and became strong, filled with wisdom; and the favour of God was upon him.

- The life of Anna was hidden away in the temple. The life of Jesus as he grew from childhood to manhood was hidden for thirty years in an obscure village. In this hidden time, Jesus grows. He becomes strong, filled with wisdom and God's favour.

- Lord, let me value the hidden quality of prayer. Let me never doubt the value of 'wasting time' hidden with you before the Father.

Friday 31 December
John 1:1–18

In the beginning was the Word, and the Word was with God, and the Word was God. He was in the beginning with God. All things came into being through him, and without him not one thing came into being. What has come into being in him was life, and the life was the light of all people. The light shines in the darkness, and the darkness did not overcome it.

There was a man sent from God, whose name was John. He came as a witness to testify to the light, so that all might believe through him. He himself was not the light, but he came to testify to the light. The true light, which enlightens everyone, was coming into the world.

He was in the world, and the world came into being through him; yet the world did not know him. He came to what was his own, and his own people did not accept him. But to all who received him, who believed in his name, he gave power to become children of God, who were born, not of blood or of the will of the flesh or of the will of man, but of God.

And the Word became flesh and lived among us, and we have seen his glory, the glory as of a father's only son, full of grace and truth. (John testified to him and cried out, 'This was he of whom I said, "He who comes after me ranks ahead of me because he was before me."') From his fullness we have all received, grace upon grace. The law indeed was given through Moses; grace and truth came through Jesus Christ. No one has ever seen God. It is God the only Son, who is close to the Father's heart, who has made him known.

• We come to the end of a year and listen to what God's word says to us. It helps us look back to learn and look forward in hope. God's word is a creative word who gives life to all, in love.

Saturday 1 January
Mary, the Mother of God
Luke 2:16–21

So they went with haste and found Mary and Joseph, and the child lying in the manger. When they saw this, they made known what had been told them about this child; and all who heard it were amazed at what the shepherds told them. But Mary treasured all these words and pondered them in her heart. The shepherds returned, glorifying and praising God for all they had heard and seen, as it had been told them.

After eight days had passed, it was time to circumcise the child; and he was called Jesus, the name given by the angel before he was conceived in the womb.

• As we begin this new year we find an amazing piece of Good News waiting to cheer our hearts! God has become human and is no longer remote or shadowy. We all feel comfortable with a baby, and when it smiles at us, our tired hearts are filled with joy. We can get in on the scene by knocking at the door and are greeted by Mary's smile. Take time to sit with the little family and the shepherds, in silent wonder.

Perhaps you forgot to bring a gift, but it doesn't matter: you've brought yourself!

- Whenever you see a baby this year, make the connection with what is happening today, and renew your sense of wonder and awe at the delightfulness of God becoming human. This will warm your heart and make you smile more.

The Second Week of Christmas
2–8 January 2022

Something to think and pray about each day this week:

What Ignatius calls disordered attachments can get the better of us – pride, greed, fear, perfectionism, the insatiable appetite for instant affirmation generated by social media, over-stimulation, the expectation of 24/7 availability, failure to realise we're stewards of creation and not its owners, obsession with prestige and status, the 'I have more than you' syndrome and all the other attractions that draw us away from God, ourselves and others, leaving us in a state of emotional turbulence, excitement and exhaustion.

My worth as a person is not determined by what I have. My material possessions, my academic attainments, my successes, my income and my bank balance do not define my worth as an invaluable and unique human person. My worth is not determined by what's outside myself. The bad spirit, the enemy of my human nature, would have me believe otherwise. I'm infinitely richer than that. It's so easy to get caught up in what we think we need and desire, but in the cold light of day we see the illusions for what they are. Solidarity with one another, rather than competition with one another, is God's idea of what life is about.

Jim Maher SJ,
Pathways to a Decision with Ignatius of Loyola

The Presence of God
Dear Jesus, today I call on you, but not to ask for anything. I'd like only to dwell in your presence. May my heart respond to your love.

Freedom
God my creator, you gave me life and the gift of freedom. Through your love I exist in this world. May I never take the gift of life for granted. May I always respect others' right to life.

Consciousness
I ask how I am today. Am I particularly tired, stressed or anxious? If any of these characteristics apply, can I try to let go of the concerns that disturb me?

The Word
The word of God comes down to us through the Scriptures. May the Holy Spirit enlighten my mind and my heart to respond to the Gospel teachings.
(Please turn to the Scripture on the following pages. Inspiration points are there, should you need them. When you are ready, return here to continue.)

Conversation
I begin to talk with Jesus about the Scripture I have just read. What part of it strikes a chord in me? Perhaps the words of a friend – or some story I have heard recently – will rise to the surface in my consciousness. If so, does the story throw light on what the Scripture passage may be saying to me?

Conclusion
Glory be to the Father, and to the Son, and to the Holy Spirit,
As it was in the beginning, is now and ever shall be,
World without end. Amen.

Sunday 2 January
Epiphany of the Lord (USA)
Matthew 2:1–12

In the time of King Herod, after Jesus was born in Bethlehem of Judea, wise men from the East came to Jerusalem, asking, 'Where is the child who has been born king of the Jews? For we observed his star at its rising, and have come to pay him homage.' When King Herod heard this, he was frightened, and all Jerusalem with him; and calling together all the chief priests and scribes of the people, he inquired of them where the Messiah was to be born. They told him, 'In Bethlehem of Judea; for so it has been written by the prophet:

"And you, Bethlehem, in the land of Judah,
are by no means least among the rulers of Judah;
for from you shall come a ruler
who is to shepherd my people Israel."'

Then Herod secretly called for the wise men and learned from them the exact time when the star had appeared. Then he sent them to Bethlehem, saying, 'Go and search diligently for the child; and when you have found him, bring me word so that I may also go and pay him homage.' When they had heard the king, they set out; and there, ahead of them, went the star that they had seen at its rising, until it stopped over the place where the child was. When they saw that the star had stopped, they were overwhelmed with joy. On entering the house, they saw the child with Mary his mother; and they knelt down and paid him homage. Then, opening their treasure-chests, they offered him gifts of gold, frankincense, and myrrh. And having been warned in a dream not to return to Herod, they left for their own country by another road.

- The story told in today's Gospel is about people being called to follow their star in order to find the fullness of life only Jesus can give. 'I came that they may have life, and have it abundantly' (John 10:10). You may not have thought much about the nature of the star you follow. With a view to clarifying this, it may be worthwhile to ask yourself what you want for your children, your family or your friends.

Monday 3 January
Matthew 4:12–17.23–25

Now when Jesus heard that John had been arrested, he withdrew to Galilee. He left Nazareth and made his home in Capernaum by the lake, in the territory of Zebulun and Naphtali, so that what had been spoken through the prophet Isaiah might be fulfilled:

'Land of Zebulun, land of Naphtali,
on the road by the sea, across the Jordan, Galilee of the Gentiles –
the people who sat in darkness
have seen a great light,
and for those who sat in the region and shadow of death
light has dawned.'
From that time Jesus began to proclaim, 'Repent, for the kingdom
of heaven has come near.'

Jesus went throughout Galilee, teaching in their synagogues and proclaiming the good news of the kingdom and curing every disease and every sickness among the people. So his fame spread throughout all Syria, and they brought to him all the sick, those who were afflicted with various diseases and pains, demoniacs, epileptics, and paralytics, and he cured them. And great crowds followed him from Galilee, the Decapolis, Jerusalem, Judea, and from beyond the Jordan.

- Jesus ventures into regions where pagan influences are felt. The 'demoniacs' were in the grip of the prince of darkness: a dark shadow hung on the lives of the epileptics; and the lives of the sick were blighted also. But Jesus, Lord of light, launches the kingdom of heaven – rolling back the darkness.

- Does some dark influence also tend at times to pull me down in spirit? I open myself to the healing light of Jesus.

Tuesday 4 January
Mark 6:34–44

As he went ashore, he saw a great crowd; and he had compassion for them, because they were like sheep without a shepherd; and he began to teach them many things. When it grew late, his disciples came to him and said,

'This is a deserted place, and the hour is now very late; send them away so that they may go into the surrounding country and villages and buy something for themselves to eat.' But he answered them, 'You give them something to eat.' They said to him, 'Are we to go and buy two hundred denarii worth of bread, and give it to them to eat?' And he said to them, 'How many loaves have you? Go and see.' When they had found out, they said, 'Five, and two fish.' Then he ordered them to get all the people to sit down in groups on the green grass. So they sat down in groups of hundreds and of fifties. Taking the five loaves and the two fish, he looked up to heaven, and blessed and broke the loaves, and gave them to his disciples to set before the people; and he divided the two fish among them all. And all ate and were filled; and they took up twelve baskets full of broken pieces and of the fish. Those who had eaten the loaves numbered five thousand men.

• Out of compassion Jesus puts the people's needs first. He calls on the Twelve to share their food, to serve these thousands and then to ensure no food is wasted. Serious lessons that, with their hard hearts, they were slow to take in.

• The actions of Jesus are exactly similar to his actions at the Last Supper. Here he anticipates the superabundant gift of the Eucharist.

Wednesday 5 January
Mark 6:45–52

Immediately he made his disciples get into the boat and go on ahead to the other side, to Bethsaida, while he dismissed the crowd. After saying farewell to them, he went up on the mountain to pray.

When evening came, the boat was out on the lake, and he was alone on the land. When he saw that they were straining at the oars against an adverse wind, he came towards them early in the morning, walking on the lake. He intended to pass them by. But when they saw him walking on the lake, they thought it was a ghost and cried out; for they all saw him and were terrified. But immediately he spoke to them and said, 'Take heart, it is I; do not be afraid.' Then he got into the boat with them and the wind ceased. And they were utterly astounded, for they did not understand about the loaves, but their hearts were hardened.

- Jesus is praying – speaking with his Father. Is he perhaps thinking about the best way to 'get through' to people regarding what his coming is really about? Is he perhaps recalling the great demonstration that was his feeding of the five thousand? However, in the minds of the people, that was seen only as the beginning of a political campaign. And the disciples were little better. So now he is about to intervene on a different level: he saves the disciples from the storm to show that he is strong enough for his 'cause' to succeed without having to rely on the popular mood.

- Jesus is strong enough to carry out his plan for my life, without having to rely on people who 'have influence'.

Thursday 6 January
The Epiphany of the Lord (IRE) – see entry for Sunday 2 January
Luke 4:14–22

Then Jesus, filled with the power of the Spirit, returned to Galilee, and a report about him spread through all the surrounding country. He began to teach in their synagogues and was praised by everyone.

When he came to Nazareth, where he had been brought up, he went to the synagogue on the sabbath day, as was his custom. He stood up to read, and the scroll of the prophet Isaiah was given to him. He unrolled the scroll and found the place where it was written:

'The Spirit of the Lord is upon me,
because he has anointed me
to bring good news to the poor.
He has sent me to proclaim release to the captives
and recovery of sight to the blind,
to let the oppressed go free,
to proclaim the year of the Lord's favour.'

And he rolled up the scroll, gave it back to the attendant, and sat down. The eyes of all in the synagogue were fixed on him. Then he began to say to them, 'Today this scripture has been fulfilled in your hearing.' All spoke well of him and were amazed at the gracious words that came from his mouth. They said, 'Is not this Joseph's son?'

- In my imagination I join the synagogue congregation, and hear this charismatic young man speaking the prophecy of Isaiah as his own mission statement. As I listen, I sense with excitement that he is reaching out to me to join him. Lord, let me be part of that unending mission, to bring good news, vision and freedom to those who need them.

Friday 7 January
Luke 5:12–16

Once, when he was in one of the cities, there was a man covered with leprosy. When he saw Jesus, he bowed with his face to the ground and begged him, 'Lord, if you choose, you can make me clean.' Then Jesus stretched out his hand, touched him, and said, 'I do choose. Be made clean.' Immediately the leprosy left him. And he ordered him to tell no one. 'Go', he said, 'and show yourself to the priest, and, as Moses commanded, make an offering for your cleansing, for a testimony to them.' But now more than ever the word about Jesus spread abroad; many crowds would gather to hear him and to be cured of their diseases. But he would withdraw to deserted places and pray.

- I am walking along happily with Jesus and his four new fishermen disciples. I draw back in horror when this man covered with repulsive sores begs for healing. No Jew would defile himself by touching a leper, but goodness flows out of Jesus and he cures him. He orders the man to observe the command of Moses.

- Jesus is uncomfortable with all the fuss and finds a quiet place where he can be alone with his Father. Have I tried silent communion with the Lord, with maybe a phrase or a single word like 'Thanks' to help focus my attention?

Saturday 8 January
John 3:22–30

After this Jesus and his disciples went into the Judean countryside, and he spent some time there with them and baptised. John also was baptising at Aenon near Salim because water was abundant there; and people kept coming and were being baptised – John, of course, had not yet been thrown into prison.

Now a discussion about purification arose between John's disciples and a Jew. They came to John and said to him, 'Rabbi, the one who was with you across the Jordan, to whom you testified, here he is baptising, and all are going to him.' John answered, 'No one can receive anything except what has been given from heaven. You yourselves are my witnesses that I said, "I am not the Messiah, but I have been sent ahead of him." He who has the bride is the bridegroom. The friend of the bridegroom, who stands and hears him, rejoices greatly at the bridegroom's voice. For this reason my joy has been fulfilled. He must increase, but I must decrease.'

- My question as I grow older is not: 'Am I qualified enough to show Jesus to people?' More and more it is: 'Am I weak enough?' Do I accept my failures and the wounds of life as more important than my strengths in witnessing to Jesus? I am a wounded healer. Like my fellow human beings, I too am searching and struggling.

The Third Week of Christmas
9–15 January 2022

Something to think and pray about each day this week:

Once a child was heard correcting an adult who said that the moon had been shining brightly the night before. The child listened and then said, 'The moon has no light of its own. It shines because it reflects the light of the sun.' Brilliant! And true.

We are like the moon. There are days when we have no light of our own. In fact, there are days when we are pretty dark. If we met ourselves on those days we'd be a bit flat and lacklustre.

There are other days when we are like the moon in another way – we have no light of our own but we do shine a bit. On these days, we reflect others' light back out into the world – the love and friendship and support we get from others. Even though we may be a bit flat or lacklustre, on these days we are lighter-feeling and hopefully others see that in us.

To have others in our lives who give us light is so important. Being connected to them keeps us going. It keeps us focused on the realities of life. It keeps our heads above water on the difficult days.

Jim Deeds & Brendan McManus SJ,
Finding God in the Mess

The Presence of God
Dear Lord, as I come to you today, fill my heart, my whole being, with the wonder of your presence. Help me remain receptive to you as I put aside the cares of this world. Fill my mind with your peace.

Freedom
Lord, grant me the grace to be free from the excesses of this life. Let me not get caught up with the desire for wealth. Keep my heart and mind free to love and serve you.

Consciousness
I exist in a web of relationships: links to nature, people, God.
I trace out these links, giving thanks for the life that flows through them.
Some links are twisted or broken; I may feel regret, anger, disappointment.
I pray for the gift of acceptance and forgiveness.

The Word
God speaks to each of us individually. I listen attentively to hear what he is saying to me. Read the text a few times, then listen.
(Please turn to the Scripture on the following pages. Inspiration points are there, should you need them. When you are ready, return here to continue.)

Conversation
Jesus, you speak to me through the words of the Gospels. May I respond to your call today. Teach me to recognise your hand at work in my daily living.

Conclusion
I thank God for these moments we have spent together and for any insights I have been given concerning the text.

Sunday 9 January
The Baptism of the Lord
Luke 3:15–16.21–22

As the people were filled with expectation, and all were questioning in their hearts concerning John, whether he might be the Messiah, John answered all of them by saying, 'I baptise you with water; but one who is more powerful than I is coming; I am not worthy to untie the thong of his sandals. He will baptise you with the Holy Spirit and fire. . . .

Now when all the people were baptised, and when Jesus also had been baptised and was praying, the heaven was opened, and the Holy Spirit descended upon him in bodily form like a dove. And a voice came from heaven, 'You are my Son, the Beloved; with you I am well pleased.'

- God always speaks to Jesus in an intimate and joyful fashion. He says: 'You are my beloved son, I am pleased with you. I love you deeply. Your whole being springs from me. I am your Father.' Jesus answers, 'Abba', 'beloved Father'. His whole life reveals trust. He hands himself over unconditionally to his Father.

- God, I ponder this love that you have also lavished upon me, calling me your child. You are the tender and compassionate Mother of my life. You are the faithful Father, the Rock on which I stand. Your love is everlasting. Your faithfulness is eternal.

Monday 10 January
Mark 1:14–20

Now after John was arrested, Jesus came to Galilee, proclaiming the good news of God, and saying, 'The time is fulfilled, and the kingdom of God has come near; repent, and believe in the good news.'

As Jesus passed along the Sea of Galilee, he saw Simon and his brother Andrew casting a net into the lake – for they were fishermen. And Jesus said to them, 'Follow me and I will make you fish for people.' And immediately they left their nets and followed him. As he went a little farther, he saw James son of Zebedee and his brother John, who were in their boat mending the nets. Immediately he called them; and they left their father Zebedee in the boat with the hired men, and followed him.

- Following his baptism and identification as the beloved Son of God, Jesus publicly proclaims the good news that the reign of God has come here and now. God makes his presence known in the person of his Son Jesus, come to establish true justice, with compassion for all of humanity. He needs help to bring this about, so he calls disciples to follow him. I marvel at Jesus' captivating personality that evoked such an immediate, unconditional response from them.

• At my baptism my godparents accepted a lighted candle on my behalf. I was 'to walk always as a child of the light' and 'keep the flame of faith alive in my heart'.

Tuesday 11 January
Mark 1:21–28

They went to Capernaum; and when the sabbath came, he entered the synagogue and taught. They were astounded at his teaching, for he taught them as one having authority, and not as the scribes. Just then there was in their synagogue a man with an unclean spirit, and he cried out, 'What have you to do with us, Jesus of Nazareth? Have you come to destroy us? I know who you are, the Holy One of God.' But Jesus rebuked him, saying, 'Be silent, and come out of him!' And the unclean spirit, throwing him into convulsions and crying with a loud voice, came out of him. They were all amazed, and they kept on asking one another, 'What is this? A new teaching – with authority! He commands even the unclean spirits, and they obey him.' At once his fame began to spread throughout the surrounding region of Galilee.

• Jesus preached the Good News not only in what he said but more so by what he did. Today's Gospel shows us a person who spoke with a courage and a wisdom that struck the ordinary people with its ring of authority.

• For a few moments of prayer let yourself notice and admire what the people were so impressed with about Jesus.

Wednesday 12 January
Mark 1:29–39

As soon as they left the synagogue, they entered the house of Simon and Andrew, with James and John. Now Simon's mother-in-law was in bed with a fever, and they told him about her at once. He came and took her by the hand and lifted her up. Then the fever left her, and she began to serve them.

That evening, at sunset, they brought to him all who were sick or possessed with demons. And the whole city was gathered around the door. And he cured many who were sick with various diseases, and cast out many demons; and he would not permit the demons to speak, because they knew him.

In the morning, while it was still very dark, he got up and went out to a deserted place, and there he prayed. And Simon and his companions hunted for him. When they found him, they said to him, 'Everyone is searching for you.' He answered, 'Let us go on to the neighbouring towns, so that I may proclaim the message there also; for that is what I came out to do.' And he went throughout Galilee, proclaiming the message in their synagogues and casting out demons.

- When Simon's mother-in-law is cured, she does what Jesus himself does. She serves those in need. She becomes a disciple. Well-being of spirit involves a willingness to serve, while spiritual sickness means that I am concerned only about myself. I ask the Lord to make me truly well.

Thursday 13 January
Mark 1:40–45

A leper came to him begging him, and kneeling he said to him, 'If you choose, you can make me clean.' Moved with pity, Jesus stretched out his hand and touched him, and said to him, 'I do choose. Be made clean!' Immediately the leprosy left him, and he was made clean. After sternly warning him he sent him away at once, saying to him, 'See that you say nothing to anyone; but go, show yourself to the priest, and offer for your cleansing what Moses commanded, as a testimony to them.' But he went out and began to proclaim it freely, and to spread the word, so that Jesus could no longer go into a town openly, but stayed out in the country; and people came to him from every quarter.

- The most painful wounds we carry with us from the past are more wounds of the spirit than of the body. Of these spiritual wounds the one that causes us the most pain is the belief that we are insignificant.

In this Gospel story we hear in Jesus' words to the leper his concern to heal this wound we carry with us from the past.

- In your prayer today tell Jesus of some way you were hurt or wounded by something people said or did to you. Listen to how sensitive and responsive he is when he is 'moved with pity' or compassion for you. Tell him how you feel about him being like this.

Friday 14 January
Mark 2:1–12

When he returned to Capernaum after some days, it was reported that he was at home. So many gathered around that there was no longer room for them, not even in front of the door; and he was speaking the word to them. Then some people came, bringing to him a paralysed man, carried by four of them. And when they could not bring him to Jesus because of the crowd, they removed the roof above him; and after having dug through it, they let down the mat on which the paralytic lay. When Jesus saw their faith, he said to the paralytic, 'Son, your sins are forgiven.' Now some of the scribes were sitting there, questioning in their hearts, 'Why does this fellow speak in this way? It is blasphemy! Who can forgive sins but God alone?' At once Jesus perceived in his spirit that they were discussing these questions among themselves; and he said to them, 'Why do you raise such questions in your hearts? Which is easier, to say to the paralytic, "Your sins are forgiven", or to say, "Stand up and take your mat and walk"? But so that you may know that the Son of Man has authority on earth to forgive sins' – he said to the paralytic – 'I say to you, stand up, take your mat and go to your home.' And he stood up, and immediately took the mat and went out before all of them; so that they were all amazed and glorified God, saying, 'We have never seen anything like this!'

- While all the people are amazed and delighted that Jesus heals the man, the religious authorities see that he is a threat to them. As we see later in the Passion, they eventually bring Jesus down, do away with him and return to the status quo in which they alone are in charge.

- I meet up with Jesus when the house is quiet and ask him to explain to me what was going on. He talks with me about the opposition I may face as a true disciple of his.

Saturday 15 January
Mark 2:13–17

Jesus went out again beside the lake; the whole crowd gathered around him, and he taught them. As he was walking along, he saw Levi son of Alphaeus sitting at the tax booth, and he said to him, 'Follow me.' And he got up and followed him.

And as he sat at dinner in Levi's house, many tax-collectors and sinners were also sitting with Jesus and his disciples – for there were many who followed him. When the scribes of the Pharisees saw that he was eating with sinners and tax-collectors, they said to his disciples, 'Why does he eat with tax-collectors and sinners?' When Jesus heard this, he said to them, 'Those who are well have no need of a physician, but those who are sick; I have come to call not the righteous but sinners.'

- In prayer, you might tell Jesus about something that you do not like about yourself. In the light of how comfortable Jesus is in relating to this side of you, see if you can let him put this fault in perspective or help you see it as a small part of the very good person he finds you to be.

The Second Week in Ordinary Time
16–22 January 2022

Something to think and pray about each day this week:

C. S. Lewis says that when he wanted to get a few days off school, he would sit close to a boy who had just got over the measles. If he wanted to get wet, he had to stand in the rain. So, if he wanted to be like God, he had to get close to Jesus. By staying close to you I can become more like you in my loving. Growing in love is hard work, but it needs to happen in me. By staying near you something of you will rub off on me: that will be a good infection indeed! Help me always to want you, like the man who said, 'I must get to him (Jesus) because he belongs to me', or the woman who said, 'If I could only touch the hem of his garment.'

This knowing of you, Jesus, is meant to be a heart-to-heart affair: the more I know how totally your heart is set on me, the more I am drawn to love you in return. You have given yourself over to me; you belong to me and I to you. Help me to believe this.

Brian Grogan SJ,
I Am Infinitely Loved

The Presence of God
God is with me, but even more astounding, God is within me.
Let me dwell for a moment on God's life-giving presence
in my body, in my mind, in my heart,
as I sit here, right now.

Freedom
Lord, may I never take the gift of freedom for granted. You gave me the
great blessing of freedom of spirit. Fill my spirit with your peace and joy.

Consciousness
I remind myself that I am in the presence of God, who is my strength in
times of weakness and my comforter in times of sorrow.

The Word
I take my time to read the word of God slowly a few times, allowing myself to dwell on anything that strikes me.
*(Please turn to the Scripture on the following pages. Inspiration points are there,
should you need them. When you are ready, return here to continue.)*

Conversation
Jesus, you always welcomed little children when you walked on this earth.
Teach me to have a childlike trust in you. Teach me to live in the knowl-
edge that you will never abandon me.

Conclusion
Glory be to the Father, and to the Son and to the Holy Spirit,
As it was in the beginning, is now and ever shall be,
World without end. Amen.

Sunday 16 January
Second Sunday in Ordinary Time
John 2:1–11

On the third day there was a wedding in Cana of Galilee, and the mother of Jesus was there. Jesus and his disciples had also been invited to the wedding. When the wine gave out, the mother of Jesus said to him, 'They have no wine.' And Jesus said to her, 'Woman, what concern is that to you and to me? My hour has not yet come.' His mother said to the servants, 'Do whatever he tells you.' Now standing there were six stone water-jars for the Jewish rites of purification, each holding twenty or thirty gallons. Jesus said to them, 'Fill the jars with water.' And they filled them up to the brim. He said to them, 'Now draw some out, and take it to the chief steward.' So they took it. When the steward tasted the water that had become wine, and did not know where it came from (though the servants who had drawn the water knew), the steward called the bridegroom and said to him, 'Everyone serves the good wine first, and then the inferior wine after the guests have become drunk. But you have kept the good wine until now.' Jesus did this, the first of his signs, in Cana of Galilee, and revealed his glory; and his disciples believed in him.

• According to the Jewish Scriptures, when the Messiah comes there shall be an abundance of new wine, a symbol of God's abundant goodness towards his people. That Jesus turns so much water into the best of wines is a 'sign' that he is in fact the long-awaited Messiah.

Monday 17 January
Mark 2:18–22

Now John's disciples and the Pharisees were fasting; and people came and said to him, 'Why do John's disciples and the disciples of the Pharisees fast, but your disciples do not fast?' Jesus said to them, 'The wedding-guests cannot fast while the bridegroom is with them, can they? As long as they have the bridegroom with them, they cannot fast. The days will come when the bridegroom is taken away from them, and then they will fast on that day.

'No one sews a piece of unshrunk cloth on an old cloak; otherwise, the patch pulls away from it, the new from the old, and a worse tear is made. And no one puts new wine into old wineskins; otherwise, the wine will burst the skins, and the wine is lost, and so are the skins; but one puts new wine into fresh wineskins.'

• People noticed the contrast between two sorts of religion: the Pharisees' preoccupation with laws and regulations, and Jesus' love of celebrations and feasts. In his parables the kingdom of heaven is often a banquet, a wedding, a party: a place of untrammelled joy, not of tight rules. It is so easy for us to reduce the interior life, and the freedom and flame of the Gospels, to a set of pieties and regulations. Jesus would measure our religiousness not in laws but in love. His images here are of freshness: new clothes, new wine. Things are different now that he is among us. A new era has begun.

Tuesday 18 January
Mark 2:23–28

One sabbath he was going through the cornfields; and as they made their way his disciples began to pluck heads of grain. The Pharisees said to him, 'Look, why are they doing what is not lawful on the sabbath?' And he said to them, 'Have you never read what David did when he and his companions were hungry and in need of food? He entered the house of God, when Abiathar was high priest, and ate the bread of the Presence, which it is not lawful for any but the priests to eat, and he gave some to his companions.' Then he said to them, 'The sabbath was made for humankind, and not humankind for the sabbath; so the Son of Man is lord even of the sabbath.'

• Lord, when human need was crying out to you, the law took second place. It seems so obvious that the sabbath, and law, are made for humankind, not vice versa, but it took courage as well as clarity of mind to state the obvious.

Wednesday 19 January
Mark 3:1–6

Again he entered the synagogue, and a man was there who had a withered hand. They watched him to see whether he would cure him on the sabbath, so that they might accuse him. And he said to the man who had the withered hand, 'Come forward.' Then he said to them, 'Is it lawful to do good or to do harm on the sabbath, to save life or to kill?' But they were silent. He looked around at them with anger; he was grieved at their hardness of heart and said to the man, 'Stretch out your hand.' He stretched it out, and his hand was restored. The Pharisees went out and immediately conspired with the Herodians against him, how to destroy him.

• Perhaps when I'm in difficulty and looking for help, people might not always go out of their way for me; they can hide behind 'red tape' and regulations. But Jesus cuts through the 'red tape' – as he did here in the synagogue – and is always ready to help me.

• Jesus can heal me, cure me; provided that I myself am not the obstacle but instead am open to his help.

Thursday 20 January
Mark 3:7–12

Jesus departed with his disciples to the lake, and a great multitude from Galilee followed him; hearing all that he was doing, they came to him in great numbers from Judea, Jerusalem, Idumea, beyond the Jordan, and the region around Tyre and Sidon. He told his disciples to have a boat ready for him because of the crowd, so that they would not crush him; for he had cured many, so that all who had diseases pressed upon him to touch him. Whenever the unclean spirits saw him, they fell down before him and shouted, 'You are the Son of God!' But he sternly ordered them not to make him known.

• Jesus did not seek popularity: he was not looking for 'likes' or 'followers' to bolster his identity. He knew who he was. My identity, too, lies in my being a child of God, in my loving relationship with the source of life.

• The people took notice of what Jesus was doing and turned to him. How does this speak to me in this time of prayer?

Friday 21 January
Mark 3:13–19

He went up the mountain and called to him those whom he wanted, and they came to him. And he appointed twelve, whom he also named apostles, to be with him, and to be sent out to proclaim the message, and to have authority to cast out demons. So he appointed the twelve: Simon (to whom he gave the name Peter); James son of Zebedee and John the brother of James (to whom he gave the name Boanerges, that is, Sons of Thunder); and Andrew, and Philip, and Bartholomew, and Matthew, and Thomas, and James son of Alphaeus, and Thaddaeus, and Simon the Cananaean, and Judas Iscariot, who betrayed him.

• The calling of the twelve is to an active sharing in the life of Jesus. As in all discipleship they are called to be with him, to listen and to learn from his words and life. Further to that, they are sent out to share in what he wants to do for the world. They will share that to their death in most cases. Our calling is similar: to spend time in prayer with the word of God and to share in our own way in the work of Jesus in the world. Each of us finds that within the cluster of our own talents and gifts from God, we are called to make the corner of the world we live in a better place for all. In prayer we can offer that desire to God – we want to be with him in this way as much as he wants us to be with him.

Saturday 22 January
Mark 3:20–21

And the crowd came together again, so that they could not even eat. When his family heard it, they went out to restrain him, for people were saying, 'He has gone out of his mind.'

• Why did people think Jesus had gone out of his mind? Because he had abandoned a secure trade as a carpenter for a wandering life; he had run into trouble with the authorities in what seemed like a deliberate way; he had gathered an odd group of disciples around him. He seemed indifferent to financial and social security and the opinion of others.

• Lord, you ask me to take risks as you did. This is not a comfortable prayer, as I think about what you have in store for me. Give me courage.

The Third Week in Ordinary Time
23–29 January 2022

Something to think and pray about each day this week:

It's in our genes to be in a relationship with God; we share the spiritual genetic make-up of Jesus, our own flesh and blood, by virtue of his sharing in our human experience. The metaphor of longing for God's house suggests all that we're looking for and all that we need. It's the intimacy of being at home with God that gives us purpose and inspires us with a sense of direction through life. Every created reality has the potential to help us grow in friendship with God. Therefore, in our day-to-day living we are required to be impartial in our choices, asking ourselves if the choices we're making serve our goal in life. If they do, we embrace them, if not, we surrender them.

In a sense, it doesn't really matter all that much what position in life we find ourselves in. We can praise God from our hospital bed to the same extent that we can when working hard in a busy airport. There are no limits to the times and places we can welcome God. The world is our oyster, providing a multiplicity of possibilities. We can embrace God as a poor person or as a wealthy person or as any other kind of person. So, if our goal is to welcome God, as Ignatius teaches, we get on with life, making the best decisions possible to implement that objective, wherever we find ourselves, and employing the unique distinctive personality traits we have inherited and developed. We don't have to be any other way than we are to praise God.

Jim Maher SJ,
Pathways to a Decision with Ignatius of Loyola

The Presence of God
God is with me, but more,
God is within me, giving me existence.
Let me dwell for a moment on God's life-giving presence
in my body, my mind, my heart,
and in the whole of my life.

Freedom
Lord, you created me to live in freedom. May your Holy Spirit guide me
to follow you freely. Instill in my heart a desire to know and love you
more each day.

Consciousness
In God's loving presence I unwind the past day,
starting from now and looking back, moment by moment.
I gather in all the goodness and light, in gratitude.
I attend to the shadows and what they say to me,
seeking healing, courage, forgiveness.

The Word
God speaks to each of us individually. I listen attentively to hear what he
is saying to me. Read the text a few times, then listen.
*(Please turn to the Scripture on the following pages. Inspiration points are there,
should you need them. When you are ready, return here to continue.)*

Conversation
Jesus, you always welcomed little children when you walked on this earth.
Teach me to have a childlike trust in you. Teach me to live in the knowledge that you will never abandon me.

Conclusion
I thank God for these moments we have spent together and for any insights I have been given concerning the text.

Sunday 23 January
Third Sunday in Ordinary Time
Luke 1:1–4; 4:14–21

Since many have undertaken to set down an orderly account of the events that have been fulfilled among us, just as they were handed on to us by those who from the beginning were eyewitnesses and servants of the word, I too decided, after investigating everything carefully from the very first, to write an orderly account for you, most excellent Theophilus, so that you may know the truth concerning the things about which you have been instructed. . . .

Then Jesus, filled with the power of the Spirit, returned to Galilee, and a report about him spread through all the surrounding country. He began to teach in their synagogues and was praised by everyone.

When he came to Nazareth, where he had been brought up, he went to the synagogue on the sabbath day, as was his custom. He stood up to read, and the scroll of the prophet Isaiah was given to him. He unrolled the scroll and found the place where it was written:

'The Spirit of the Lord is upon me,
because he has anointed me
to bring good news to the poor.
He has sent me to proclaim release to the captives
and recovery of sight to the blind,
to let the oppressed go free,
to proclaim the year of the Lord's favour.'

And he rolled up the scroll, gave it back to the attendant, and sat down. The eyes of all in the synagogue were fixed on him. Then he began to say to them, 'Today this scripture has been fulfilled in your hearing.'

- A 'year of favour' was a season when God would 'visit his people' – God would come and overturn a situation where his people had been at the mercy of enemies. He would relieve the oppressed, set free the imprisoned, cure the disabled and those who had succumbed to illness. It would be a whole new age – God would lift his people out of their distress.

- Jesus tells his hearers that, with his own coming, God is visiting his people right now. And he's visiting every single one of his people, from that day to this.

Monday 24 January
Mark 3:22–30

And the scribes who came down from Jerusalem said, 'He has Beelzebul, and by the ruler of the demons he casts out demons.' And he called them to him, and spoke to them in parables, 'How can Satan cast out Satan? If a kingdom is divided against itself, that kingdom cannot stand. And if a house is divided against itself, that house will not be able to stand. And if Satan has risen up against himself and is divided, he cannot stand, but his end has come. But no one can enter a strong man's house and plunder his property without first tying up the strong man; then indeed the house can be plundered.

'Truly I tell you, people will be forgiven for their sins and whatever blasphemies they utter; but whoever blasphemes against the Holy Spirit can never have forgiveness, but is guilty of an eternal sin' – for they had said, 'He has an unclean spirit.'

- Passages such as this remind us that the world-view shared by Jesus and his critics was very different from ours in the twenty-first century. We may need to ask, even more insistently than usual, for grace to understand how the story is relevant for us today. Always remember that Mark and the other evangelists are trying to explain who Jesus is and what it means to call him Saviour. That is the heart of the Gospel.

Tuesday 25 January
The Conversion of Saint Paul, Apostle
Mark 16:15–18

And he said to them, 'Go into all the world and proclaim the good news to the whole creation. The one who believes and is baptised will be saved; but the one who does not believe will be condemned. And these signs will accompany those who believe: by using my name they will cast out demons; they will speak in new tongues; they will pick up snakes in their hands, and if they drink any deadly thing, it will not hurt them; they will lay their hands on the sick, and they will recover.'

- Today the Church celebrates the conversion of Saint Paul, the Apostle to the Gentiles. That dramatic event is recorded in the Acts of the Apostles, Chapters 9 and 22.

- Verses 15–18 above are a late addition to Mark's Gospel. In verse 14 Jesus reproached the apostles for not believing the witnesses to his Resurrection, Mary Magdalene or the two disciples at Emmaus. Here he is addressing them and all of us baptised believers. Each one is called by the Lord to 'go and proclaim the good news' of the long-awaited reign of God. I bring justice, respect and goodness to all I live with, work with or meet in the course of my day.

Wednesday 26 January
Mark 4:1–20

Again he began to teach beside the lake. Such a very large crowd gathered around him that he got into a boat on the lake and sat there, while the whole crowd was beside the lake on the land. He began to teach them many things in parables, and in his teaching he said to them: 'Listen! A sower went out to sow. And as he sowed, some seed fell on the path, and the birds came and ate it up. Other seed fell on rocky ground, where it did not have much soil, and it sprang up quickly, since it had no depth of soil. And when the sun rose, it was scorched; and since it had no root, it withered away. Other seed fell among thorns, and the thorns grew up and choked it, and it yielded no grain. Other seed fell into good soil and brought forth grain, growing up and increasing and yielding thirty and sixty and a hundredfold.' And he said, 'Let anyone with ears to hear listen!'

When he was alone, those who were around him along with the twelve asked him about the parables. And he said to them, 'To you has been given the secret of the kingdom of God, but for those outside, everything comes in parables; in order that

"they may indeed look, but not perceive,
and may indeed listen, but not understand;
so that they may not turn again and be forgiven." '

And he said to them, 'Do you not understand this parable? Then how will you understand all the parables? The sower sows the word. These are the ones on the path where the word is sown: when they hear, Satan immediately comes and takes away the word that is sown in them. And these are the ones sown on rocky ground: when they hear the word, they immediately receive it with joy. But they have no root, and endure only for a while; then, when trouble or persecution arises on account of the word, immediately they fall away. And others are those sown among the thorns: these are the ones who hear the word, but the cares of the world, and the lure of wealth, and the desire for other things come in and choke the word, and it yields nothing. And these are the ones sown on the good soil: they hear the word and accept it and bear fruit, thirty and sixty and a hundredfold.'

- In Mark's explanation the seed is the 'word'. Do you recall other biblical references to the 'word'? In what contexts do they occur? Remember Isaiah: 'For as the rain and the snow come down from heaven, and do not return there until they have watered the earth … so shall my word be that goes out from my mouth; it shall not return to me empty … ' (Isaiah 55:10–11). Both Isaiah and Mark associate the word with fruitfulness. Do you see this mystery at work in your own life? In the world around you?

Thursday 27 January
Mark 4:21–25

He said to them, 'Is a lamp brought in to be put under the bushel basket, or under the bed, and not on the lampstand? For there is nothing hidden, except to be disclosed; nor is anything secret, except to come to light. Let anyone with ears to hear listen!' And he said to them, 'Pay attention to what you hear; the measure you give will be the measure you get, and still more will be given you. For to those who have, more will be given; and from those who have nothing, even what they have will be taken away.'

- We understand first that Jesus wants his close followers to let the light of his teaching shine out. Others may choose to remain in the dark, indifferent or hostile.

- The second half of the passage is obscure. It seems to mean that just as the wealthy keep accumulating riches and the poor are consistently deprived, so those with spiritual insight will be further enlightened, while those without it will only fall into worse ignorance.

- Do I allow the light of Christ to shine out before others?

Friday 28 January
Mark 4:26–34

He also said, 'The kingdom of God is as if someone would scatter seed on the ground, and would sleep and rise night and day, and the seed would sprout and grow, he does not know how. The earth produces of itself, first the stalk, then the head, then the full grain in the head. But when the grain is ripe, at once he goes in with his sickle, because the harvest has come.

He also said, 'With what can we compare the kingdom of God, or what parable will we use for it? It is like a mustard seed, which, when sown upon the ground, is the smallest of all the seeds on earth; yet when it is sown it grows up and becomes the greatest of all shrubs, and puts forth large branches, so that the birds of the air can make nests in its shade.'

With many such parables he spoke the word to them, as they were able to hear it; he did not speak to them except in parables, but he explained everything in private to his disciples.

• The mustard seed becomes a tree for all; the kingdom of God is for every man, woman and child. Have you ever brought something of the kingdom of God – of love and peace, prayer and faith, justice and hope – when you didn't recognise it? Let that fill your mind and heart with gratitude as you pray.

Saturday 29 January
Mark 4:35–41

On that day, when evening had come, he said to them, 'Let us go across to the other side.' And leaving the crowd behind, they took him with them in the boat, just as he was. Other boats were with him. A great gale arose, and the waves beat into the boat, so that the boat was already being swamped. But he was in the stern, asleep on the cushion; and they woke him up and said to him, 'Teacher, do you not care that we are perishing?' He woke up and rebuked the wind, and said to the sea, 'Peace! Be still!' Then the wind ceased, and there was a dead calm. He said to them, 'Why are you afraid? Have you still no faith?' And they were filled with great awe and said to one another, 'Who then is this, that even the wind and the sea obey him?'

- In this dramatic episode Mark is warning us that we are moving into a new depth of discipleship. The hostility of Jesus' enemies grows more intense, and will play itself out in his passion and death, when all the disciples will desert him and flee (Mark 14:50). I beg that my faith in him will keep me close to him in the storms that threaten to swamp not only me but the Church, the world and nature itself.

30 January–5 February 2022

Something to think and pray about each day this week:

Like Abraham, who had shown his willingness to sacrifice his son Isaac, Mary offered the life of Jesus to the Father. The difference was that although Abraham did not have to go through with his sacrifice, Mary did. Mary's offering was made at the Presentation, and would eventually be fulfilled on Calvary. In the silence of Mary's heart, something deep, beautiful and heroic was unfolding. That's because Mary lived love, and the heart of love is to give ourselves. She gave fully of herself, already, in advance, thus imitating the sacrificial love of Jesus. We could all learn from this gentle woman to give of ourselves more and more generously to God.

Despite the sorrow Mary felt at this moment, there is no suggestion that she was a sorrowful kind of person, or that she had a disheartening influence upon her son. Her sorrowful experiences did not burden her with a pessimistic outlook, and they did not make her unequal to the various challenges she had to face over the course of her life. Mary was a woman of hope. Just as Jesus would later turn water into wine at Mary's request, God seems to have given this most blessed among women the disarming grace of transforming even sorrow into joy. She needed this kind of resilience, because she was about to be completely uprooted from her country, culture and people.

Thomas Casey SJ,
Smile of Joy: Mary of Nazareth

The Presence of God

I pause for a moment and think of the love and the grace that God showers on me. I am created in the image and likeness of God; I am God's dwelling place.

Freedom

I am free. When I look at these words in writing, they seem to create in me a feeling of awe. Yes, a wonderful feeling of freedom. Thank you, God.

Consciousness

In the presence of my loving Creator, I look honestly at my feelings over the past day: the highs, the lows and the level ground. Can I see where the Lord has been present?

The Word

I read the word of God slowly, a few times over, and I listen to what God is saying to me.

(Please turn to the Scripture on the following pages. Inspiration points are there, should you need them. When you are ready, return here to continue.)

Conversation

Remembering that I am still in God's presence,
I imagine Jesus standing or sitting beside me,
and I say whatever is on my mind, whatever is in my heart,
speaking as one friend to another.

Conclusion

Glory be to the Father, and to the Son, and to the Holy Spirit,
As it was in the beginning, is now and ever shall be,
World without end. Amen.

Sunday 30 January
Fourth Sunday in Ordinary Time
Luke 4:21–30

Then he began to say to them, 'Today this scripture has been fulfilled in your hearing.' All spoke well of him and were amazed at the gracious words that came from his mouth. They said, 'Is not this Joseph's son?' He said to them, 'Doubtless you will quote to me this proverb, "Doctor, cure yourself!" And you will say, "Do here also in your home town the things that we have heard you did at Capernaum."' And he said, 'Truly I tell you, no prophet is accepted in the prophet's home town. But the truth is, there were many widows in Israel in the time of Elijah, when the heaven was shut up for three years and six months, and there was a severe famine over all the land; yet Elijah was sent to none of them except to a widow at Zarephath in Sidon. There were also many lepers in Israel in the time of the prophet Elisha, and none of them was cleansed except Naaman the Syrian.' When they heard this, all in the synagogue were filled with rage. They got up, drove him out of the town, and led him to the brow of the hill on which their town was built, so that they might hurl him off the cliff. But he passed through the midst of them and went on his way.

• Why did the assembly turn on Jesus? Simply because what he said about the prophets Elijah and Elisha implied that God's offer of salvation was no longer restricted to Jews but extended to Gentiles as well. Such an implication was anathema to those who thought of themselves as God's 'chosen people'.

• Is my Christian belief so restricted that I fail to see that God's choice is wider than mine?

Monday 31 January
Mark 5:1–20

They came to the other side of the lake, to the country of the Gerasenes. And when he had stepped out of the boat, immediately a man out of the tombs with an unclean spirit met him. He lived among the tombs; and no one could restrain him any more, even with a chain; for he had often been restrained with shackles and chains, but the chains he wrenched apart, and the shackles he broke in pieces; and no one had the strength to subdue him. Night and day among the tombs and on the mountains he was always howling and bruising himself with stones. When he saw Jesus from a distance, he ran and bowed down before him; and he shouted at the top of his voice, 'What have you to do with me, Jesus, Son of the Most High God? I adjure you by God, do not torment me.' For he had said to him, 'Come out of the man, you unclean spirit!' Then Jesus asked him, 'What is your name?' He replied, 'My name is Legion; for we are many.' He begged him earnestly not to send them out of the country. Now there on the hillside a great herd of swine was feeding; and the unclean spirits begged him, 'Send us into the swine; let us enter them.' So he gave them permission. And the unclean spirits came out and entered the swine; and the herd, numbering about two thousand, rushed down the steep bank into the lake, and were drowned in the lake.

The swineherds ran off and told it in the city and in the country. Then people came to see what it was that had happened. They came to Jesus and saw the demoniac sitting there, clothed and in his right mind, the very man who had had the legion; and they were afraid. Those who had seen what had happened to the demoniac and to the swine reported it. Then they began to beg Jesus to leave their neighbourhood. As he was getting into the boat, the man who had been possessed by demons begged him that he might be with him. But Jesus refused, and said to him, 'Go home to your friends, and tell them how much the Lord has done for you, and what mercy he has shown you.' And he went away and began to proclaim in the Decapolis how much Jesus had done for him; and everyone was amazed.

- How might a person pray with this Gospel? Remember to keep your attention on Jesus. As he exercises his power over evil spirits he is revealing who he really is. That is the main point of the story. And if you find yourself uncomprehending or disturbed by some of the details, bring your reactions to Jesus and ask him to enlighten you. He is the source, not only of power, but of compassion.

Tuesday 1 February
Mark 5:21–43

When Jesus had crossed again in the boat to the other side, a great crowd gathered round him; and he was by the lake. Then one of the leaders of the synagogue named Jairus came and, when he saw him, fell at his feet and begged him repeatedly, 'My little daughter is at the point of death. Come and lay your hands on her, so that she may be made well, and live.' So he went with him.

And a large crowd followed him and pressed in on him. Now there was a woman who had been suffering from haemorrhages for twelve years. She had endured much under many physicians, and had spent all that she had; and she was no better, but rather grew worse. She had heard about Jesus, and came up behind him in the crowd and touched his cloak, for she said, 'If I but touch his clothes, I will be made well.' Immediately her haemorrhage stopped; and she felt in her body that she was healed of her disease. Immediately aware that power had gone forth from him, Jesus turned about in the crowd and said, 'Who touched my clothes?' And his disciples said to him, 'You see the crowd pressing in on you; how can you say, "Who touched me?"' He looked all round to see who had done it. But the woman, knowing what had happened to her, came in fear and trembling, fell down before him, and told him the whole truth. He said to her, 'Daughter, your faith has made you well; go in peace, and be healed of your disease.'

While he was still speaking, some people came from the leader's house to say, 'Your daughter is dead. Why trouble the teacher any further?' But overhearing what they said, Jesus said to the leader of the synagogue, 'Do not fear, only believe.' He allowed no one to follow him except Peter, James, and John, the brother of James. When they came to the house of the leader of the synagogue, he saw a commotion, people weeping and wailing loudly. When he had entered, he said to them, 'Why do you make a commotion and weep? The child is not dead but sleeping.' And they laughed at him. Then he put them all outside, and took the child's father and mother and those who were with him, and went in where the child was. He took her by the hand and said to her, 'Talitha cum', which means, 'Little girl, get up!' And immediately the girl got up and began to walk about (she was twelve years of age). At this they were overcome with amazement. He strictly ordered them that no one should know this, and told them to give her something to eat.

• What strikes us about Jesus in this reading is his willingness to help those who are in need of his help. He is always sensitive to where people are and to what they need and is most practical in his concern for us.

- If you wish to dwell with Jesus being like this for you now, you might let him be tuned into where you are in a sensitive way. Likewise you might allow yourself to be with him as one who is attuned to your needs and does not impose his desires on you.

Wednesday 2 February
The Presentation of the Lord
Luke 2:22–40

When the time came for their purification according to the law of Moses, they brought him up to Jerusalem to present him to the Lord (as it is written in the law of the Lord, 'Every firstborn male shall be designated as holy to the Lord'), and they offered a sacrifice according to what is stated in the law of the Lord, 'a pair of turtle-doves or two young pigeons'.

Now there was a man in Jerusalem whose name was Simeon; this man was righteous and devout, looking forward to the consolation of Israel, and the Holy Spirit rested on him. It had been revealed to him by the Holy Spirit that he would not see death before he had seen the Lord's Messiah. Guided by the Spirit, Simeon came into the temple; and when the parents brought in the child Jesus, to do for him what was customary under the law, Simeon took him in his arms and praised God, saying,

> 'Master, now you are dismissing your servant in peace,
> according to your word;
> for my eyes have seen your salvation,
> which you have prepared in the presence of all peoples,
> a light for revelation to the Gentiles
> and for glory to your people Israel.'

And the child's father and mother were amazed at what was being said about him. Then Simeon blessed them and said to his mother Mary, 'This child is destined for the falling and the rising of many in Israel, and to be a sign that will be opposed so that the inner thoughts of many will be revealed – and a sword will pierce your own soul too.'

There was also a prophet, Anna the daughter of Phanuel, of the tribe of Asher. She was of a great age, having lived with her husband for seven years after her marriage, then as a widow to the age of eighty-four. She never left the temple but worshipped there with fasting and prayer night and day. At that moment she came, and began to praise God and to speak about the child to all who were looking for the redemption of Jerusalem.

When they had finished everything required by the law of the Lord, they returned to Galilee, to their own town of Nazareth. The child grew and became strong, filled with wisdom; and the favour of God was upon him.

- The mixture of the old and the young: Mary and Joseph left the temple with a greater idea of what their son would be. He would be a light for the world, and glory for his people. The light would come from the darkness of death and the glory from the newness of risen life. With those words of hope for their child, and also indeed future suffering, they went back home. Almost thirty years of the Lord's life is described here in just one line.

Thursday 3 February
Mark 6:7–13

He called the twelve and began to send them out two by two, and gave them authority over the unclean spirits. He ordered them to take nothing for their journey except a staff; no bread, no bag, no money in their belts; but to wear sandals and not to put on two tunics. He said to them, 'Wherever you enter a house, stay there until you leave the place. If any place will not welcome you and they refuse to hear you, as you leave, shake off the dust that is on your feet as a testimony against them.' So they went out and proclaimed that all should repent. They cast out many demons, and anointed with oil many who were sick and cured them.

- The teaching that God's love is present in welcoming strangers and neighbours has been a strong belief in many cultures. The Indian writer Rabindranath Tagore tells us that when people left his hut, he found 'God's footsteps on the floor'. The divine lives in each of us, and when we welcome each other we welcome God, and Jesus the Son of God. This is the welcome of the Church to all. Too often the Church has been choosy about who to welcome or not welcome to the table of the Lord or even to the community. Our country can be overly particular in welcoming the stranger in need. A call to the Church today is to welcome all and be enriched by the variety of prayer, friendship and worship that all can bring.

Friday 4 February
Mark 6:14–29

King Herod heard of it, for Jesus' name had become known. Some were saying, 'John the baptiser has been raised from the dead; and for this reason these powers are at work in him.' But others said, 'It is Elijah.' And others said, 'It is a prophet, like one of the prophets of old.' But when Herod heard of it, he said, 'John, whom I beheaded, has been raised.'

For Herod himself had sent men who arrested John, bound him, and put him in prison on account of Herodias, his brother Philip's wife, because Herod had married her. For John had been telling Herod, 'It is not lawful for you to have your brother's wife.' And Herodias had a grudge against him, and wanted to kill him. But she could not, for Herod feared John, knowing that he was a righteous and holy man, and he protected him. When he heard him, he was greatly perplexed; and yet he liked to listen to him. But an opportunity came when Herod on his birthday gave a banquet for his courtiers and officers and for the leaders of Galilee. When the daughter of Herodias came in and danced, she pleased Herod and his guests; and the king said to the girl, 'Ask me for whatever you wish, and I will give it.' And he solemnly swore to her, 'Whatever you ask me, I will give you, even half of my kingdom.' She went out and said to her mother, 'What should I ask for?' She replied, 'The head of John the baptiser.' Immediately she rushed back to the king and requested, 'I want you to give me at once the head of John the Baptist on a platter.' The king was deeply grieved; yet out of regard for his oaths and for the guests, he did not want to refuse her. Immediately the king sent a soldier of the guard with orders to bring John's head. He went and beheaded him in the prison, brought his head on a platter, and gave it to the girl. Then the girl gave it to her mother. When his disciples heard about it, they came and took his body, and laid it in a tomb.

• The only response to this story is horror. We think of how Jesus must have felt – John was beheaded because of his name becoming known. This horror reminds us of the persecution of many people today in the name of Jesus. May our hearts reach out in compassion for all who are imprisoned or tortured or separated from family in the cause of what is right and good.

Saturday 5 February
Mark 6:30–34

The apostles gathered around Jesus, and told him all that they had done and taught. He said to them, 'Come away to a deserted place all by yourselves and rest a while.' For many were coming and going, and they had no leisure even to eat. And they went away in the boat to a deserted place by themselves. Now many saw them going and recognised them, and they hurried there on foot from all the towns and arrived ahead of them. As he went ashore, he saw a great crowd; and he had compassion for them, because they were like sheep without a shepherd; and he began to teach them many things.

• He searched for them with compassion. This is a big word in the kingdom of God. Compassion received and offered out of personal knowledge. Compassion is entering into the joyful and sad world of another so that we feel with them. We may not know exactly how others feel, but we can accompany them.

The Fifth Week in Ordinary Time
6–12 February 2022

Something to think and pray about each day this week:

In the vast expanse of the universe, we are tiny insignificant specks of dust. Our lives are eighty or ninety years. Set against the estimated 13.8 billion years of the existence of this universe, that is a brief moment. In truth, there is nothing intrinsically significant about what we are, who we are, how we live or why we live. *The Hitchhiker's Guide to the Galaxy* famously described our entire planet in a single word – 'harmless'.

What Jesus offers is the converse of that: a relationship with God, the creator and sustainer of this entire universe. A relationship that gives us our place in the world, in the whole cosmos; we are baptised, anointed children of the creator God. That is the only credible source of hope in our feeble and passing world, our only reasonable expectation that the little we have and the little we are can actually mean something worthwhile. Ultimately, it is the only thing in this world that is actually worth having.

Paul O'Reilly SJ,
Hope in All Things

The Presence of God

I pause for a moment and think of the love and the grace that God showers on me. I am created in the image and likeness of God; I am God's dwelling place.

Freedom

Lord, you granted me the great gift of freedom. In these times, O Lord, grant that I may be free from any form of racism or intolerance. Remind me that we are all equal in your loving eyes.

Consciousness

Knowing that God loves me unconditionally, I can afford to be honest about how I am.
How has the day been, and how do I feel now? I share my feelings openly with the Lord.

The Word

I take my time to read the word of God slowly, a few times, allowing myself to dwell on anything that strikes me.
(Please turn to the Scripture on the following pages. Inspiration points are there, should you need them. When you are ready, return here to continue.)

Conversation

Sometimes I wonder what I might say if I were to meet you in person, Lord. I think I might say, 'Thank you' because you are always there for me.

Conclusion

I thank God for these moments we have spent together and for any insights I have been given concerning the text.

Sunday 6 February
Fifth Sunday in Ordinary Time
Luke 5:1–11

Once while Jesus was standing beside the lake of Gennesaret, and the crowd was pressing in on him to hear the word of God, he saw two boats there at the shore of the lake; the fishermen had gone out of them and were washing their nets. He got into one of the boats, the one belonging to Simon, and asked him to put out a little way from the shore. Then he sat down and taught the crowds from the boat. When he had finished speaking, he said to Simon, 'Put out into the deep water and let down your nets for a catch.' Simon answered, 'Master, we have worked all night long but have caught nothing. Yet if you say so, I will let down the nets.' When they had done this, they caught so many fish that their nets were beginning to break. So they signalled to their partners in the other boat to come and help them. And they came and filled both boats, so that they began to sink. But when Simon Peter saw it, he fell down at Jesus' knees, saying, 'Go away from me, Lord, for I am a sinful man!' For he and all who were with him were amazed at the catch of fish that they had taken; and so also were James and John, sons of Zebedee, who were partners with Simon. Then Jesus said to Simon, 'Do not be afraid; from now on you will be catching people.' When they had brought their boats to shore, they left everything and followed him.

- Peter knows better than Jesus. Are there occasions when I believe that life should be different for myself or others; that God should have arranged things differently? Think of occasions when you were thinking in this way and speak to the Lord about them.

Monday 7 February
Mark 6:53–56

When they had crossed over, they came to land at Gennesaret and moored the boat. When they got out of the boat, people at once recognised him, and rushed about that whole region and began to bring the sick on mats to wherever they heard he was. And wherever he went, into villages or cities or farms, they laid the sick in the market-places, and begged him that they might touch even the fringe of his cloak; and all who touched it were healed.

- They came to him in their numbers because they wanted something from him, a cure for themselves or their sick. We come to prayer often with our needs. We can come to prayer also to know what we might do for Jesus, or what he might do through us. Discipleship brings us into both friendship and partnership. We are grateful for both these callings, knowing that every time we meet the Lord, we are healed and strengthened.

Tuesday 8 February
Mark 7:1–13

Now when the Pharisees and some of the scribes who had come from Jerusalem gathered around him, they noticed that some of his disciples were eating with defiled hands, that is, without washing them. (For the Pharisees, and all the Jews, do not eat unless they thoroughly wash their hands, thus observing the tradition of the elders; and they do not eat anything from the market unless they wash it; and there are also many other traditions that they observe, the washing of cups, pots, and bronze kettles.) So the Pharisees and the scribes asked him, 'Why do your disciples not live according to the tradition of the elders, but eat with defiled hands?' He said to them, 'Isaiah prophesied rightly about you hypocrites, as it is written,

"This people honours me with their lips,
but their hearts are far from me;
in vain do they worship me,
teaching human precepts as doctrines.'
You abandon the commandment of God and hold to human
 tradition."'

Then he said to them, 'You have a fine way of rejecting the commandment of God in order to keep your tradition! For Moses said, "Honour your father and your mother"; and, "Whoever speaks evil of father or mother must surely die." But you say that if anyone tells father or mother, "Whatever support you might have had from me is Corban" (that is, an offering to God) – then you no longer permit doing anything for a father or mother, thus making void the word of God through your tradition that you have handed on. And you do many things like this.'

- Let's just pray at the end of this Gospel – a way of honouring our parents is to be grateful for them, for the gift of life and all the best things in life we learned from them and from our family. Sometime today, perhaps you could make a 'thanks list' and present this in prayer to God.

Wednesday 9 February
Mark 7:14–23

Then he called the crowd again and said to them, 'Listen to me, all of you, and understand: there is nothing outside a person that by going in can defile, but the things that come out are what defile.'

When he had left the crowd and entered the house, his disciples asked him about the parable. He said to them, 'Then do you also fail to understand? Do you not see that whatever goes into a person from outside cannot defile, since it enters, not the heart but the stomach, and goes out into the sewer?' (Thus he declared all foods clean.) And he said, 'It is what comes out of a person that defiles. For it is from within, from the human heart, that evil intentions come: fornication, theft, murder, adultery, avarice, wickedness, deceit, licentiousness, envy, slander, pride, folly. All these evil things come from within, and they defile a person.'

- For Jesus, the battlefield between good and evil is the human heart, and my heart is included! How clean is my heart? In Psalm 51 I ask God to create in me a clean heart. It is not something I can do on my own, much as I try to be respectable before I meet with God in prayer.

- Lord, you list twelve 'evil intentions' that defile a person. Reveal to me the one I need to address right now!

Thursday 10 February
Mark 7:24–30

From there he set out and went away to the region of Tyre. He entered a house and did not want anyone to know he was there. Yet he could not escape notice, but a woman whose little daughter had an unclean spirit immediately heard about him, and she came and bowed down at his feet. Now the woman was a Gentile, of Syrophoenician origin. She begged him to cast the demon out of her daughter. He said to her, 'Let the children be fed first, for it is not fair to take the children's food and throw it to the dogs.' But she answered him, 'Sir, even the dogs under the table eat the children's crumbs.' Then he said to her, 'For saying that, you may go – the demon has left your daughter.' So she went home, found the child lying on the bed, and the demon gone.

- The theologian Karl Rahner SJ was once asked whether he believed in miracles. His answer: 'I don't believe in them, I rely on them to get through each day!' Indeed, miracles are always present within our lives, miracles of birth, of love and of hope. The way people can let go of hurt and forgive. Someone giving a lot from the little they have. It is the world of mystery – of little miracles. A miracle is not against nature – it is something that causes faith and love.

Friday 11 February
Mark 7:31–37

Then he returned from the region of Tyre, and went by way of Sidon towards the Sea of Galilee, in the region of the Decapolis. They brought to him a deaf man who had an impediment in his speech; and they begged him to lay his hand on him. He took him aside in private, away from the crowd, and put his fingers into his ears, and he spat and touched his tongue. Then looking up to heaven, he sighed and said to him, 'Ephphatha', that is, 'Be opened.' And immediately his ears were opened, his tongue was released, and he spoke plainly. Then Jesus ordered them to tell no one; but the more he ordered them, the more zealously they proclaimed it. They were astounded beyond measure, saying, 'He has done everything well; he even makes the deaf to hear and the mute to speak.'

- Most of Jesus' life is about the ordinary and is lived among people who are sick, depressed, worried about the future, hiding their shame of the past, losing faith and getting it back. People who lose a loved one in death, or who are involved in family misunderstandings, hungry and thirsty people etc. Imagine Jesus touches your ear. He clears resistance and you hear love, for the touch of Jesus on your ear is the touch of love, of life, of new hearing. His touch on the tongue gave the life of new speech and new freedom to a stammering man.

Saturday 12 February
Mark 8:1–10

In those days when there was again a great crowd without anything to eat, he called his disciples and said to them, 'I have compassion for the crowd, because they have been with me now for three days and have nothing to eat. If I send them away hungry to their homes, they will faint on the way – and some of them have come from a great distance.' His disciples replied, 'How can one feed these people with bread here in the desert?' He asked them, 'How many loaves do you have?' They said, 'Seven.' Then he ordered the crowd to sit down on the ground; and he took the seven loaves, and after giving thanks he broke them and gave them to his disciples to distribute; and they distributed them to the crowd. They had also a few small fish; and after blessing them, he ordered that these too should be distributed. They ate and were filled; and they took up the broken pieces left over, seven baskets full. Now there were about four thousand people. And he sent them away. And immediately he got into the boat with his disciples and went to the district of Dalmanutha.

- We are still being fed with the leftovers! Jesus feeds us with his word and with his body and blood. His word is the truth that enlightens our minds and at times sets us free. His body is our food for the journey of life, drawing us into the closest tender intimacy possible. Give thanks today for your favourite gift from Jesus in today's Gospel – a phrase, a word, a sentence, something that encourages and gives meaning to your life.

The Sixth Week in Ordinary Time
13–19 February 2022

Something to think and pray about each day this week:

Faith gives an answer to questions like: why do we exist? What is the meaning of life? Why is there something instead of nothing? Nuclear physics, chemistry or mathematics can't answer those questions. That is not their domain. The question the scientist wants to answer is *how* our world works. For centuries people thought and believed that they could find the answer to that question in the Bible. It has only been a few centuries since Christians started to disassemble these questions, an unravelling that is still going on.

Many people say that they believed as a child, but that they lost their faith when they discovered science. One of the reasons for this is that many people's knowledge of faith has been limited to the knowledge they had of it when they were children. It is not surprising that such a belief is undermined by the confrontation with scientific thinking. For others, it is precisely the practice of science that is the starting point of a path of faith: who or what is at the origin of this incredibly beautiful cosmos?

Nikolaas Sintobin SJ,
Did Jesus Really Exist? And 51 Other Questions

The Presence of God
I pause for a moment
and reflect on God's life-giving presence
in every part of my body,
in everything around me,
in the whole of my life.

Freedom
Many countries are at this moment suffering the agonies of war. I bow my head in thanksgiving for my freedom. I pray for all prisoners and captives.

Consciousness
Knowing that God loves me unconditionally, I look honestly over the past day, its events and my feelings. Do I have something to be grateful for? Then I give thanks. Is there something I am sorry for? Then I ask forgiveness.

The Word
Now I turn to the Scripture set out for me this day. I read slowly over the words and see if any sentence or sentiment appeals to me.
(Please turn to the Scripture on the following pages. Inspiration points are there, should you need them. When you are ready, return here to continue.)

Conversation
I know with certainty that there were times when you carried me, Lord. There were times when it was through your strength that I got through the dark times in my life.

Conclusion
Glory be to the Father, and to the Son, and to the Holy Spirit,
As it was in the beginning, is now and ever shall be,
World without end. Amen.

Sunday 13 February
Sixth Sunday in Ordinary time
Luke 6:17.20–26

He came down with them and stood on a level place, with a great crowd of his disciples and a great multitude of people from all Judea, Jerusalem, and the coast of Tyre and Sidon. . . .
    Then he looked up at his disciples and said:

    'Blessed are you who are poor,
        for yours is the kingdom of God.
    'Blessed are you who are hungry now,
        for you will be filled.
    'Blessed are you who weep now,
        for you will laugh.
    'Blessed are you when people hate you, and when they exclude you, revile you, and defame you on account of the Son of Man. Rejoice on that day and leap for joy, for surely your reward is great in heaven; for that is what their ancestors did to the prophets.
    'But woe to you who are rich,
        for you have received your consolation.
    'Woe to you who are full now,
        for you will be hungry.
    'Woe to you who are laughing now,
        for you will mourn and weep.
    'Woe to you when all speak well of you, for that is what their ancestors did to the false prophets.'

- Happy are the unhappy, Jesus seems to be saying! What can he mean? 'Blessed' means the condition of being righteous before God, of living as one should before God. The poor are not only those who are economically poor, but include those who have been marginalised in any way in society. They are blessed because God is on their side, as opposed to the 'rich', who often hold them in contempt and oppress them. Jesus is appealing for love and respect for all those who are outside one's social milieu.

Monday 14 February
Mark 8:11–13

The Pharisees came and began to argue with him, asking him for a sign from heaven, to test him. And he sighed deeply in his spirit and said, 'Why does this generation ask for a sign? Truly I tell you, no sign will be given to this generation.' And he left them, and getting into the boat again, he went across to the other side.

- Lord, do we make you 'sigh deeply'? You do everything for us, and still we want more. First, you love us limitlessly. Pope Francis reminds us of this: 'When everything is said and done, we are infinitely loved.' How about that! Next, each of us is a brother or sister for whom you willingly died. Next, you are with us always: everything that is good in our lives comes from you. Finally, you have breathtaking and glorious plans for our future after death.

- Lord, let me see everything that is good around me, including nature, as the signs that I was seeking. Let me be grateful and use my energy in building the better world I desire.

Tuesday 15 February
Mark 8:14–21

Now the disciples had forgotten to bring any bread; and they had only one loaf with them in the boat. And he cautioned them, saying, 'Watch out – beware of the yeast of the Pharisees and the yeast of Herod.' They said to one another, 'It is because we have no bread.' And becoming aware of it, Jesus said to them, 'Why are you talking about having no bread? Do you still not perceive or understand? Are your hearts hardened? Do you have eyes, and fail to see? Do you have ears, and fail to hear? And do you not remember? When I broke the five loaves for the five thousand, how many baskets full of broken pieces did you collect?' They said to him, 'Twelve.' 'And the seven for the four thousand, how many baskets full of broken pieces did you collect?' And they said to him, 'Seven.' Then he said to them, 'Do you not yet understand?'

- The disciples seem to still have one-track minds – fantasising scenes of future political glory which seemed to be heralded by the popularity of Jesus in the wake of the miracle of the feeding the four thousand. When he tries to warn them against the expectations raised by the

Pharisees and by Herod (yeast was the raising agent used in baking), they can hear his words only as something like a warning against themselves again running short of bread.

• What they are missing out on is this: The only real future is the future that has already arrived before their eyes (and not any good-time future offered by politicians). The Lord Of The Future is already present among them: how else is one to explain the sheer liberality of the mass feeding that has happened before their very eyes?

Wednesday 16 February
Mark 8:22–26

They came to Bethsaida. Some people brought a blind man to him and begged him to touch him. He took the blind man by the hand and led him out of the village; and when he had put saliva on his eyes and laid his hands on him, he asked him, 'Can you see anything?' And the man looked up and said, 'I can see people, but they look like trees, walking.' Then Jesus laid his hands on his eyes again; and he looked intently and his sight was restored, and he saw everything clearly. Then he sent him away to his home, saying, 'Do not even go into the village.'

• Jesus is beginning to teach his disciples that he will soon be put to death, but the disciples cannot take in this bad news. Mark's stories about blind people and their cures suggest that disciples may only slowly come to see that Jesus cannot be understood or appreciated apart from the mystery of his cross.

• With this in mind, you can identify with this blind man. Ask Jesus to help you to see him properly; allow him to minister to you as he did to this blind man. Then beg him to help you to accept the mystery of the passion – in his life, in your own life and in the story of the world.

Thursday 17 February
Mark 8:27–33

Jesus went on with his disciples to the villages of Caesarea Philippi; and on the way he asked his disciples, 'Who do people say that I am?' And they answered him, 'John the Baptist; and others, Elijah; and still others, one of the prophets.' He asked them, 'But who do you say that I am?'

Peter answered him, 'You are the Messiah.' And he sternly ordered them not to tell anyone about him.

Then he began to teach them that the Son of Man must undergo great suffering, and be rejected by the elders, the chief priests, and the scribes, and be killed, and after three days rise again. He said all this quite openly. And Peter took him aside and began to rebuke him. But turning and looking at his disciples, he rebuked Peter and said, 'Get behind me, Satan! For you are setting your mind not on divine things but on human things.'

- Lord, when I fail to understand your ways, don't lose hope in me. May I heed your call to 'get behind you' like a good disciple following the Master. Strengthen me in times of suffering: may I patiently bear unavoidable suffering, as you did. May I believe that what I endure helps in the saving of the world.

Friday 18 February

Mark 8:34–9:1

He called the crowd with his disciples, and said to them, 'If any want to become my followers, let them deny themselves and take up their cross and follow me. For those who want to save their life will lose it, and those who lose their life for my sake, and for the sake of the Gospel, will save it. For what will it profit them to gain the whole world and forfeit their life? Indeed, what can they give in return for their life? Those who are ashamed of me and of my words in this adulterous and sinful generation, of them the Son of Man will also be ashamed when he comes in the glory of his Father with the holy angels.' And he said to them, 'Truly I tell you, there are some standing here who will not taste death until they see that the kingdom of God has come with power.'

- Two crosses await each of us in this life: the cross of the world and the cross of Christ. We have to choose. The cross of the world has an insidious appeal. It appears as a shortcut to happiness and, at the start, easily carried. But it becomes heavy and more disappointing as time passes. The cross of Christ appears difficult and challenging at the start. But it gets easier, if carried faithfully, over the years. Eventually, it will bring us to a happiness without end.

Saturday 19 February
Mark 9:2–13

Six days later, Jesus took with him Peter and James and John, and led them up a high mountain apart, by themselves. And he was transfigured before them, and his clothes became dazzling white, such as no one on earth could bleach them. And there appeared to them Elijah with Moses, who were talking with Jesus. Then Peter said to Jesus, 'Rabbi, it is good for us to be here; let us make three dwellings, one for you, one for Moses, and one for Elijah.' He did not know what to say, for they were terrified. Then a cloud overshadowed them, and from the cloud there came a voice, 'This is my Son, the Beloved; listen to him!' Suddenly when they looked around, they saw no one with them any more, but only Jesus.

As they were coming down the mountain, he ordered them to tell no one about what they had seen, until after the Son of Man had risen from the dead. So they kept the matter to themselves, questioning what this rising from the dead could mean. Then they asked him, 'Why do the scribes say that Elijah must come first?' He said to them, 'Elijah is indeed coming first to restore all things. How then is it written about the Son of Man, that he is to go through many sufferings and be treated with contempt? But I tell you that Elijah has come, and they did to him whatever they pleased, as it is written about him.'

- This incident on the mountain gets us to look forward either to the resurrection of Jesus or the glory of the second coming. Peter's reaction also gets us to look forward to life with God, so that we will say in eternity, 'It is good for us to be here'. In prayer we can rest at times and just be glad, happy and content to be with Jesus, in his presence and in his love. The transfiguration was for the benefit of the disciples, for their faith and confidence in the lasting glory of Jesus at bad times. It can be the same for each of us in prayer.

20–26 February 2022

Something to think and pray about each day this week:

The theologian Karl Rahner remarked in the 1980s that the Christian of the future will be a mystic or will not be a Christian at all. Are you becoming a mini-mystic by now? It is important that you are, and it is also a thrilling development in you.

The popular image of a mystic is of someone who spends a lot of time alone in solitary prayer, cut off from the distracting world. The mysticism of nature, however, is a gift for everyone in the audience! You may not be a person who spends much time alone with God but as you contemplate nature are you growing in wonder, in awareness that every bit of creation is singing a song to you, and is inviting you to catch on to its melody? Do feelings of awe arise in you as you spend little moments now and then marvelling at what nature keeps coming up with? When you worry about the messiness of life can you envelop it in gratitude for the steadiness of nature's laws of growth? Can you hope that perhaps God hasn't abandoned this chaotic world of ours to its own destructive devices but is creatively at work to bring it to its intended beauty?

All you have to do is to look long and lovingly at creation, and let it speak to your heart. Do this for a while today, and you will experience what it is like 'to live joyfully in God's love and hope'. Every garden is a divine schoolroom.

Brian Grogan SJ,
Finding God in a Leaf: The Mysticism of Laudato Si'

The Presence of God
I remind myself that I am in the presence of God, who is my strength in times of weakness and my comforter in times of sorrow.

Freedom
Saint Ignatius thought that a thick and shapeless tree trunk would never believe that it could become a statue, admired as a miracle of sculpture, and would never submit itself to the chisel of the sculptor, who sees by her genius what she can make of it. I ask for the grace to let myself be shaped by my loving Creator.

Consciousness
Dear Lord, help me to remember that you gave me life. Teach me to slow down, to be still and enjoy the pleasures created for me. To be aware of the beauty that surrounds me: the marvel of mountains, the calmness of lakes, the fragility of a flower petal. I need to remember that all these things come from you.

The Word
In this expectant state of mind, please turn to the text for the day with confidence. Believe that the Holy Spirit is present and may reveal whatever the passage has to say to you. Read reflectively, listening with a third ear to what may be going on in your heart.
(Please turn to the Scripture on the following pages. Inspiration points are there, should you need them. When you are ready, return here to continue.)

Conversation
What feelings are rising in me as I pray and reflect on God's word? I imagine Jesus himself sitting or standing near me, and I open my heart to him.

Conclusion
I thank God for these moments we have spent together and for any insights I have been given concerning the text.

Sunday 20 February
Seventh Sunday in Ordinary Time
Luke 6:27–38

'But I say to you that listen, Love your enemies, do good to those who hate you, bless those who curse you, pray for those who abuse you. If anyone strikes you on the cheek, offer the other also; and from anyone who takes away your coat do not withhold even your shirt. Give to everyone who begs from you; and if anyone takes away your goods, do not ask for them again. Do to others as you would have them do to you.

'If you love those who love you, what credit is that to you? For even sinners love those who love them. If you do good to those who do good to you, what credit is that to you? For even sinners do the same. If you lend to those from whom you hope to receive, what credit is that to you? Even sinners lend to sinners, to receive as much again. But love your enemies, do good, and lend, expecting nothing in return. Your reward will be great, and you will be children of the Most High; for he is kind to the ungrateful and the wicked. Be merciful, just as your Father is merciful.

'Do not judge, and you will not be judged; do not condemn, and you will not be condemned. Forgive, and you will be forgiven; give, and it will be given to you. A good measure, pressed down, shaken together, running over, will be put into your lap; for the measure you give will be the measure you get back.'

* Perhaps it is not so much that I am asked to imitate God's compassion as to be a channel for it. I pray that I may be open, transparent and free in letting the image of God in which I am created be seen and experienced.

Monday 21 February
Mark 9:14–29

When they came to the disciples, they saw a great crowd around them, and some scribes arguing with them. When the whole crowd saw him, they were immediately overcome with awe, and they ran forward to greet him. He asked them, 'What are you arguing about with them?' Someone from the crowd answered him, 'Teacher, I brought you my son; he has a spirit that makes him unable to speak; and whenever it seizes him, it dashes him down; and he foams and grinds his teeth and becomes rigid; and I asked your disciples to cast it out, but they could not do so.' He answered them, 'You faithless generation, how much longer must I be among you? How much longer must I put up with you? Bring him to me.' And they brought the boy to him. When the spirit saw him, immediately it threw the boy into convulsions, and he fell on the ground and rolled about, foaming at the mouth. Jesus asked the father, 'How long has this been happening to him?' And he said, 'From childhood. It has often cast him into the fire and into the water, to destroy him; but if you are able to do anything, have pity on us and help us.' Jesus said to him, 'If you are able! – All things can be done for the one who believes.' Immediately the father of the child cried out, 'I believe; help my unbelief!' When Jesus saw that a crowd came running together, he rebuked the unclean spirit, saying to it, 'You spirit that keep this boy from speaking and hearing, I command you, come out of him, and never enter him again!' After crying out and convulsing him terribly, it came out, and the boy was like a corpse, so that most of them said, 'He is dead.' But Jesus took him by the hand and lifted him up, and he was able to stand. When he had entered the house, his disciples asked him privately, 'Why could we not cast it out?' He said to them, 'This kind can come out only through prayer.'

• The poor father's cry, 'I believe, help my unbelief', is one of the best-loved human statements in the Gospels. Does it express the reality of your own struggle to believe? It has been said humorously that most of us are atheists before breakfast, but perhaps we are half-atheists for most of the day? It is also said that most people live lives of quiet desperation. When you experience things getting beyond you, do as the father did and bring your problems to Jesus. Be honest with him; beg his help. You will, he promises, find rest for your aching heart.

Tuesday 22 February
St Peter's Chair
Matthew 16:13–19

Now when Jesus came into the district of Caesarea Philippi, he asked his disciples, 'Who do people say that the Son of Man is?' And they said, 'Some say John the Baptist, but others Elijah, and still others Jeremiah or one of the prophets.' He said to them, 'But who do you say that I am?' Simon Peter answered, 'You are the Messiah, the Son of the living

God.' And Jesus answered him, 'Blessed are you, Simon son of Jonah! For flesh and blood has not revealed this to you, but my Father in heaven. And I tell you, you are Peter, and on this rock I will build my church, and the gates of Hades will not prevail against it. I will give you the keys of the kingdom of heaven, and whatever you bind on earth will be bound in heaven, and whatever you loose on earth will be loosed in heaven.'

- Each of us is called to be a foundation stone for the building up of the lives of those around us. Saint John tells us in the Apocalypse that each of us will receive a new name when we reach heaven. Let us do all we can to prepare ourselves, here on earth, to receive joyfully that mysterious new name.

Wednesday 23 February
Mark 9:38–40

John said to him, 'Teacher, we saw someone casting out demons in your name, and we tried to stop him, because he was not following us.' But Jesus said, 'Do not stop him; for no one who does a deed of power in my name will be able soon afterwards to speak evil of me. Whoever is not against us is for us.'

- Gathering and belonging are important human needs but Jesus shows us how we can lead ourselves astray. The reign of God is advanced wherever good is done, where truth is spoken, when love wins out. Lord, help me not to be narrow-minded or judgemental but to give thanks to you for all that is good.

Thursday 24 February
Mark 9:41–50

For truly I tell you, whoever gives you a cup of water to drink because you bear the name of Christ will by no means lose the reward.

'If any of you put a stumbling-block before one of these little ones who believe in me, it would be better for you if a great millstone were hung around your neck and you were thrown into the sea. If your hand causes you to stumble, cut it off; it is better for you to enter life maimed than to have two hands and to go to hell, to the unquenchable fire. And if your foot causes you to stumble, cut it off; it is better for you to enter life lame than to have two feet and to be thrown into hell. And if your eye causes you to stumble, tear it out; it is better for you to enter the kingdom of God with one eye than to have two eyes and to be thrown into hell, where their worm never dies, and the fire is never quenched.

'For everyone will be salted with fire. Salt is good; but if salt has lost its saltiness, how can you season it? Have salt in yourselves, and be at peace with one another.'

- As a Christian, I bear the name of Christ. I strive to think and feel and act as he might. I pray that today, and every day, I may see with his eyes, listen with his ears, speak with his words and touch with his hands.

Friday 25 February
Mark 10:1–12

He left that place and went to the region of Judea and beyond the Jordan. And crowds again gathered around him; and, as was his custom, he again taught them.

Some Pharisees came, and to test him they asked, 'Is it lawful for a man to divorce his wife?' He answered them, 'What did Moses command you?' They said, 'Moses allowed a man to write a certificate of dismissal and to divorce her.' But Jesus said to them, 'Because of your hardness of heart he wrote this commandment for you. But from the beginning of creation, "God made them male and female." "For this reason a man shall leave his father and mother and be joined to his wife, and the two shall become one flesh." So they are no longer two, but one flesh. Therefore what God has joined together, let no one separate.'

Then in the house the disciples asked him again about this matter. He said to them, 'Whoever divorces his wife and marries another commits adultery against her; and if she divorces her husband and marries another, she commits adultery.'

- Jesus calls us back to the original vision that God has for creation. He sets out the ideal for marriage: a loving and faithful union of mutual respect. In words repeated in the marriage rite he says, 'What God has joined together, let no one separate.'

- Speak with Jesus about how this passage sits with me. Is there an invitation here for me to love, to be compassionate? 'Be merciful, just as your Father is merciful' (Luke 6:36).

Saturday 26 February
Mark 10:13–16

People were bringing little children to him in order that he might touch them; and the disciples spoke sternly to them. But when Jesus saw this, he was indignant and said to them, 'Let the little children come to me; do not stop them; for it is to such as these that the kingdom of God belongs. Truly I tell you, whoever does not receive the kingdom of God as a little child will never enter it.' And he took them up in his arms, laid his hands on them, and blessed them.

- I am like a child in the arms of Jesus; I want to trust him with my life; I want him to be close to me in joys and sorrows. I ask him for this, and ask it for all who are in my circle of life. Jesus wants closeness to each of us, as we want a close friendship with him. Let the child in me trust, ask and simply enjoy being loved by him.

The Eighth Week in Ordinary Time
27 February–5 March 2022

Something to think and pray about each day this week:

'Love your enemy' is easy for some people. There are those who cannot live without an enemy. They learn to feed off negativity. They can make others appear to be horrendous human beings who lack basic goodness. This creation is often a figment of their imagination but necessary to sustain their own warped sense of self-worth and their drive. They love the presence of an enemy because without one, they'd have to consider their own heart and soul and this is too difficult for them. An enemy gives justification to a world-view that distracts from personal well-being.

Jesus suffered under such people. He was made to be an enemy of the people to suit those in power. May we be protected from such people and the damage they do. The heart is too tender a space to be wasted on such negativity.

'Jesus said, "Father, forgive them, for they do not know what they are doing." And they divided up his clothes by casting lots.' (Luke 23:34)

Alan Hilliard,
Dipping into Lent

The Presence of God

I remind myself that, as I sit here now,
God is gazing on me with love and holding me in being.
I pause for a moment and think of this.

Freedom

'There are very few people who realise what God would make of them
if they abandoned themselves into his hands, and let themselves be
formed by his grace' (Saint Ignatius). I ask for the grace to trust myself
totally to God's love.

Consciousness

Where do I sense hope, encouragement and growth in my life? By looking
back over the past few months, I may be able to see which activities and
occasions have produced rich fruit. If I do notice such areas, I will determine to give those areas both time and space in the future.

The Word

Lord Jesus, you became human to communicate with me.
You walked and worked on this earth.
You endured the heat and struggled with the cold.
All your time on this earth was spent in caring for humanity.
You healed the sick, you raised the dead.
Most important of all, you saved me from death.
*(Please turn to the Scripture on the following pages. Inspiration points are there,
should you need them. When you are ready, return here to continue.)*

Conversation

What is stirring in me as I pray? Am I consoled, troubled, left cold? I
imagine Jesus standing or sitting at my side, and I share my feelings with
him.

Conclusion

Glory be to the Father, and to the Son, and to the Holy Spirit,
As it was in the beginning, is now and ever shall be,
World without end. Amen.

Sunday 27 February
Eighth Sunday in Ordinary Time
Luke 6:39–45

He also told them a parable: 'Can a blind person guide a blind person? Will not both fall into a pit? A disciple is not above the teacher, but everyone who is fully qualified will be like the teacher. Why do you see the speck in your neighbour's eye, but do not notice the log in your own eye? Or how can you say to your neighbour, "Friend, let me take out the speck in your eye", when you yourself do not see the log in your own eye? You hypocrite, first take the log out of your own eye, and then you will see clearly to take the speck out of your neighbour's eye.

'No good tree bears bad fruit, nor again does a bad tree bear good fruit; for each tree is known by its own fruit. Figs are not gathered from thorns, nor are grapes picked from a bramble bush. The good person out of the good treasure of the heart produces good, and the evil person out of evil treasure produces evil; for it is out of the abundance of the heart that the mouth speaks.

• Lord, when you tell me to hold off criticism until I have cleared my own slate, you are telling me not to criticise at all, because I am never above criticism myself. In the story of the adulterous woman, when you said: 'Let the one without sin cast the first stone', what happened? They went out, beginning with the eldest. Throwing stones, or bad-mouthing others, is an ignoble business. Taking apart is the trade of those who cannot construct.

Monday 28 February
Mark 10:17–27

As he was setting out on a journey, a man ran up and knelt before him, and asked him, 'Good Teacher, what must I do to inherit eternal life?' Jesus said to him, 'Why do you call me good? No one is good but God alone. You know the commandments: "You shall not murder; You shall not commit adultery; You shall not steal; You shall not bear false witness; You shall not defraud; Honour your father and mother."' He said to him, 'Teacher, I have kept all these since my youth.' Jesus, looking at him, loved him and said, 'You lack one thing; go, sell what you own, and give the money to the poor, and you will have treasure in heaven; then come, follow me.' When he heard this, he was shocked and went away grieving, for he had many possessions.

Then Jesus looked around and said to his disciples, 'How hard it will be for those who have wealth to enter the kingdom of God!' And the disciples were perplexed at these words. But Jesus said to them again, 'Children, how hard it is to enter the kingdom of God! It is easier for a camel to go through the eye of a needle than for someone who is rich to enter the kingdom of God.' They were greatly astounded and said to one another, 'Then who can be saved?' Jesus looked at them and said, 'For mortals it is impossible, but not for God; for God all things are possible.'

- I consider this scene and wonder what it was that Jesus loved about the young man. I allow myself time to think about what he loves about me – and I don't move on until I do!

Tuesday 1 March
Mark 10:28–31

Peter began to say to him, 'Look, we have left everything and followed you.' Jesus said, 'Truly I tell you, there is no one who has left house or brothers or sisters or mother or father or children or fields, for my sake and for the sake of the good news, who will not receive a hundredfold now in this age – houses, brothers and sisters, mothers and children, and fields, with persecutions – and in the age to come eternal life. But many who are first will be last, and the last will be first.'

- What God offers to us, and what Jesus offers to his disciples, is a gift of God, not our right. Whatever place we think we have with God, is God's to give. In other places he promises the sheer generous gift of his love to all. Maybe last and first will be the same after all, and it's only humans that talk in such terms! Pray in thanks that all of us belong to God.

Wednesday 2 March
Ash Wednesday
Matthew 6:1–6.16–18

'Beware of practising your piety before others in order to be seen by them; for then you have no reward from your Father in heaven.

'So whenever you give alms, do not sound a trumpet before you, as the hypocrites do in the synagogues and in the streets, so that they may be praised by others. Truly I tell you, they have received their reward. But when you give alms, do not let your left hand know what your right hand is doing, so that your alms may be done in secret; and your Father who sees in secret will reward you.

'And whenever you pray, do not be like the hypocrites; for they love to stand and pray in the synagogues and at the street corners, so that they may be seen by others. Truly I tell you, they have received their reward. But whenever you pray, go into your room and shut the door and pray to your Father who is in secret; and your Father who sees in secret will reward you. . . .

'And whenever you fast, do not look dismal, like the hypocrites, for they disfigure their faces so as to show others that they are fasting. Truly I tell you, they have received their reward. But when you fast, put oil on your head and wash your face, so that your fasting may be seen not by others but by your Father who is in secret; and your Father who sees in secret will reward you.

- Jesus calls for generosity – Give! Share! Lend! When somebody is looking for help, do we pass by on the other side, like the priest in the parable of the Good Samaritan? Pope Francis calls on us not to ignore anybody begging on the street, and says the way one reaches out to the person looking for help must be done 'by looking them in the eyes and touching their hands'.

Thursday 3 March
Luke 9:22–25

'The Son of Man must undergo great suffering, and be rejected by the elders, chief priests, and scribes, and be killed, and on the third day be raised.'

Then he said to them all, 'If any want to become my followers, let them deny themselves and take up their cross daily and follow me. For those who want to save their life will lose it, and those who lose their life for my sake will save it. What does it profit them if they gain the whole world, but lose or forfeit themselves?

- Jesus is often presented in the Gospel as giving his life over to his Father. His convictions and preaching would lead to his death. His future resurrection was in the power of his Father. Much of what we want to hold on to in life can be swiftly taken away – our good health, our security of wealth, even our good name. What we share in love and in God cannot be taken away. Ask in prayer to value love, and to offer your life now and always in love and for love.

Friday 4 March
Matthew 9:14–15

Then the disciples of John came to him, saying, 'Why do we and the Pharisees fast often, but your disciples do not fast?' And Jesus said to them, 'The wedding-guests cannot mourn as long as the bridegroom is with them, can they? The days will come when the bridegroom is taken away from them, and then they will fast.'

- Spend some time each day allowing the joy of God to fill your heart. Spend a little time mourning with him also as joy is lost for so many. Any fasting is to remind us that the Lord of all joy suffers in his people, maybe those near to us. True prayer brings us near to others and near to God, especially near to those in any type of pain. It also brings us near to ourselves – our hopes, desires and anything about the mystery of ourselves.

Saturday 5 March
Luke 5:27–32

After this he went out and saw a tax-collector named Levi, sitting at the tax booth; and he said to him, 'Follow me.' And he got up, left everything, and followed him.

Then Levi gave a great banquet for him in his house; and there was a large crowd of tax-collectors and others sitting at the table with them. The Pharisees and their scribes were complaining to his disciples, saying, 'Why do you eat and drink with tax-collectors and sinners?' Jesus answered, 'Those who are well have no need of a physician, but those who are sick; I have come to call not the righteous but sinners to repentance.'

- Who Jesus eats and drinks with is a distraction from what his mission is – to call us into a change of life. When we are focused on Jesus, we can eat and drink with anyone. If we focus on Jesus nobody can take away what is best in life – his love and his word. We can invite anyone into our prayer and allow prayer to be a time of healing and forgiveness.

The First Week of Lent
6–12 March 2022

Something to think and pray about each day this week:

For the Christian, the season of Lent and Easter tells of a God who intervened in human history in an unimaginable way. He didn't come to a perfect time or a perfect place. In some sense, I'd love if he intervened in our times to show us how to deal with the challenges of the Internet and social media! The one thing for sure though, is that he entered the chaos of people's lives and the chaos of our world.

Let us not be afraid of the chaos that is often around us and within us. In particular, let us not be afraid of the chaos we see in the lives of others: the homeless person, the refugee, the person who is recovering in hospital. If God entered our chaos let us not be afraid to step into the chaos of those we serve and love.

Alan Hilliard,
Dipping into Lent

The Presence of God

Lord, help me to be fully alive to your holy presence. Enfold me in your love. Let my heart become one with yours.

My soul longs for your presence, Lord. When I turn my thoughts to you, I find peace and contentment.

Freedom

Your death on the cross has set me free. I can live joyously and freely without fear of death. Your mercy knows no bounds.

Consciousness

At this moment, Lord, I turn my thoughts to you.

I will leave aside my chores and preoccupations.

I will take rest and refreshment in your presence.

The Word

The word of God comes down to us through the Scriptures.

May the Holy Spirit enlighten my mind and my heart

to respond to the Gospel teachings:

to love my neighbour as myself,

to care for my sisters and brothers in Christ.

(Please turn to the Scripture on the following pages. Inspiration points are there, should you need them. When you are ready, return here to continue.)

Conversation

Begin to talk to Jesus about the Scripture you have just read. What part of it strikes a chord in you? Perhaps the words of a friend – or some story you have heard recently – will slowly rise to the surface of your consciousness. If so, does the story throw light on what the Scripture passage may be saying to you?

Conclusion

I thank God for these moments we have spent together and for any insights I have been given concerning the text.

Sunday 6 March
First Sunday of Lent
Luke 4:1–13

Jesus, full of the Holy Spirit, returned from the Jordan and was led by the Spirit in the wilderness, where for forty days he was tempted by the devil. He ate nothing at all during those days, and when they were over, he was famished. The devil said to him, 'If you are the Son of God, command this stone to become a loaf of bread.' Jesus answered him, 'It is written, "One does not live by bread alone."'

Then the devil led him up and showed him in an instant all the kingdoms of the world. And the devil said to him, 'To you I will give their glory and all this authority; for it has been given over to me, and I give it to anyone I please. If you, then, will worship me, it will all be yours.' Jesus answered him, 'It is written,

"Worship the Lord your God,
and serve only him."'

Then the devil took him to Jerusalem, and placed him on the pinnacle of the temple, saying to him,

'If you are the Son of God, throw yourself down from here, for it is written,

"He will command his angels concerning you,
to protect you",

and

"On their hands they will bear you up,
so that you will not dash your foot against a stone."'

Jesus answered him, 'It is said, "Do not put the Lord your God to the test."' When the devil had finished every test, he departed from him until an opportune time.

- That Jesus was tested throughout his ministry was widely held in early Christianity. The Letter to the Hebrews tells us, 'For we do not have a high priest (Jesus) who is unable to sympathise with our weakness, but we have one who in every respect has been tested as we are, yet without sin.'

Monday 7 March
Matthew 25:31–46

'When the Son of Man comes in his glory, and all the angels with him, then he will sit on the throne of his glory. All the nations will be gathered before him, and he will separate people one from another as a shepherd separates the sheep from the goats, and he will put the sheep at his right hand and the goats at the left. Then the king will say to those at his right hand, "Come, you that are blessed by my Father, inherit the kingdom prepared for you from the foundation of the world; for I was hungry and you gave me food, I was thirsty and you gave me something to drink, I was a stranger and you welcomed me, I was naked and you gave me clothing, I was sick and you took care of me, I was in prison and you visited me." Then the righteous will answer him, "Lord, when was it that we saw you hungry and gave you food, or thirsty and gave you something to drink? And when was it that we saw you a stranger and welcomed you, or naked and gave you clothing? And when was it that we saw you sick or in prison and visited you?" And the king will answer them, "Truly I tell you, just as you did it to one of the least of these who are members of my family, you did it to me." Then he will say to those at his left hand, "You that are accursed, depart from me into the eternal fire prepared for the devil and his angels; for I was hungry and you gave me no food, I was thirsty and you gave me nothing to drink, I was a stranger and you did not welcome me, naked and you did not give me clothing, sick and in prison and you did not visit me." Then they also will answer, "Lord, when was it that we saw you hungry or thirsty or a stranger or naked or sick or in prison, and did not take care of you?" Then he will answer them, "Truly I tell you, just as you did not do it to one of the least of these, you did not do it to me." And these will go away into eternal punishment, but the righteous into eternal life.'

- This parable of the sheep and the goats is not about the future, but about opening my eyes here and now to the needs of my neighbour – the hungry, the homeless, the refugee, the isolated lonely ones. Jesus identifies with each one. If I turn away from my brothers and sisters in need, I am turning away from my brother Jesus.

Tuesday 8 March
Matthew 6:7–15

'When you are praying, do not heap up empty phrases as the Gentiles do; for they think that they will be heard because of their many words. Do not be like them, for your Father knows what you need before you ask him.

'Pray then in this way:

Our Father in heaven,
hallowed be your name.
Your kingdom come.
Your will be done,
on earth as it is in heaven.
Give us this day our daily bread.
And forgive us our debts,
as we also have forgiven our debtors.
And do not bring us to the time of trial,
but rescue us from the evil one.
For if you forgive others their trespasses, your heavenly Father will also forgive you; but if you do not forgive others, neither will your Father forgive your trespasses.'

• Are you having difficulty praying just now? Maybe you are confused, annoyed, daydreaming. Try to be still for a few moments. Do you not know what to say? Try the prayer that Jesus offers here, the Our Father, praying it slowly, or just be still and silent in the Lord's presence. Prayer is a time of relaxing into the mystery of God's love, letting go of tensions and worries for this period of time.

Wednesday 9 March
Luke 11:29–32

When the crowds were increasing, he began to say, 'This generation is an evil generation; it asks for a sign, but no sign will be given to it except the sign of Jonah. For just as Jonah became a sign to the people of Nineveh, so the Son of Man will be to this generation. The queen of the South will rise at the judgement with the people of this generation and condemn them, because she came from the ends of the earth to listen to the wisdom of Solomon, and see, something greater than Solomon is here! The people of Nineveh will rise up at the judgement with this generation and condemn it, because they repented at the proclamation of Jonah, and see, something greater than Jonah is here!'

- Jonah is the sign of God's care for all. His call was to go to a far country that did not know him or his God. He is also a sign of God's care for us individually – his care was for Jonah's safety. Jonah's strength was in his trust in God. Prayer is a time of allowing trust in God to grow and become a central part of our being.

Thursday 10 March
Matthew 7:7–12

'Ask, and it will be given to you; search, and you will find; knock, and the door will be opened for you. For everyone who asks receives, and everyone who searches finds, and for everyone who knocks, the door will be opened. Is there anyone among you who, if your child asks for bread, will give a stone? Or if the child asks for a fish, will give a snake? If you then, who are evil, know how to give good gifts to your children, how much more will your Father in heaven give good things to those who ask him!

'In everything do to others as you would have them do to you; for this is the law and the prophets.'

- Prayer time is never wasted. Good things come in prayer even if they are maybe not what we asked for. Prayer opens the heart to good things from God. Be grateful at the end of prayer for time spent with God. Prayer time is always productive by making us people of more love. True prayer brings peace of mind and heart. It also brings the peace of knowing we are loved and of being called into following the Lord.

Friday 11 March
Matthew 5:20–26

For I tell you, unless your righteousness exceeds that of the scribes and Pharisees, you will never enter the kingdom of heaven.

'You have heard that it was said to those of ancient times, "You shall not murder"; and "whoever murders shall be liable to judgement." But I say to you that if you are angry with a brother or sister, you will be liable to judgement; and if you insult a brother or sister, you will be liable to the council; and if you say, "You fool", you will be liable to the hell of fire. So when you are offering your gift at the altar, if you remember that your brother or sister has something against you, leave your gift there before the altar and go; first be reconciled to your brother or sister, and then come and offer your gift. Come to terms quickly with your accuser while you are on the way to court with him, or your accuser may hand you over to the judge, and the judge to the guard, and you will be thrown into prison. Truly I tell you, you will never get out until you have paid the last penny.'

- True religion is the religion of the heart. Jesus saw the good in the Pharisees but challenged them against any hypocrisy. He goes on to encourage us to live by one of the most difficult spiritual principles – to forgive and be reconciled with others.

- Pay attention to the way we deal with each other; seek reconciliation with each other above all.

Saturday 12 March
Matthew 5:43–48

'You have heard that it was said, "You shall love your neighbour and hate your enemy." But I say to you, Love your enemies and pray for those who persecute you, so that you may be children of your Father in heaven; for he makes his sun rise on the evil and on the good, and sends rain on the righteous and on the unrighteous. For if you love those who love you, what reward do you have? Do not even the tax-collectors do the same? And if you greet only your brothers and sisters, what more are you doing than others? Do not even the Gentiles do the same? Be perfect, therefore, as your heavenly Father is perfect.'

- The love Jesus lived by and encourages is a freeing love. We may find it hard to forgive, but the beginnings of forgiveness can be to pray for those we need to forgive. We may love only those who return our love, but the beginning of real love is to expect and want nothing in return. Let us pray that our love may be like the sunshine, which shines equally on all, 'neighbour and enemy'.

The Second Week of Lent
13–19 March 2022

Something to think and pray about each day this week:

The big truth of Jesus is that he is intimately united to God the Father. So following him is not just action, but prayer that leads to action. We say someone is a great Christian – he or she helps the poor. Christianity is more – it is also prayer and the Eucharist. While we are thankful for the good lives of many people, we also can say that the full Christian life includes prayer and Mass.

It also involves community – the three were called to witness and help each other remember the Lord Jesus. Community brings the word of God alive in a real way. The community of the Church brings us to fuller faith.

Prayer leads to action for others, and action leads back to prayer. We can be so close to heavenly things that we are no earthly good! Lent brings us into this mystery of the death and resurrection of the Lord – we are part of this, and we try to make life a grace for others. We can transfigure the lives of others, or disfigure. Let's be people of the transfiguration.

Donal Neary SJ,
Gospel Reflections for Sundays of Year C: Luke

The Presence of God
The more we call on God, the more we can feel God's presence. Day by day we are drawn closer to the loving heart of God.

Freedom
I am free. When I look at these words in writing, they seem to create in me a feeling of awe. Yes, a wonderful feeling of freedom. Thank you, God.

Consciousness
Help me, Lord, become more conscious of your presence. Teach me to recognise your presence in others. Fill my heart with gratitude for the times your love has been shown to me through the care of others.

The Word
The word of God comes down to us through the Scriptures. May the Holy Spirit enlighten my mind and my heart to respond to the Gospel teachings.
(Please turn to the Scripture on the following pages. Inspiration points are there, should you need them. When you are ready, return here to continue.)

Conversation
Conversation requires talking and listening.
As I talk to Jesus, may I also learn to pause and listen.
I picture the gentleness in his eyes and the love in his smile.
I can be totally honest with Jesus as I tell him my worries and cares.
I will open my heart to Jesus as I tell him my fears and doubts.
I will ask him to help me place myself fully in his care, knowing that he always desires good for me.

Conclusion
Glory be to the Father, and to the Son, and to the Holy Spirit,
As it was in the beginning, is now and ever shall be,
World without end. Amen.

Sunday 13 March
Second Sunday of Lent
Luke 9:28b–36

Jesus took with him Peter and John and James, and went up on the mountain to pray. And while he was praying, the appearance of his face changed, and his clothes became dazzling white. Suddenly they saw two men, Moses and Elijah, talking to him. They appeared in glory and were speaking of his departure, which he was about to accomplish at Jerusalem. Now Peter and his companions were weighed down with sleep; but since they had stayed awake, they saw his glory and the two men who stood with him. Just as they were leaving him, Peter said to Jesus, 'Master, it is good for us to be here; let us make three dwellings, one for you, one for Moses, and one for Elijah' – not knowing what he said. While he was saying this, a cloud came and overshadowed them; and they were terrified as they entered the cloud. Then from the cloud came a voice that said, 'This is my Son, my Chosen; listen to him!' When the voice had spoken, Jesus was found alone. And they kept silent and in those days told no one any of the things they had seen.

• In our journey towards God we experience high moments, spots when we find ourselves on holy ground and God shows himself. That was the state of Saint Peter as he witnessed the Transfiguration of Jesus: 'Lord, let us build here three dwellings, for you, for Moses and for Elijah'. Peter wanted the party to go on for ever. Jesus brought him down to earth, led him down the mountain, told him to stop talking about the vision and instead be ready for Calvary.

Monday 14 March
Luke 6:36–38

Be merciful, just as your Father is merciful.

'Do not judge, and you will not be judged; do not condemn, and you will not be condemned. Forgive, and you will be forgiven; give, and it will be given to you. A good measure, pressed down, shaken together, running over, will be put into your lap; for the measure you give will be the measure you get back.'

• Jesus stresses once again the primary importance of good relationships with others. The world would be a different place if we were merciful and non-condemning. Help me to stop despising, hating, judging other people.

- Lord, my poor heart is very small, and it can also be very hard. Your heart is large and also very tender and compassionate. When I try to forgive others, my heart becomes a bit more like yours, and you swamp me with your overflowing generosity. I like that!

Tuesday 15 March
Matthew 23:1–12

Then Jesus said to the crowds and to his disciples, 'The scribes and the Pharisees sit on Moses' seat; therefore, do whatever they teach you and follow it; but do not do as they do, for they do not practise what they teach. They tie up heavy burdens, hard to bear, and lay them on the shoulders of others; but they themselves are unwilling to lift a finger to move them. They do all their deeds to be seen by others; for they make their phylacteries broad and their fringes long. They love to have the place of honour at banquets and the best seats in the synagogues, and to be greeted with respect in the market-places, and to have people call them rabbi. But you are not to be called rabbi, for you have one teacher, and you are all students. And call no one your father on earth, for you have one Father – the one in heaven. Nor are you to be called instructors, for you have one instructor, the Messiah. The greatest among you will be your servant. All who exalt themselves will be humbled, and all who humble themselves will be exalted.

- Jesus' disciples are not to make a big display of religion, nor are they to seek honourable titles like 'father' and 'teacher' and 'rabbi'. Our teacher is God, and the true disciple learns only from God. I think of what it would be like for me to assume the lowest place, to really take to heart what Jesus says about humility. I begin my prayer by asking God for the help I need, humbly and sincerely.

Wednesday 16 March
Matthew 20:17–28

While Jesus was going up to Jerusalem, he took the twelve disciples aside by themselves, and said to them on the way, 'See, we are going up to Jerusalem, and the Son of Man will be handed over to the chief priests and scribes, and they will condemn him to death; then they will hand him over to the Gentiles to be mocked and flogged and crucified; and on the third day he will be raised.'

Then the mother of the sons of Zebedee came to him with her sons, and kneeling before him, she asked a favour of him. And he said to her, 'What do you want?' She said to him, 'Declare that these two sons of mine will sit, one at your right hand and one at your left, in your kingdom.' But Jesus answered, 'You do not know what you are asking. Are you able to drink the cup that I am about to drink?' They said to him, 'We are able.' He said to them, 'You will indeed drink my cup, but to sit at my right hand and at my left, this is not mine to grant, but it is for those for whom it has been prepared by my Father.'

When the ten heard it, they were angry with the two brothers. But Jesus called them to him and said, 'You know that the rulers of the Gentiles lord it over them, and their great ones are tyrants over them. It will not be so among you; but whoever wishes to be great among you must be your servant, and whoever wishes to be first among you must be your slave; just as the Son of Man came not to be served but to serve, and to give his life a ransom for many.'

- Saint Matthew elsewhere brings up this topic of what we might call 'promotion to high office': 'The disciples came to Jesus and asked, "Who is the greatest in the kingdom of heaven?"' (Matthew 18:1). And the answer is always the same: a child. A child, ideally, is never 'pushy', elbowing others out of the way; a child, ideally, is just thankful for whatever comes. Any lording it over others, Jesus warns, is only typical of what happens among the pagans.

Thursday 17 March
Saint Patrick, Bishop and Patron of Ireland
Luke 16:19–31

'There was a rich man who was dressed in purple and fine linen and who feasted sumptuously every day. And at his gate lay a poor man named Lazarus, covered with sores, who longed to satisfy his hunger with what fell from the rich man's table; even the dogs would come and lick his sores. The poor man died and was carried away by the angels to be with Abraham. The rich man also died and was buried. In Hades, where he was being tormented, he looked up and saw Abraham far away with Lazarus by his side. He called out, "Father Abraham, have mercy on me, and send Lazarus to dip the tip of his finger in water and cool my tongue; for I am in agony in these flames." But Abraham said, "Child, remember that during your lifetime you received your good things, and Lazarus in like manner evil things; but now he is comforted here, and you are in agony. Besides all this, between you and us a great chasm has been fixed, so that those who might want to pass from here to you cannot do so, and no one can cross from there to us." He said, "Then, father, I beg you to send him to my father's house – for I have five brothers – that he may warn them, so that they will not also come into this place of torment." Abraham replied, "They have Moses and the prophets; they should listen to them." He said, "No, father Abraham; but if someone goes to them from the dead, they will repent." He said to him, "If they do not listen to Moses and the prophets, neither will they be convinced even if someone rises from the dead."'

- Without an eye for the needy around us, our life becomes self-centred and callous. Jesus is asking his listeners to open their eyes to what is around them, and to open their ears to the simple commands of the Gospel: love your neighbour.

Friday 18 March
Matthew 21:33–43.45–46

'Listen to another parable. There was a landowner who planted a vineyard, put a fence around it, dug a wine press in it, and built a watch-tower. Then he leased it to tenants and went to another country. When the harvest time had come, he sent his slaves to the tenants to collect his produce. But the tenants seized his slaves and beat one, killed another, and stoned another. Again he sent other slaves, more than the first; and they treated them in the same way. Finally he sent his son to them, saying, "They will respect my son." But when the tenants saw the son, they said to themselves, "This is the heir; come, let us kill him and get his inheritance." So they seized him, threw him out of the vineyard, and killed him. Now when the owner of the vineyard comes, what will he do to those tenants?' They said to him, 'He will put those wretches to a miserable death, and lease the vineyard to other tenants who will give him the produce at the harvest time.'

Jesus said to them, 'Have you never read in the scriptures:
"The stone that the builders rejected
has become the cornerstone;
this was the Lord's doing,
and it is amazing in our eyes"?
'Therefore I tell you, the kingdom of God will be taken away
from you and given to a people that produces the fruits of the
kingdom.' . . .

When the chief priests and the Pharisees heard his parables, they realised that he was speaking about them. They wanted to arrest him, but
they feared the crowds, because they regarded him as a prophet.

• One of the saddest statements in the Gospels is this innocent comment
of the father: 'They will respect my son.' I am frightened to think what
would happen if Jesus came into our world today. His message about
the kingdom of God would put him in direct opposition to so many
other kingdoms. He would become an enemy to be got rid of.

Saturday 19 March
Saint Joseph, Spouse of the Blessed Virgin Mary
Matthew 1:16.18–21.24

. . . and Jacob the father of Joseph the husband of Mary, of whom Jesus
was born, who is called the Messiah. . . .

Now the birth of Jesus the Messiah took place in this way. When his
mother Mary had been engaged to Joseph, but before they lived together,
she was found to be with child from the Holy Spirit. Her husband Joseph,
being a righteous man and unwilling to expose her to public disgrace,
planned to dismiss her quietly. But just when he had resolved to do this,
an angel of the Lord appeared to him in a dream and said, 'Joseph, son of
David, do not be afraid to take Mary as your wife, for the child conceived
in her is from the Holy Spirit. She will bear a son, and you are to name
him Jesus, for he will save his people from their sins.' . . . When Joseph
awoke from sleep, he did as the angel of the Lord commanded him; he
took her as his wife.

• Matthew invites us to ponder the birth of Jesus from the perspective
of Joseph, the husband of Mary. He finds himself in a moral dilemma

when he learns of Mary's pregnancy, which had come about 'before they lived together'. He is a righteous man who wants to do what is best for everyone and what is in harmony with the will of God. An angel is sent to enlighten him.

- Not all the decisions we face in life are clearly between right and wrong. We may have to operate in morally grey areas, or in so-called 'no-win' situations (where we will be misunderstood no matter what choice we make). We need to tap into the experience of others and pray for the wisdom of God's Holy Spirit.

The Third Week of Lent
20–26 March 2022

Something to think and pray about each day this week:

Without denying the reality of human shortcoming and sinfulness, holiness is a positive prospect. The pursuit of holiness does not rob persons of their 'energy, vitality or joy' (*GE*, 32). On the contrary, it enhances these qualities to a degree of excellence that exceeds human efforts. Holiness holds out the hope of becoming what 'the Father had in mind when he created you' (*GE*, 32). Francis declares that this is the dignity of the 'deepest self'. Like a seed lying in the ground, this self needs to be nurtured and brought to blossom through the cooperation of nature and grace. This is the holy self which is never hindered by the Holy Spirit but, on the contrary, is helped and even healed in the course of a person's life history. The search for truth, beauty and goodness in a person's life is an invitation not to be fearful but a call to deeper faith, to trust that God takes nothing that is truly human from us. Growth in holiness always augments the greater good of the world and all who live within it. We need not be afraid of holiness because we are worth it in God's eyes and what the Father wants.

Kevin O'Gorman SMA,
Journeying in Joy and Gladness

The Presence of God

'Be still, and know that I am God!' Lord, your words lead us to the calmness and greatness of your presence.

Freedom

'In these days, God taught me as a schoolteacher teaches a pupil' (Saint Ignatius). I remind myself that there are things God has to teach me yet, and I ask for the grace to hear them and let them change me.

Consciousness

How am I really feeling? Lighthearted? Heavyhearted? I may be very much at peace, happy to be here.

Equally, I may be frustrated, worried or angry.

I acknowledge how I really am. It is the real me whom the Lord loves.

The Word

God speaks to each of us individually. I listen attentively to hear what he is saying to me. Read the text a few times, then listen.

(Please turn to the Scripture on the following pages. Inspiration points are there, should you need them. When you are ready, return here to continue.)

Conversation

Do I notice myself reacting as I pray with the word of God? Do I feel challenged, comforted, angry? Imagining Jesus sitting or standing by me, I speak out my feelings, as one trusted friend to another.

Conclusion

I thank God for these moments we have spent together and for any insights I have been given concerning the text.

Sunday 20 March
Third Sunday of Lent
Luke 13:1–9

At that very time there were some present who told him about the Galileans whose blood Pilate had mingled with their sacrifices. He asked them, 'Do you think that because these Galileans suffered in this way they were worse sinners than all other Galileans? No, I tell you; but unless you repent, you will all perish as they did. Or those eighteen who were killed when the tower of Siloam fell on them – do you think that they were worse offenders than all the others living in Jerusalem? No, I tell you; but unless you repent, you will all perish just as they did.'

Then he told this parable: 'A man had a fig tree planted in his vine-yard; and he came looking for fruit on it and found none. So he said to the gardener, "See here! For three years I have come looking for fruit on this fig tree, and still I find none. Cut it down! Why should it be wasting the soil?" He replied, "Sir, let it alone for one more year, until I dig round it and put manure on it. If it bears fruit next year, well and good; but if not, you can cut it down."'

• 'Unless you repent you will all perish as they did.' Some clear words of warning from Jesus, who alerts us to the risk of feeling too satisfied with ourselves and our ways. Is there something I feel called to change, an area in my relationships I do not feel satisfied with? I ask Jesus to let me hear his words as addressed to me.

Monday 21 March
John 4:5–42

So he came to a Samaritan city called Sychar, near the plot of ground that Jacob had given to his son Joseph. Jacob's well was there, and Jesus, tired out by his journey, was sitting by the well. It was about noon.

A Samaritan woman came to draw water, and Jesus said to her, 'Give me a drink'. (His disciples had gone to the city to buy food.) The Samaritan woman said to him, 'How is it that you, a Jew, ask a drink of me, a woman of Samaria?' (Jews do not share things in common with Samaritans.) Jesus answered her, 'If you knew the gift of God, and who it is that is saying to you, "Give me a drink", you would have asked him, and he would have given you living water.' The woman said to him, 'Sir, you have no bucket, and the well is deep. Where do you get that living water? Are you greater than our ancestor Jacob, who gave us the well, and with his sons and his flocks drank from it?' Jesus said to her, 'Everyone who drinks of this water will be thirsty again, but those who drink of the water that I will give them will never be thirsty. The water that I will give will become in them a spring of water gushing up to eternal life.' The woman said to him, 'Sir, give me this water, so that I may never be thirsty or have to keep coming here to draw water.'

Jesus said to her, 'Go, call your husband, and come back.' The woman answered him, 'I have no husband.' Jesus said to her, 'You are right in saying, "I have no husband"; for you have had five husbands, and the one you have now is not your husband. What you have said is true!' The woman said to him, 'Sir, I see that you are a prophet. Our ancestors worshipped on this mountain, but you say that the place where people must worship is in Jerusalem.' Jesus said to her, 'Woman, believe me, the hour is coming when you will worship the Father neither on this mountain nor in Jerusalem. You worship what you do not know; we worship what we know, for salvation is from the Jews. But the hour is coming, and is now here, when the true worshippers will worship the Father in spirit and truth, for the Father seeks such as these to worship him. God is spirit, and those who worship him must worship in spirit and truth.' The woman said to him, 'I know that Messiah is coming' (who is called Christ). 'When he comes, he will proclaim all things to us.' Jesus said to her, 'I am he, the one who is speaking to you.'

Just then his disciples came. They were astonished that he was speaking with a woman, but no one said, 'What do you want?' or, 'Why are you speaking with her?' Then the woman left her water-jar and went back to the city. She said to the people, 'Come and see a man who told me everything I have ever done! He cannot be the Messiah, can he?' They left the city and were on their way to him.

Meanwhile the disciples were urging him, 'Rabbi, eat something.' But he said to them, 'I have food to eat that you do not know about.' So the disciples said to one another, 'Surely no one has brought him something to eat?' Jesus said to them, 'My food is to do the will of him who sent me and to complete his work. Do you not say, "Four months more, then comes the harvest"? But I tell you, look around you, and see how the fields are ripe for harvesting. The reaper is already receiving wages and is gathering fruit for eternal life, so that sower and reaper may rejoice together. For here the saying holds true, "One sows and another reaps." I sent you to reap that for which you did not labour. Others have laboured, and you have entered into their labour.'

Many Samaritans from that city believed in him because of the woman's testimony, 'He told me everything I have ever done.' So when the Samaritans came to him, they asked him to stay with them; and he stayed there for two days. And many more believed because of his word. They said to the woman, 'It is no longer because of what you said that we believe, for we have heard for ourselves, and we know that this is truly the Saviour of the world.'

• Lord, I am going about my business like the Samarian woman, and am taken aback when you accost me at the well. You interrupt my business, my getting and spending, and the routines of my day. Let me savour this encounter, imagine you probing my desires, showing you know the waywardness of my heart. At the end, like her, I am moved with such joy at meeting you that I cannot keep it to myself. 'Lift up your eyes and see how the fields are already white for harvest.'

Tuesday 22 March
Matthew 18:21–35

Then Peter came and said to him, 'Lord, if another member of the church sins against me, how often should I forgive? As many as seven times?' Jesus said to him, 'Not seven times, but, I tell you, seventy-seven times.

'For this reason the kingdom of heaven may be compared to a king who wished to settle accounts with his slaves. When he began the reckoning, one who owed him ten thousand talents was brought to him; and, as he could not pay, his lord ordered him to be sold, together with his wife and children and all his possessions, and payment to be made. So the slave fell on his knees before him, saying, "Have patience with me, and I will pay you everything." And out of pity for him, the lord of that slave released him and forgave him the debt. But that same slave, as he went out, came upon one of his fellow-slaves who owed him a hundred denarii; and seizing him by the throat, he said, "Pay what you owe." Then his fellow-slave fell down and pleaded with him, "Have patience with me, and I will pay you." But he refused; then he went and threw him into prison until he should pay the debt. When his fellow-slaves saw what had happened, they were greatly distressed, and they went and reported to their lord all that had taken place. Then his lord summoned him and said to him, "You wicked slave! I forgave you all that debt because you pleaded with me. Should you not have had mercy on your fellow-slave, as I had mercy on you?" And in anger his lord handed him over to be tortured until he should pay his entire debt. So my heavenly Father will also do to every one of you, if you do not forgive your brother or sister from your heart.'

- This parable is about the mercy of God, which is one of the strongest divine qualities, if we may put it like that. Nothing except mercy born of compassion cancels a debt like the one referred to in the story. It further ends by calling us to be merciful as we have received mercy. Mercy is deeper than forgiveness; it sees into the heart of the other and walks around for a while in the other's shoes. It includes compassion and active healing. Shakespeare's description still resounds, '[Mercy] is twice blessed: it blesseth him that gives and him that takes.' To live in an environment of mercy is to live in an atmosphere of peace, healing and growth.

Wednesday 23 March
Matthew 5:17–19

'Do not think that I have come to abolish the law or the prophets; I have come not to abolish but to fulfil. For truly I tell you, until heaven and earth pass away, not one letter, not one stroke of a letter, will pass from the law until all is accomplished. Therefore, whoever breaks one of the least of these commandments, and teaches others to do the same, will be called least in the kingdom of heaven; but whoever does them and teaches them will be called great in the kingdom of heaven.'

- Jesus teaches by word and action, by saying and doing. His example of life is our guide and our encouragement. There is a link between what we say and what we do, and when this link is strong, we are strong in the kingdom of God. We are 'to walk it as we talk it'. Sincerity and integrity of life are what we are called to.

Thursday 24 March
Luke 11:14–23

Now he was casting out a demon that was mute; when the demon had gone out, the one who had been mute spoke, and the crowds were amazed. But some of them said, 'He casts out demons by Beelzebul, the ruler of the demons.' Others, to test him, kept demanding from him a sign from heaven. But he knew what they were thinking and said to them, 'Every kingdom divided against itself becomes a desert, and house falls on house. If Satan also is divided against himself, how will his kingdom stand? – for you say that I cast out the demons by Beelzebul. Now if I cast out the demons by Beelzebul, by whom do your exorcists cast them out? Therefore they will be your judges. But if it is by the finger of God that I cast out the demons, then the kingdom of God has come to you. When a strong man, fully armed, guards his castle, his property is safe. But when one stronger than he attacks him and overpowers him, he takes away his armour in which he trusted and divides his plunder. Whoever is not with me is against me, and whoever does not gather with me scatters.'

- Some listeners, who have just witnessed Jesus curing a dumb man, refuse to think well of him, and invent a slanderous story. It prods me: do I think ill of others more readily than I credit them with good? Lord, give me the grace to see the best in others, as I'd wish them to see the best in me.

Friday 25 March
The Annunciation of the Lord
Luke 1:26–38

In the sixth month the angel Gabriel was sent by God to a town in Galilee called Nazareth, to a virgin engaged to a man whose name was Joseph, of the house of David. The virgin's name was Mary. And he came to her and said, 'Greetings, favoured one! The Lord is with you.' But she was much perplexed by his words and pondered what sort of greeting this might be. The angel said to her, 'Do not be afraid, Mary, for you have found favour with God. And now, you will conceive in your womb and bear a son, and you will name him Jesus. He will be great, and will be called the Son of the Most High, and the Lord God will give to him the throne of his ancestor David. He will reign over the house of Jacob for ever, and of his kingdom there will be no end.' Mary said to the angel, 'How can this be, since I am a virgin?' The angel said to her, 'The Holy Spirit will come upon you, and the power of the Most High will overshadow you; therefore the child to be born will be holy; he will be called Son of God. And now, your relative Elizabeth in her old age has also conceived a son; and this is the sixth month for her who was said to be barren. For nothing will be impossible with God.' Then Mary said, 'Here am I, the servant of the Lord; let it be with me according to your word.' Then the angel departed from her.

- Scripture leaves us in no doubt about God being a long-range planner – he can determine a whole series of events to come to maturity in his own good time. In fact, he has done this for the benefit of us all – planning, even before the beginning of the world, for us to become sisters and brothers of Jesus.

- For the grand plan to come to completion, the cooperation of Mary was needed. And that is why the devotion of the faithful has long believed that Mary had to be specially privileged – namely, through being herself exempted from any touch of inherited sin.

Saturday 26 March
Luke 18:9–14

He also told this parable to some who trusted in themselves that they were righteous and regarded others with contempt: 'Two men went up to the temple to pray, one a Pharisee and the other a tax-collector. The Pharisee, standing by himself, was praying thus, "God, I thank you that I am not like other people: thieves, rogues, adulterers, or even like this tax-collector. I fast twice a week; I give a tenth of all my income." But the tax-collector, standing far off, would not even look up to heaven, but was beating his breast and saying, "God, be merciful to me, a sinner!" I tell you, this man went down to his home justified rather than the other; for all who exalt themselves will be humbled, but all who humble themselves will be exalted.'

- Both men who went up to the temple to pray were good men. The Pharisee could rightly list his qualities, but unfortunately he regarded himself as better than others. None of us can say before the Almighty that I am superior to anyone.

- The tax-collector stayed at the back. He was conscious before God that he was a sinner, but pleaded for mercy. He felt humble and unworthy before the greatness of the Almighty.

- Pope Francis continually reminds us that God never tires of forgiving us, but that we tire of asking him for forgiveness.

The Fourth Week of Lent
27 March–2 April 2022

Something to think and pray about each day this week:

The front pages of the newspapers and our online newsfeeds make the world appear as if it is falling apart. God seems to be more absent than present to the world. A person of faith may begin to wonder if God's wish for the world is mere fantasy.

There are days when I pray for God's intervention in the world. The selfish satisfaction would be immense if I could just look into the eyes of those who scoff and sneer and say 'told you so'. But God seems silent and I am not getting my way.

There are occasions, I admit, when God has broken through silence. When I visited Rwanda to hear the story of people of faith who survived the genocide, I heard lots of silence broken open. One religious sister who experienced horrendous brutality and personal suffering was inspiring. I asked the obvious question, 'How did you feel about God when all this murder and brutality was going on around you – should he have intervened to stop it?' She replied without even thinking as the answer was deep within her. 'I would not put blame for this on the shoulders of God.'

Alan Hilliard,
Dipping into Lent

The Presence of God
To be present is to arrive as one is and open up to the other.
At this instant, as I arrive here, God is present, waiting for me.
God always arrives before me, desiring to connect with me
even more than my most intimate friend.
I take a moment and greet my loving God.

Freedom
Leave me here freely all alone. / In cell where never sunlight shone. /
Should no one ever speak to me. / This golden silence makes me free!
– Part of a poem by Bl. Titus Brandsma, written while he was a prisoner
at Dachau concentration camp

Consciousness
Where am I with God? With others?
Do I have something to be grateful for? Then I give thanks.
Is there something I am sorry for? Then I ask forgiveness.

The Word
I take my time to read the word of God slowly, a few times, allowing
myself to dwell on anything that strikes me.
*(Please turn to the Scripture on the following pages. Inspiration points are there,
should you need them. When you are ready, return here to continue.)*

Conversation
How has God's word moved me? Has it left me cold?
Has it consoled me or moved me to act in a new way?
I imagine Jesus standing or sitting beside me;
I turn and share my feelings with him.

Conclusion
Glory be to the Father, and to the Son, and to the Holy Spirit,
As it was in the beginning, is now and ever shall be,
World without end. Amen.

Sunday 27 March
Fourth Sunday of Lent
Luke 15:1–3.11–32

Now all the tax-collectors and sinners were coming near to listen to him. And the Pharisees and the scribes were grumbling and saying, 'This fellow welcomes sinners and eats with them.'

So he told them this parable: . . .

Then Jesus said, 'There was a man who had two sons. The younger of them said to his father, "Father, give me the share of the property that will belong to me." So he divided his property between them. A few days later the younger son gathered all he had and travelled to a distant country, and there he squandered his property in dissolute living. When he had spent everything, a severe famine took place throughout that country, and he began to be in need. So he went and hired himself out to one of the citizens of that country, who sent him to his fields to feed the pigs. He would gladly have filled himself with the pods that the pigs were eating; and no one gave him anything. But when he came to himself he said, "How many of my father's hired hands have bread enough and to spare, but here I am dying of hunger! I will get up and go to my father, and I will say to him, 'Father, I have sinned against heaven and before you; I am no longer worthy to be called your son; treat me like one of your hired hands.' " So he set off and went to his father. But while he was still far off, his father saw him and was filled with compassion; he ran and put his arms around him and kissed him. Then the son said to him, "Father, I have sinned against heaven and before you; I am no longer worthy to be called your son." But the father said to his slaves, "Quickly, bring out a robe – the best one – and put it on him; put a ring on his finger and sandals on his feet. And get the fatted calf and kill it, and let us eat and celebrate; for this son of mine was dead and is alive again; he was lost and is found!" And they began to celebrate.

'Now his elder son was in the field; and when he came and approached the house, he heard music and dancing. He called one of the slaves and asked what was going on. He replied, "Your brother has come, and your father has killed the fatted calf, because he has got him back safe and sound." Then he became angry and refused to go in. His father came out and began to plead with him. But he answered his father, "Listen! For all these years I have been working like a slave for you, and I have never disobeyed your command; yet you have never given me even a young goat so that I might celebrate with my friends. But when this son of yours came back, who has devoured your property with prostitutes, you killed the fatted calf for him!" Then the father said to him, "Son, you are always with me, and all that is mine is yours. But we had to celebrate and rejoice, because this brother of yours was dead and has come to life; he was lost and has been found."'

- The parable of the Prodigal Son gives me a picture of the steadfast love of God. There, Lord, you show how your heavenly father would appear in human form. When he welcomes back his lost son with tears of delight, kills the fatted calf, brings out the best robe, and throws a great party, it is not to please other people, but to give expression to his own overwhelming pleasure that his child has come home. You delight in me.

- Time and again God promises me goodness. I pray that my eyes may be opened to appreciate where God is working in my life.

Monday 28 March
John 4:43–54

When the two days were over, he went from that place to Galilee (for Jesus himself had testified that a prophet has no honour in the prophet's own country). When he came to Galilee, the Galileans welcomed him, since they had seen all that he had done in Jerusalem at the festival; for they too had gone to the festival.

Then he came again to Cana in Galilee where he had changed the water into wine. Now there was a royal official whose son lay ill in Capernaum. When he heard that Jesus had come from Judea to Galilee, he went and begged him to come down and heal his son, for he was at the point of death. Then Jesus said to him, 'Unless you see signs and wonders you will not believe.' The official said to him, 'Sir, come down before my little boy dies.' Jesus said to him, 'Go; your son will live.' The man believed the word that Jesus spoke to him and started on his way. As he was going down, his slaves met him and told him that his child was alive. So he asked them the hour when he began to recover, and they said to him, 'Yesterday at one in the afternoon the fever left him.' The father realised that this was the hour when Jesus had said to him, 'Your son will live.' So he himself believed, along with his whole household. Now this was the second sign that Jesus did after coming from Judea to Galilee.

• Think of the sick people for whom you have prayed. Perhaps your prayer and that of others played its part in their recovery or had no visible result. Yet no prayer is made in vain. Prayer for another strengthens bonds, softens hearts and is heard by God.

• For whom do you want to pray now? Be sure that the Lord will answer your prayer in the way that is best.

Tuesday 29 March
John 5:1–16

After this there was a festival of the Jews, and Jesus went up to Jerusalem.

Now in Jerusalem by the Sheep Gate there is a pool, called in Hebrew Beth-zatha, which has five porticoes. In these lay many invalids – blind, lame, and paralysed. One man was there who had been ill for thirty-eight years. When Jesus saw him lying there and knew that he had been there a long time, he said to him, 'Do you want to be made well?' The sick man answered him, 'Sir, I have no one to put me into the pool when the water is stirred up; and while I am making my way, someone else steps down ahead of me.' Jesus said to him, 'Stand up, take your mat and walk.' At once the man was made well, and he took up his mat and began to walk.

Now that day was a sabbath. So the Jews said to the man who had been cured, 'It is the sabbath; it is not lawful for you to carry your mat.' But he answered them, 'The man who made me well said to me, "Take up your mat and walk."' They asked him, 'Who is the man who said to you, "Take it up and walk"?' Now the man who had been healed did not know who it was, for Jesus had disappeared in the crowd that was there. Later Jesus found him in the temple and said to him, 'See, you have been made well! Do not sin any more, so that nothing worse happens to you.' The man went away and told the Jews that it was Jesus who had made him well. Therefore the Jews started persecuting Jesus, because he was doing such things on the sabbath.

• Are there sick people in your family, among your friends? Bring them one by one, before the Lord, asking him to do what is best for them.

Maybe you are worried about your own health? Tell the Lord of your anxieties and leave them with him. 'Cast all your anxiety on him, because he cares for you' (1 Peter 5:7).

Wednesday 30 March
John 5:17–30

But Jesus answered them, 'My Father is still working, and I also am working.' For this reason the Jews were seeking all the more to kill him, because he was not only breaking the sabbath, but was also calling God his own Father, thereby making himself equal to God.

Jesus said to them, 'Very truly, I tell you, the Son can do nothing on his own, but only what he sees the Father doing; for whatever the Father does, the Son does likewise. The Father loves the Son and shows him all that he himself is doing; and he will show him greater works than these, so that you will be astonished. Indeed, just as the Father raises the dead and gives them life, so also the Son gives life to whomsoever he wishes. The Father judges no one but has given all judgement to the Son, so that all may honour the Son just as they honour the Father. Anyone who does not honour the Son does not honour the Father who sent him. Very truly, I tell you, anyone who hears my word and believes him who sent me has eternal life, and does not come under judgement, but has passed from death to life.

'Very truly, I tell you, the hour is coming, and is now here, when the dead will hear the voice of the Son of God, and those who hear will live. For just as the Father has life in himself, so he has granted the Son also to have life in himself; and he has given him authority to execute judgement, because he is the Son of Man. Do not be astonished at this; for the hour is coming when all who are in their graves will hear his voice and will come out – those who have done good, to the resurrection of life, and those who have done evil, to the resurrection of condemnation.

'I can do nothing on my own. As I hear, I judge; and my judgement is just, because I seek to do not my own will but the will of him who sent me.'

- The relationship between Jesus and his heavenly Father is the topic of this enigmatic passage. Jesus traces everything in his being and in his choices to their source in the Father. 'I can do nothing on my own.'

'I seek to do not my own will but the will of him who sent me' (the Father). He and his Father are intertwined in every way, so much so that they are one (John 10:30). Honour Jesus and you will be honouring the Father.

Thursday 31 March
John 5:31–47

'If I testify about myself, my testimony is not true. There is another who testifies on my behalf, and I know that his testimony to me is true. You sent messengers to John, and he testified to the truth. Not that I accept such human testimony, but I say these things so that you may be saved. He was a burning and shining lamp, and you were willing to rejoice for a while in his light. But I have a testimony greater than John's. The works that the Father has given me to complete, the very works that I am doing, testify on my behalf that the Father has sent me. And the Father who sent me has himself testified on my behalf. You have never heard his voice or seen his form, and you do not have his word abiding in you, because you do not believe him whom he has sent.

'You search the scriptures because you think that in them you have eternal life; and it is they that testify on my behalf. Yet you refuse to come to me to have life. I do not accept glory from human beings. But I know that you do not have the love of God in you. I have come in my Father's name, and you do not accept me; if another comes in his own name, you will accept him. How can you believe when you accept glory from one another and do not seek the glory that comes from the one who alone is God? Do not think that I will accuse you before the Father; your accuser is Moses, on whom you have set your hope. If you believed Moses, you would believe me, for he wrote about me. But if you do not believe what he wrote, how will you believe what I say?'

• John the Baptist fulfilled Isaiah's prophecy, that a voice would cry in the wilderness 'Prepare the way of the Lord; make straight in the desert a highway for our God'. As we make our Lenten journey, let us reflect on what we are doing to make our own crooked ways straight.

Friday 1 April

John 7:1–2.10.25–30

After this Jesus went about in Galilee. He did not wish to go about in Judea because the Jews were looking for an opportunity to kill him. Now the Jewish festival of Booths was near.

But after his brothers had gone to the festival, then he also went, not publicly but as it were in secret.

Now some of the people of Jerusalem were saying, 'Is not this the man whom they are trying to kill? And here he is, speaking openly, but they say nothing to him! Can it be that the authorities really know that this is the Messiah? Yet we know where this man is from; but when the Messiah comes, no one will know where he is from.' Then Jesus cried out as he was teaching in the temple, 'You know me, and you know where I am from. I have not come on my own. But the one who sent me is true, and you do not know him. I know him, because I am from him, and he sent me.' Then they tried to arrest him, but no one laid hands on him, because his hour had not yet come.

- How do you pray on a text like this? (1) Enter into the way Jesus must have felt within himself in his frustration and their refusal to hear his good news. This helps us to better understand the human aspect of his life and brings us closer to him as we realise how much he is like us. (2) How do you manage when people reject you and criticise you when you mean well? It can be a great help to turn to the Lord as someone who understands you from his own experience and who supports you by his friendship.

Saturday 2 April

John 7:40–53

When they heard these words, some in the crowd said, 'This is really the prophet.' Others said, 'This is the Messiah.' But some asked, 'Surely the Messiah does not come from Galilee, does he? Has not the scripture said that the Messiah is descended from David and comes from Bethlehem, the village where David lived?' So there was a division in the crowd because of him. Some of them wanted to arrest him, but no one laid hands on him.

Then the temple police went back to the chief priests and Pharisees, who asked them, 'Why did you not arrest him?' The police answered, 'Never has anyone spoken like this!' Then the Pharisees replied, 'Surely you have not been deceived too, have you? Has any one of the authorities or of the Pharisees believed in him? But this crowd, which does not know the law – they are accursed.' Nicodemus, who had gone to Jesus before, and who was one of them, asked, 'Our law does not judge people without first giving them a hearing to find out what they are doing, does it?' They replied, 'Surely you are not also from Galilee, are you? Search and you will see that no prophet is to arise from Galilee.'

Then each of them went home.

- There is a wide range of views among the Jewish people as to who Jesus really is. Notice the constant appeal to the Old Testament. We may be more convinced by what the temple police report: 'Never has anyone spoken like this!' Jesus speaks with integrity, with wisdom, and with authority. This impresses these unsophisticated men. They are able to recognise the goodness of Jesus, which was hidden from the religious leaders.

- Pope Francis teaches that we must listen to the poor and the marginalised because they have a special insight into the reality of the world and of God.

The Fifth Week of Lent
3–9 April 2020

Something to think and pray about each day this week:

[Jesus] has been betrayed, cast aside and rejected by most of humanity. He has suffered the most awful physical and emotional torture. He can see no way forward and cries out to his Father to rescue him from the ignominy of the cross. This must be one of the most heartfelt cries of anguish or loneliness that must ever have been heard on the face of the earth; it will have gone right to the heart of God. However, Jesus acknowledges his son-ship and wishes to uphold the mission of the Father for the salvation of the world. He surrenders his own will to the will of the Father and in this he finds the courage to go on, to complete the salvation story and to win true peace for himself and all humankind.

In this he has left us an example to follow – when our wills are in union with the will of the Father, we too receive the grace to live through any loneliness and to come to a new and deeper peace at the core of our souls.

Siobhán O'Keeffe SHJM,
I Am with You Always

The Presence of God

What is present to me is what has a hold on my becoming.
I reflect on the presence of God always there in love.
I pause and pray that I may let God
affect my becoming in this precise moment.

Freedom

By God's grace I was born to live in freedom. Free to enjoy the pleasures
he created for me. Dear Lord, grant that I may live as you intended, with
complete confidence in your loving care.

Consciousness

To be conscious about something is to be aware of it.
Dear Lord, help me to remember that you gave me life.
Thank you for the gift of life.
Teach me to slow down, to be still and enjoy the pleasures created for me.
To be aware of the beauty that surrounds me: the marvel of mountains,
the calmness of lakes, the fragility of a flower petal. I need to remember
that all these things come from you.

The Word

God speaks to each of us individually. I listen attentively to hear what he
is saying to me. Read the text a few times, then listen.
*(Please turn to the Scripture on the following pages. Inspiration points are there,
should you need them. When you are ready, return here to continue.)*

Conversation

I begin to talk with Jesus about the Scripture I have just read. What part
of it strikes a chord in me? Perhaps the words of a friend – or some story
I have heard recently – will rise to the surface in my consciousness. If so,
does the story throw light on what the Scripture passage may be saying
to me?

Conclusion

Glory be to the Father, and to the Son, and to the Holy Spirit,
As it was in the beginning, is now and ever shall be,
World without end. Amen.

Sunday 3 April
Fifth Sunday of Lent
John 8:2–11

Early in the morning he came again to the temple. All the people came to him and he sat down and began to teach them. The scribes and the Pharisees brought a woman who had been caught in adultery; and making her stand before all of them, they said to him, 'Teacher, this woman was caught in the very act of committing adultery. Now in the law Moses commanded us to stone such women. Now what do you say?' They said this to test him, so that they might have some charge to bring against him. Jesus bent down and wrote with his finger on the ground. When they kept on questioning him, he straightened up and said to them, 'Let anyone among you who is without sin be the first to throw a stone at her.' And once again he bent down and wrote on the ground. When they heard it, they went away, one by one, beginning with the elders; and Jesus was left alone with the woman standing before him. Jesus straightened up and said to her, 'Woman, where are they? Has no one condemned you?' She said, 'No one, sir.' And Jesus said, 'Neither do I condemn you. Go your way, and from now on do not sin again.'

• A meeting with Jesus is always a life-giving experience, as he himself has said, 'I am the Way, the Truth and the Life'.

Monday 4 April
John 8:12–20

Again Jesus spoke to them, saying, 'I am the light of the world. Whoever follows me will never walk in darkness but will have the light of life.' Then the Pharisees said to him, 'You are testifying on your own behalf; your testimony is not valid.' Jesus answered, 'Even if I testify on my own behalf, my testimony is valid because I know where I have come from and where I am going, but you do not know where I come from or where I am going. You judge by human standards; I judge no one. Yet even if I do judge, my judgement is valid; for it is not I alone who judge, but I and the Father who sent me. In your law it is written that the testimony of two witnesses is valid. I testify on my own behalf, and the Father who sent me testifies on my behalf.' Then they said to him, 'Where is your Father?' Jesus answered, 'You know neither me nor my Father. If you knew me, you would know my Father also.' He spoke these words while he was teaching in the treasury of the temple, but no one arrested him, because his hour had not yet come.

- No matter how dark things may seem, I remind myself that darkness can never overpower light. I turn to Christ, the light of the world.

- I pray in the words of Saint Benedict: 'O gracious and Holy Father, give us wisdom to perceive you, diligence to seek you, patience to wait for you, eyes to behold you, a heart to meditate upon you, and a life to proclaim you; through the power of the Spirit of Jesus Christ our Lord.'

Tuesday 5 April
John 8:21–30

Again he said to them, 'I am going away, and you will search for me, but you will die in your sin. Where I am going, you cannot come.' Then the Jews said, 'Is he going to kill himself? Is that what he means by saying, "Where I am going, you cannot come"?' He said to them, 'You are from below, I am from above; you are of this world, I am not of this world. I told you that you would die in your sins, for you will die in your sins unless you believe that I am he.' They said to him, 'Who are you?' Jesus said to them, 'Why do I speak to you at all? I have much to say about you and much to condemn; but the one who sent me is true, and I declare to the world what I have heard from him.' They did not understand that he was speaking to them about the Father. So Jesus said, 'When you have lifted up the Son of Man, then you will realise that I am he, and that I do nothing on my own, but I speak these things as the Father instructed me. And the one who sent me is with me; he has not left me alone, for I always do what is pleasing to him.' As he was saying these things, many believed in him.

- The Father is all truth and so is the Son, who speaks only what he has learned from the source of all. Jesus was totally in tune with his Father, in his thinking and doing. The harmony between them is total and divine.

- Jesus is aware that only when he is lifted up on the cross will his followers realise who he is. The cross reveals God to us.

Wednesday 6 April

John 8:31–42

Then Jesus said to the Jews who had believed in him, 'If you continue in my word, you are truly my disciples; and you will know the truth, and the truth will make you free.' They answered him, 'We are descendants of Abraham and have never been slaves to anyone. What do you mean by saying, "You will be made free"?'

Jesus answered them, 'Very truly, I tell you, everyone who commits sin is a slave to sin. The slave does not have a permanent place in the household; the son has a place there for ever. So if the Son makes you free, you will be free indeed. I know that you are descendants of Abraham; yet you look for an opportunity to kill me, because there is no place in you for my word. I declare what I have seen in the Father's presence; as for you, you should do what you have heard from the Father.'

They answered him, 'Abraham is our father.' Jesus said to them, 'If you were Abraham's children, you would be doing what Abraham did, but now you are trying to kill me, a man who has told you the truth that I heard from God. This is not what Abraham did. You are indeed doing what your father does.' They said to him, 'We are not illegitimate children; we have one father, God himself.' Jesus said to them, 'If God were your Father, you would love me, for I came from God and now I am here. I did not come on my own, but he sent me.'

• John shows the people who listened to Jesus as being prickly and precious, quick to defend their religion and righteousness. Jesus' replies show them that they have forgotten love and relationship.

Thursday 7 April

John 8:51–59

'Very truly, I tell you, whoever keeps my word will never see death.' The Jews said to him, 'Now we know that you have a demon. Abraham died, and so did the prophets; yet you say, "Whoever keeps my word will never taste death." Are you greater than our father Abraham, who died? The prophets also died. Who do you claim to be?' Jesus answered, 'If I glorify myself, my glory is nothing. It is my Father who glorifies me, he of whom you say, "He is our God", though you do not know him. But I know him; if I were to say that I do not know him, I would be a liar like you. But I do know him and I keep his word. Your ancestor Abraham rejoiced that he would see my day; he saw it and was glad.' Then the Jews said to him, 'You are not yet fifty years old, and have you seen Abraham?' Jesus said to them, 'Very truly, I tell you, before Abraham was, I am.' So they picked up stones to throw at him, but Jesus hid himself and went out of the temple.

• Abraham's life marks the beginning of salvation history. His immense journey through the wilderness was made in response to God's call. The biblical desert was a place of passage and purification. In our own passage to the Promised Land, we must learn that God is with us at every stage of the journey, as he was with Abraham.

• Only by making ourselves vulnerable to our own pain and fear can we make ourselves open to the experience of loving and being loved.

Friday 8 April
John 10:31–42

The Jews took up stones again to stone him. Jesus replied, 'I have shown you many good works from the Father. For which of these are you going to stone me?' The Jews answered, 'It is not for a good work that we are going to stone you, but for blasphemy, because you, though only a human being, are making yourself God.' Jesus answered, 'Is it not written in your law, "I said, you are gods"? If those to whom the word of God came were called "gods" – and the scripture cannot be annulled – can you say that the one whom the Father has sanctified and sent into the world is blaspheming because I said, "I am God's Son"? If I am not doing the works of my Father, then do not believe me. But if I do them, even though you do not believe me, believe the works, so that you may know and understand that the Father is in me and I am in the Father.' Then they tried to arrest him again, but he escaped from their hands.

He went away again across the Jordan to the place where John had been baptising earlier, and he remained there. Many came to him, and they were saying, 'John performed no sign, but everything that John said about this man was true.' And many believed in him there.

• The people in today's reading condemn Jesus because of their particular image of God. What is my image of God? The best image is to see God as Pure Love. Have I ever condemned someone because I nursed a warped image of God?

Saturday 9 April

John 11:45–56

Many of the Jews therefore, who had come with Mary and had seen what Jesus did, believed in him. But some of them went to the Pharisees and told them what he had done. So the chief priests and the Pharisees called a meeting of the council, and said, 'What are we to do? This man is performing many signs. If we let him go on like this, everyone will believe in him, and the Romans will come and destroy both our holy place and our nation.' But one of them, Caiaphas, who was high priest that year, said to them, 'You know nothing at all! You do not understand that it is better for you to have one man die for the people than to have the whole nation destroyed.' He did not say this on his own, but being high priest that year he prophesied that Jesus was about to die for the nation, and not for the nation only, but to gather into one the dispersed children of God. So from that day on they planned to put him to death.

Jesus therefore no longer walked about openly among the Jews, but went from there to a town called Ephraim in the region near the wilderness; and he remained there with the disciples.

Now the Passover of the Jews was near, and many went up from the country to Jerusalem before the Passover to purify themselves. They were looking for Jesus and were asking one another as they stood in the temple, 'What do you think? Surely he will not come to the festival, will he?'

- Pope Francis, reflecting on this text, noted that Jesus died for his people and for everyone. But this, the pope stressed, must not be applied generically; it means that Jesus died specifically for each and every one of us individually. And this is the ultimate expression of Jesus' love for all people.

10–16 April 2022

Something to think and pray about each day this week:

Icons of Christ usually show him wearing a blue mantle over a red robe. Red signifies his humanity, the colour of the reddish earth from which Adam was made (Genesis 25:25). His humanity is in essence with his divinity, generally represented as blue, sometimes using crushed *lapis lazuli,* a most expensive mineral, at that time mined only in Afghanistan. There is little difference between the red and the blue, as though the humanity is showing through in greater clarity. As well as symbolising life, blood, passion and love in iconography in general, red has also come to symbolise the life-blood of Christ, poured out for us. The resurrection, too, is associated with red to proclaim Christ's victory of life over death. The iconographer invites us to contemplate the resurrection and the offer of eternal life to all people, extending beyond the Jewish people, although we know that God's promise to them is never rescinded and God's relationship with them remains true for all time.

Magdalen Lawler SND,
Well of Living Water: Jesus and the Samaritan Woman

The Presence of God

'Be still, and know that I am God!' Lord, your words lead us to the calmness and greatness of your presence.

Freedom

Everything has the potential to draw forth from me a fuller love and life. Yet my desires are often fixed, caught, on illusions of fulfilment. I ask that God, through my freedom, may orchestrate my desires in a vibrant loving melody rich in harmony.

Consciousness

I exist in a web of relationships: links to nature, people, God.
I trace out these links, giving thanks for the life that flows through them.
Some links are twisted or broken; I may feel regret, anger, disappointment.
I pray for the gift of acceptance and forgiveness.

The Word

I read the word of God slowly, a few times over, and I listen to what God is saying to me.

(Please turn to the Scripture on the following pages. Inspiration points are there, should you need them. When you are ready, return here to continue.)

Conversation

Jesus, you speak to me through the words of the Gospels. May I respond to your call today. Teach me to recognise your hand at work in my daily living.

Conclusion

I thank God for these moments we have spent together and for any insights I have been given concerning the text.

Sunday 10 April
Palm Sunday of the Passion of the Lord
Luke 22:14–23:56

When the hour came, he took his place at the table, and the apostles with him. He said to them, 'I have eagerly desired to eat this Passover with you before I suffer; for I tell you, I will not eat it until it is fulfilled in the kingdom of God.' Then he took a cup, and after giving thanks he said, 'Take this and divide it among yourselves; for I tell you that from now on I will not drink of the fruit of the vine until the kingdom of God comes.' Then he took a loaf of bread, and when he had given thanks, he broke it and gave it to them, saying, 'This is my body, which is given for you. Do this in remembrance of me.' And he did the same with the cup after supper, saying, 'This cup that is poured out for you is the new covenant in my blood. But see, the one who betrays me is with me, and his hand is on the table. For the Son of Man is going as it has been determined, but woe to that one by whom he is betrayed!' Then they began to ask one another which one of them it could be who would do this.

A dispute also arose among them as to which one of them was to be regarded as the greatest. But he said to them, 'The kings of the Gentiles lord it over them; and those in authority over them are called benefactors. But not so with you; rather the greatest among you must become like the youngest, and the leader like one who serves. For who is greater, the one who is at the table or the one who serves? Is it not the one at the table? But I am among you as one who serves.

'You are those who have stood by me in my trials; and I confer on you, just as my Father has conferred on me, a kingdom, so that you may eat and drink at my table in my kingdom, and you will sit on thrones judging the twelve tribes of Israel.

'Simon, Simon, listen! Satan has demanded to sift all of you like wheat, but I have prayed for you that your own faith may not fail; and you, when once you have turned back, strengthen your brothers.' And he said to him, 'Lord, I am ready to go with you to prison and to death!' Jesus said, 'I tell you, Peter, the cock will not crow this day, until you have denied three times that you know me.'

He said to them, 'When I sent you out without a purse, bag, or sandals, did you lack anything?' They said, 'No, not a thing.' He said to them,

'But now, the one who has a purse must take it, and likewise a bag. And the one who has no sword must sell his cloak and buy one. For I tell you, this scripture must be fulfilled in me, "And he was counted among the lawless"; and indeed what is written about me is being fulfilled.' They said, 'Lord, look, here are two swords.' He replied, 'It is enough.'

He came out and went, as was his custom, to the Mount of Olives; and the disciples followed him. When he reached the place, he said to them, 'Pray that you may not come into the time of trial.' Then he withdrew from them about a stone's throw, knelt down, and prayed, 'Father, if you are willing, remove this cup from me; yet, not my will but yours be done.' [Then an angel from heaven appeared to him and gave him strength. In his anguish he prayed more earnestly, and his sweat became like great drops of blood falling down on the ground.] When he got up from prayer, he came to the disciples and found them sleeping because of grief, and he said to them, 'Why are you sleeping? Get up and pray that you may not come into the time of trial.'

While he was still speaking, suddenly a crowd came, and the one called Judas, one of the twelve, was leading them. He approached Jesus to kiss him; but Jesus said to him, 'Judas, is it with a kiss that you are betraying the Son of Man?' When those who were around him saw what was coming, they asked, 'Lord, should we strike with the sword?' Then one of them struck the slave of the high priest and cut off his right ear. But Jesus said, 'No more of this!' And he touched his ear and healed him. Then Jesus said to the chief priests, the officers of the temple police, and the elders who had come for him, 'Have you come out with swords and clubs as if I were a bandit? When I was with you day after day in the temple, you did not lay hands on me. But this is your hour, and the power of darkness!'

Then they seized him and led him away, bringing him into the high priest's house. But Peter was following at a distance. When they had kindled a fire in the middle of the courtyard and sat down together, Peter sat among them. Then a servant-girl, seeing him in the firelight, stared at him and said, 'This man also was with him.' But he denied it, saying, 'Woman, I do not know him.' A little later someone else, on seeing him, said, 'You also are one of them.' But Peter said, 'Man, I am not!' Then about an hour later yet another kept insisting, 'Surely this man also was with him; for he is a Galilean.' But Peter said, 'Man, I do not know what you are talking about!' At that moment, while he was still speaking, the cock crowed. The Lord turned and looked at Peter. Then Peter remembered the word of the Lord, how he had said to him, 'Before the cock crows today, you will deny me three times.' And he went out and wept bitterly.

Now the men who were holding Jesus began to mock him and beat him; they also blindfolded him and kept asking him, 'Prophesy! Who is it that struck you?' They kept heaping many other insults on him.

When day came, the assembly of the elders of the people, both chief priests and scribes, gathered together, and they brought him to their council. They said, 'If you are the Messiah, tell us.' He replied, 'If I tell you, you will not believe; and if I question you, you will not answer. But from now on the Son of Man will be seated at the right hand of the power of God.' All of them asked, 'Are you, then, the Son of God?' He said to them, 'You say that I am.' Then they said, 'What further testimony do we need? We have heard it ourselves from his own lips!'

Then the assembly rose as a body and brought Jesus before Pilate. They began to accuse him, saying, 'We found this man perverting our nation, forbidding us to pay taxes to the emperor, and saying that he himself is the Messiah, a king.' Then Pilate asked him, 'Are you the king of the Jews?' He answered, 'You say so.' Then Pilate said to the chief priests and the crowds, 'I find no basis for an accusation against this man.' But they were insistent and said, 'He stirs up the people by teaching throughout all Judea, from Galilee where he began even to this place.'

When Pilate heard this, he asked whether the man was a Galilean. And when he learned that he was under Herod's jurisdiction, he sent him off to Herod, who was himself in Jerusalem at that time. When Herod saw Jesus, he was very glad, for he had been wanting to see him for a long time, because he had heard about him and was hoping to see him perform some sign. He questioned him at some length, but Jesus gave him no answer. The chief priests and the scribes stood by, vehemently accusing him. Even Herod with his soldiers treated him with contempt and mocked him; then he put an elegant robe on him, and sent him back to Pilate. That same day Herod and Pilate became friends with each other; before this they had been enemies.

Pilate then called together the chief priests, the leaders, and the people, and said to them, 'You brought me this man as one who was perverting the people; and here I have examined him in your presence and have not found this man guilty of any of your charges against him. Neither has Herod, for he sent him back to us. Indeed, he has done nothing to deserve death. I will therefore have him flogged and release him.'

Then they all shouted out together, 'Away with this fellow! Release Barabbas for us!' (This was a man who had been put in prison for an insurrection that had taken place in the city, and for murder.) Pilate, wanting to release Jesus, addressed them again; but they kept shouting, 'Crucify, crucify him!' A third time he said to them, 'Why, what evil has he done? I have found in him no ground for the sentence of death; I will therefore have him flogged and then release him.' But they kept urgently demanding with loud shouts that he should be crucified; and their voices prevailed. So Pilate gave his verdict that their demand should be granted. He released the man they asked for, the one who had been put in prison for insurrection and murder, and he handed Jesus over as they wished.

As they led him away, they seized a man, Simon of Cyrene, who was coming from the country, and they laid the cross on him, and made him carry it behind Jesus. A great number of the people followed him, and among them were women who were beating their breasts and wailing for him. But Jesus turned to them and said, 'Daughters of Jerusalem, do not weep for me, but weep for yourselves and for your children. For the days are surely coming when they will say, "Blessed are the barren, and the wombs that never bore, and the breasts that never nursed." Then they will begin to say to the mountains, "Fall on us"; and to the hills, "Cover us." For if they do this when the wood is green, what will happen when it is dry?'

Two others also, who were criminals, were led away to be put to death with him. When they came to the place that is called The Skull, they crucified Jesus there with the criminals, one on his right and one on his left. [Then Jesus said, 'Father, forgive them; for they do not know what they are doing.'] And they cast lots to divide his clothing. And the people stood by, watching; but the leaders scoffed at him, saying, 'He saved others; let him save himself if he is the Messiah of God, his chosen one!' The soldiers also mocked him, coming up and offering him sour wine, and saying, 'If you are the King of the Jews, save yourself!' There was also an inscription over him, 'This is the King of the Jews.'

One of the criminals who were hanged there kept deriding him and saying, 'Are you not the Messiah? Save yourself and us!' But the other rebuked him, saying, 'Do you not fear God, since you are under the same sentence of condemnation? And we indeed have been condemned justly, for we are getting what we deserve for our deeds, but this man has done nothing wrong.' Then he said, 'Jesus, remember me when you come into your kingdom.' He replied, 'Truly I tell you, today you will be with me in Paradise.'

It was now about noon, and darkness came over the whole land until three in the afternoon, while the sun's light failed; and the curtain of the temple was torn in two. Then Jesus, crying with a loud voice, said, 'Father, into your hands I commend my spirit.' Having said this, he breathed his last. When the centurion saw what had taken place, he praised God and said, 'Certainly this man was innocent.' And when all the crowds who had gathered there for this spectacle saw what had taken place, they returned home, beating their breasts. But all his acquaintances, including the women who had followed him from Galilee, stood at a distance, watching these things.

Now there was a good and righteous man named Joseph, who, though a member of the council, had not agreed to their plan and action. He came from the Jewish town of Arimathea, and he was waiting expectantly for the kingdom of God. This man went to Pilate and asked for the body of Jesus. Then he took it down, wrapped it in a linen cloth, and laid it in a rock-hewn tomb where no one had ever been laid. It was the day of Preparation, and the sabbath was beginning. The women who had come with him from Galilee followed, and they saw the tomb and how his body was laid. Then they returned, and prepared spices and ointments.

On the sabbath they rested according to the commandment.

• As we go through this day and this week, let us look very carefully at Jesus our Saviour. We watch not just to admire but also to learn, to penetrate the mind, the thinking, the attitudes and the values of Jesus so that we, in the very different circumstances of our own lives, may walk in his footsteps.

Monday 11 April
Luke 4:16–21

When he came to Nazareth, where he had been brought up, he went to the synagogue on the sabbath day, as was his custom. He stood up to read, and the scroll of the prophet Isaiah was given to him. He unrolled the scroll and found the place where it was written:

> 'The Spirit of the Lord is upon me,
> because he has anointed me
> to bring good news to the poor.
> He has sent me to proclaim release to the captives
> and recovery of sight to the blind,
> to let the oppressed go free,
> to proclaim the year of the Lord's favour.'

And he rolled up the scroll, gave it back to the attendant, and sat down. The eyes of all in the synagogue were fixed on him. Then he began to say to them, 'Today this scripture has been fulfilled in your hearing.'

- Jesus lists his priorities: all who are restricted or confined are invited to freedom. I realise that I am included, called to new liberty and life. What does Jesus have in mind for me? Where is he calling me to freedom, to life?

- Jesus lived among people whose vision was narrow and who found it difficult to accept his inspired words – they were ready even to kill him. Yet he remained part of them, going to pray with them 'as was his custom'.

Tuesday 12 April
John 13:21–33.36–38

After saying this Jesus was troubled in spirit, and declared, 'Very truly, I tell you, one of you will betray me.' The disciples looked at one another, uncertain of whom he was speaking. One of his disciples – the one whom Jesus loved – was reclining next to him; Simon Peter therefore motioned to him to ask Jesus of whom he was speaking. So while reclining next to Jesus, he asked him, 'Lord, who is it?' Jesus answered, 'It is the one to whom I give this piece of bread when I have dipped it in the dish.' So when he had dipped the piece of bread, he gave it to Judas son of Simon Iscariot. After he received the piece of bread, Satan entered into him. Jesus said to him, 'Do quickly what you are going to do.' Now no one at the table knew why he said this to him. Some thought that, because Judas had the common purse, Jesus was telling him, 'Buy what we need for the festival'; or, that he should give something to the poor. So, after receiving the piece of bread, he immediately went out. And it was night.

When he had gone out, Jesus said, 'Now the Son of Man has been glorified, and God has been glorified in him. If God has been glorified in him, God will also glorify him in himself and will glorify him at once. Little children, I am with you only a little longer. You will look for me; and as I said to the Jews so now I say to you, "Where I am going, you cannot come." ' . . .

Simon Peter said to him, 'Lord, where are you going?' Jesus answered, 'Where I am going, you cannot follow me now; but you will follow afterwards.' Peter said to him, 'Lord, why can I not follow you now? I will lay down my life for you.' Jesus answered, 'Will you lay down your life for me? Very truly, I tell you, before the cock crows, you will have denied me three times.'

- We rightly hesitate to answer affirmatively the question, 'Will you lay down your life for me?' But there is no ambivalence in Jesus – he has already decided to lay down his life for us, in purest love.

Wednesday 13 April
Matthew 26:14–25

Then one of the twelve, who was called Judas Iscariot, went to the chief priests and said, 'What will you give me if I betray him to you?' They paid him thirty pieces of silver. And from that moment he began to look for an opportunity to betray him.

On the first day of Unleavened Bread the disciples came to Jesus, saying, 'Where do you want us to make the preparations for you to eat the Passover?' He said, 'Go into the city to a certain man, and say to him, "The Teacher says, My time is near; I will keep the Passover at your house with my disciples."' So the disciples did as Jesus had directed them, and they prepared the Passover meal.

When it was evening, he took his place with the twelve; and while they were eating, he said, 'Truly I tell you, one of you will betray me.' And they became greatly distressed and began to say to him one after another, 'Surely not I, Lord?' He answered, 'The one who has dipped his hand into the bowl with me will betray me. The Son of Man goes as it is written of him, but woe to that one by whom the Son of Man is betrayed! It would have been better for that one not to have been born.' Judas, who betrayed him, said, 'Surely not I, Rabbi?' He replied, 'You have said so.'

- This highlights the depth of love that Jesus shows. He 'goes to his fate', but he is loyal all the way. He does not retaliate, no matter how shamefully he is treated. A higher love – divine love – keeps him going. I thank him for his greatness of heart, and ask that I may never betray him or his values. He promises to help me.

Thursday 14 April
Holy Thursday
John 13:1–15

Now before the festival of the Passover, Jesus knew that his hour had come to depart from this world and go to the Father. Having loved his own who were in the world, he loved them to the end. The devil had already put it into the heart of Judas son of Simon Iscariot to betray him. And during supper Jesus, knowing that the Father had given all things into his hands, and that he had come from God and was going to God, got up from the table, took off his outer robe, and tied a towel around himself. Then he poured water into a basin and began to wash the disciples' feet and to wipe them with the towel that was tied around him. He came to Simon Peter, who said to him, 'Lord, are you going to wash my feet?' Jesus answered, 'You do not know now what I am doing, but later you will understand.' Peter said to him, 'You will never wash my feet.' Jesus answered, 'Unless I wash you, you have no share with me.' Simon Peter said to him, 'Lord, not my feet only but also my hands and my head!' Jesus said to him, 'One who has bathed does not need to wash, except for the feet, but is entirely clean. And you are clean, though not all of you.' For he knew who was to betray him; for this reason he said, 'Not all of you are clean.'

After he had washed their feet, had put on his robe, and had returned to the table, he said to them, 'Do you know what I have done to you? You call me Teacher and Lord – and you are right, for that is what I am. So if I, your Lord and Teacher, have washed your feet, you also ought to wash one another's feet. For I have set you an example, that you also should do as I have done to you.

- Jesus' instruction – to do to others what he does to us – was not intended to stop at the church door. How can I bear witness to a servant God in my life today?

Friday 15 April
Good Friday
John 18:1–19:42

After Jesus had spoken these words, he went out with his disciples across the Kidron valley to a place where there was a garden, which he and his disciples entered. Now Judas, who betrayed him, also knew the place, because Jesus often met there with his disciples. So Judas brought a detachment of soldiers together with police from the chief priests and the Pharisees, and they came there with lanterns and torches and weapons. Then Jesus, knowing all that was to happen to him, came forward and asked them, 'For whom are you looking?' They answered, 'Jesus of Nazareth.' Jesus replied, 'I am he.' Judas, who betrayed him, was standing with them. When Jesus said to them, 'I am he', they stepped back and fell to the ground. Again he asked them, 'For whom are you looking?' And they said, 'Jesus of Nazareth.' Jesus answered, 'I told you that I am he. So if you are looking for me, let these men go.' This was to fulfil the word that he had spoken, 'I did not lose a single one of those whom you gave me.' Then Simon Peter, who had a sword, drew it, struck the high priest's slave, and cut off his right ear. The slave's name was Malchus. Jesus said to Peter, 'Put your sword back into its sheath. Am I not to drink the cup that the Father has given me?'

So the soldiers, their officer, and the Jewish police arrested Jesus and bound him. First they took him to Annas, who was the father-in-law of Caiaphas, the high priest that year. Caiaphas was the one who had advised the Jews that it was better to have one person die for the people.

Simon Peter and another disciple followed Jesus. Since that disciple was known to the high priest, he went with Jesus into the courtyard of the high priest, but Peter was standing outside at the gate. So the other disciple, who was known to the high priest, went out, spoke to the woman who guarded the gate, and brought Peter in. The woman said to Peter, 'You are not also one of this man's disciples, are you?' He said, 'I am not.' Now the slaves and the police had made a charcoal fire because it was cold, and they were standing round it and warming themselves. Peter also was standing with them and warming himself.

Then the high priest questioned Jesus about his disciples and about his teaching. Jesus answered, 'I have spoken openly to the world; I have always taught in synagogues and in the temple, where all the Jews come together. I have said nothing in secret. Why do you ask me? Ask those who heard what I said to them; they know what I said.' When he had said this, one of the police standing nearby struck Jesus on the face, saying, 'Is that how you answer the high priest?' Jesus answered, 'If I have spoken wrongly, testify to the wrong. But if I have spoken rightly, why do you strike me?' Then Annas sent him bound to Caiaphas the high priest.

Now Simon Peter was standing and warming himself. They asked him, 'You are not also one of his disciples, are you?' He denied it and said, 'I am not.' One of the slaves of the high priest, a relative of the man whose ear Peter had cut off, asked, 'Did I not see you in the garden with him?' Again Peter denied it, and at that moment the cock crowed.

Then they took Jesus from Caiaphas to Pilate's headquarters. It was early in the morning. They themselves did not enter the headquarters, so as to avoid ritual defilement and to be able to eat the Passover. So Pilate went out to them and said, 'What accusation do you bring against this man?' They answered, 'If this man were not a criminal, we would not have handed him over to you.' Pilate said to them, 'Take him yourselves and judge him according to your law.' The Jews replied, 'We are not permitted to put anyone to death.' (This was to fulfil what Jesus had said when he indicated the kind of death he was to die.)

Then Pilate entered the headquarters again, summoned Jesus, and asked him, 'Are you the King of the Jews?' Jesus answered, 'Do you ask this on your own, or did others tell you about me?' Pilate replied, 'I am not a Jew, am I? Your own nation and the chief priests have handed you over to me. What have you done?' Jesus answered, 'My kingdom is not from this world. If my kingdom were from this world, my followers would be fighting to keep me from being handed over to the Jews. But as it is, my kingdom is not from here.' Pilate asked him, 'So you are a king?' Jesus answered, 'You say that I am a king. For this I was born, and for this I came into the world, to testify to the truth. Everyone who belongs to the truth listens to my voice.' Pilate asked him, 'What is truth?'

After he had said this, he went out to the Jews again and told them, 'I find no case against him. But you have a custom that I release someone for you at the Passover. Do you want me to release for you the King of the Jews?' They shouted in reply, 'Not this man, but Barabbas!' Now Barabbas was a bandit.

Then Pilate took Jesus and had him flogged. And the soldiers wove a crown of thorns and put it on his head, and they dressed him in a purple robe. They kept coming up to him, saying, 'Hail, King of the Jews!' and striking him on the face. Pilate went out again and said to them, 'Look, I am bringing him out to you to let you know that I find no case against him.' So Jesus came out, wearing the crown of thorns and the purple robe. Pilate said to them, 'Here is the man!' When the chief priests and the police saw him, they shouted, 'Crucify him! Crucify him!' Pilate said to them, 'Take him yourselves and crucify him; I find no case against him.' The Jews answered him, 'We have a law, and according to that law he ought to die because he has claimed to be the Son of God.'

Now when Pilate heard this, he was more afraid than ever. He entered his headquarters again and asked Jesus, 'Where are you from?' But Jesus gave him no answer. Pilate therefore said to him, 'Do you refuse to speak to me? Do you not know that I have power to release you, and power to crucify you?' Jesus answered him, 'You would have no power over me unless it had been given you from above; therefore the one who handed me over to you is guilty of a greater sin.' From then on Pilate tried to release him, but the Jews cried out, 'If you release this man, you are no friend of the emperor. Everyone who claims to be a king sets himself against the emperor.'

When Pilate heard these words, he brought Jesus outside and sat on the judge's bench at a place called The Stone Pavement, or in Hebrew Gabbatha. Now it was the day of Preparation for the Passover; and it was about noon. He said to the Jews, 'Here is your King!' They cried out, 'Away with him! Away with him! Crucify him!' Pilate asked them, 'Shall I crucify your King?' The chief priests answered, 'We have no king but the emperor.' Then he handed him over to them to be crucified.

So they took Jesus; and carrying the cross by himself, he went out to what is called The Place of the Skull, which in Hebrew is called Golgotha. There they crucified him, and with him two others, one on either side, with Jesus between them. Pilate also had an inscription written and put on the cross. It read, 'Jesus of Nazareth, the King of the Jews.' Many of the Jews read this inscription, because the place where Jesus was crucified was near the city; and it was written in Hebrew, in Latin, and in Greek. Then the chief priests of the Jews said to Pilate, 'Do not write, "The King of the Jews", but, "This man said, I am King of the Jews."' Pilate answered, 'What I have written I have written.' When the soldiers had crucified Jesus, they took his clothes and divided them into four parts, one for each soldier. They also took his tunic; now the tunic was seamless, woven in one piece from the top. So they said to one another, 'Let us not tear it, but cast lots for it to see who will get it.' This was to fulfil what the scripture says,

'They divided my clothes among themselves,
and for my clothing they cast lots.'
And that is what the soldiers did.

Meanwhile, standing near the cross of Jesus were his mother, and his mother's sister, Mary the wife of Clopas, and Mary Magdalene. When Jesus saw his mother and the disciple whom he loved standing beside her, he said to his mother, 'Woman, here is your son.' Then he said to the disciple, 'Here is your mother.' And from that hour the disciple took her into his own home.

After this, when Jesus knew that all was now finished, he said (in order to fulfil the scripture), 'I am thirsty.' A jar full of sour wine was standing there. So they put a sponge full of the wine on a branch of hyssop and held it to his mouth. When Jesus had received the wine, he said, 'It is finished.' Then he bowed his head and gave up his spirit.

Since it was the day of Preparation, the Jews did not want the bodies left on the cross during the sabbath, especially because that sabbath was a day of great solemnity. So they asked Pilate to have the legs of the crucified men broken and the bodies removed. Then the soldiers came and broke the legs of the first and of the other who had been crucified with him. But when they came to Jesus and saw that he was already dead, they did not break his legs. Instead, one of the soldiers pierced his side with a spear, and at once blood and water came out. (He who saw this has testified so that you also may believe. His testimony is true, and he knows that he tells the truth.) These things occurred so that the scripture might be fulfilled, 'None of his bones shall be broken.' And again another passage of scripture says, 'They will look on the one whom they have pierced.'

After these things, Joseph of Arimathea, who was a disciple of Jesus, though a secret one because of his fear of the Jews, asked Pilate to let him take away the body of Jesus. Pilate gave him permission; so he came and removed his body. Nicodemus, who had at first come to Jesus by night, also came, bringing a mixture of myrrh and aloes, weighing about a hundred pounds. They took the body of Jesus and wrapped it with the spices in linen cloths, according to the burial custom of the Jews. Now there was a garden in the place where he was crucified, and in the garden there was a new tomb in which no one had ever been laid. And so, because it was the Jewish day of Preparation, and the tomb was nearby, they laid Jesus there.

• Good Friday puts the cross before me and challenges me not to look away. If I have followed Jesus' footsteps to Calvary, I do not have to fear because I, like him, am confident in God's enduring presence. Wherever there is suffering or pain, I look again, seeking the face of Jesus. I ask him for the strength I need to be a sign of hope wherever there is despair, to be a presence of love wherever it is most needed.

Saturday 16 April
Holy Saturday
Luke 24:1–12

But on the first day of the week, at early dawn, they came to the tomb, taking the spices that they had prepared. They found the stone rolled away from the tomb, but when they went in, they did not find the body. While were perplexed about this, suddenly two men in dazzling clothes stood beside them. The women were terrified and bowed their faces to the ground, but the men said to them, 'Why do you look for the living among the dead? He is not here, but has risen. Remember how he told you, while he was still in Galilee, that the Son of Man must be handed over to sinners, and be crucified, and on the third day rise again.' Then they remembered his words, and returning from the tomb, they told all this to the eleven and to all the rest. Now it was Mary Magdalene, Joanna, Mary the mother of James, and the other women with them who told this to the apostles. But these words seemed to them an idle tale, and they did not believe them. But Peter got up and ran to the tomb; stooping and looking in, he saw the linen cloths by themselves; then he went home, amazed at what had happened.

• We must not skip lightly over Holy Saturday. It is a time of waiting. I wait with Mary: we chat and pray as Jesus descends into the world of the dead. He holds the keys to Death and the Underworld. Theologians suggest that this means that Jesus went in search of the dead, especially hardened sinners. These in their despair find his footprints on their lonely path, and come face to face with the crucified One, who invites them to accept the forgiving love of God. He goes to the dark limits of human experience and brings them Easter light.

Octave of Easter
17–23 April 2022

Something to think and pray about each day this week:

The Easter season is itself the great season of encounter, of dialogue, as different New Testament figures come to faith in Jesus risen from the dead. An ancient Easter greeting found especially in the ancient churches of the East goes likes this: Christ is risen, he is truly risen! We need to hear this acclamation more than ever before, for it announces something momentous: Evil, death and destruction are not the final word on each of us or on our lives or on our world, in spite of evidence to the contrary. This conviction is grounded in the proclamation of Christ risen, victorious over death, setting us free even from the fear of death itself. In the elevated vision of Gerard Manley Hopkins SJ,

> I am all at once what Christ is,
> since he was what I am, and
> This Jack, joke, poor potsherd,
> patch, matchwood, immortal diamond,
> Is immortal diamond.

This is so good, so exactly what we need to hear as 'hearers of the word', it has to be true!

Kieran J. O'Mahony OSA,
Hearers of the Word: Easter & Pentecost Year A

The Presence of God

'Come to me, all you who are weary and are carrying heavy burdens, and I will give you rest.' Here I am, Lord. I come to seek your presence. I long for your healing power.

Freedom

God is not foreign to my freedom. The Spirit breathes life into my most intimate desires, gently nudging me towards all that is good. I ask for the grace to let myself be enfolded by the Spirit.

Consciousness

I remind myself that I am in the presence of the Lord. I will take refuge in his loving heart. He is my strength in times of weakness. He is my comforter in times of sorrow.

The Word

I take my time to read the word of God slowly, a few times, allowing myself to dwell on anything that strikes me.

(Please turn to the Scripture on the following pages. Inspiration points are there, should you need them. When you are ready, return here to continue.)

Conversation

Jesus, you always welcomed little children when you walked on this earth. Teach me to have a childlike trust in you. Teach me to live in the knowledge that you will never abandon me.

Conclusion

Glory be to the Father, and to the Son and to the Holy Spirit,
As it was in the beginning, is now and ever shall be,
World without end. Amen.

Sunday 17 April
Easter Sunday of the Resurrection of the Lord
John 20:1–9

Early on the first day of the week, while it was still dark, Mary Magdalene came to the tomb and saw that the stone had been removed from the tomb. So she ran and went to Simon Peter and the other disciple, the one whom Jesus loved, and said to them, 'They have taken the Lord out of the tomb, and we do not know where they have laid him.' Then Peter and the other disciple set out and went towards the tomb. The two were running together, but the other disciple outran Peter and reached the tomb first. He bent down to look in and saw the linen wrappings lying there, but he did not go in. Then Simon Peter came, following him, and went into the tomb. He saw the linen wrappings lying there, and the cloth that had been on Jesus' head, not lying with the linen wrappings but rolled up in a place by itself. Then the other disciple, who reached the tomb first, also went in, and he saw and believed; for as yet they did not understand the scripture, that he must rise from the dead.

- The great gifts of Easter are hope and faith. Hope: which makes us have that confidence in God, in his ultimate triumph, and in his goodness and love, which nothing can shake. Faith: the belief that Christ has triumphed over evil despite appearances and that the resurrection is the definitive act in human history.

- So, we celebrate the mystery of the resurrection, proclaim our faith and hope, and give thanks for these gifts.

Monday 18 April
Matthew 28:8–15

So they left the tomb quickly with fear and great joy, and ran to tell his disciples. Suddenly Jesus met them and said, 'Greetings!' And they came to him, took hold of his feet, and worshipped him. Then Jesus said to them, 'Do not be afraid; go and tell my brothers to go to Galilee; there they will see me.'

While they were going, some of the guard went into the city and told the chief priests everything that had happened. After the priests had assembled with the elders, they devised a plan to give a large sum of money to the soldiers, telling them, 'You must say, "His disciples came by night and stole him away while we were asleep." If this comes to the governor's ears, we will satisfy him and keep you out of trouble.' So they took the money and did as they were directed. And this story is still told among the Jews to this day.

- This incident of the guards and the conspiracy is unique to Matthew. Why were the guards there at all? While the disciples of the Lord had no recollection of his saying that he would be put to death and would rise again, his enemies remembered this very well and so put guards at the tomb to prevent his disciples stealing the body and proclaiming that he had risen.

- What has given the Christian version the edge is not the meticulous historical work of scholars or the arguments of theologians but the fact that the proponents of the Christian version and their followers have been and still are prepared to die for that version. The witness of the Christian life lived to the full is the best apologetic for the resurrection.

Tuesday 19 April
John 20:11–18

But Mary stood weeping outside the tomb. As she wept, she bent over to look into the tomb; and she saw two angels in white, sitting where the body of Jesus had been lying, one at the head and the other at the feet. They said to her, 'Woman, why are you weeping?' She said to them, 'They have taken away my Lord, and I do not know where they have laid him.' When she had said this, she turned round and saw Jesus standing there, but she did not know that it was Jesus. Jesus said to her, 'Woman, why are you weeping? For whom are you looking?' Supposing him to be the gardener, she said to him, 'Sir, if you have carried him away, tell me where you have laid him, and I will take him away.' Jesus said to her, 'Mary!' She turned and said to him in Hebrew, 'Rabbouni!' (which means Teacher). Jesus said to her, 'Do not hold on to me, because I have not yet ascended to the Father. But go to my brothers and say to them, "I am ascending to my Father and your Father, to my God and your God."' Mary Magdalene went and announced to the disciples, 'I have seen the Lord'; and she told them that he had said these things to her.

- Lord, you offer me a parable of your dealings with me. Like Mary I am looking for you, following the call of love, but not recognising you because I am too caught up in my own emotions. But all the time you are looking at me, and it is when you call me by my name, and reach me with some intimately personal experience, that I recognise you with joy as my Rabbouni.

Wednesday 20 April
Luke 24:13–35

Now on that same day two of them were going to a village called Emmaus, about seven miles from Jerusalem, and talking with each other about all these things that had happened. While they were talking and discussing, Jesus himself came near and went with them, but their eyes were kept from recognising him. And he said to them, 'What are you discussing with each other while you walk along?' They stood still, looking sad. Then one of them, whose name was Cleopas, answered him, 'Are you the only stranger in Jerusalem who does not know the things that have taken place there in these days?' He asked them, 'What things?' They replied, 'The things about Jesus of Nazareth, who was a prophet mighty in deed and word before God and all the people, and how our chief priests and leaders handed him over to be condemned to death and crucified him. But we had hoped that he was the one to redeem Israel. Yes, and besides all this, it is now the third day since these things took place. Moreover, some women of our group astounded us. They were at the tomb early this morning, and when they did not find his body there, they came back and told us that they had indeed seen a vision of angels who said that he was alive. Some of those who were with us went to the tomb and found it just as the women had said; but they did not see him.' Then he said to them, 'Oh, how foolish you are, and how slow of heart to believe all that the prophets have declared! Was it not necessary that the Messiah should suffer these things and then enter into his glory?' Then beginning with Moses and all the prophets, he interpreted to them the things about himself in all the scriptures.

As they came near the village to which they were going, he walked ahead as if he were going on. But they urged him strongly, saying, 'Stay with us, because it is almost evening and the day is now nearly over.' So he went in to stay with them. When he was at the table with them, he took bread, blessed and broke it, and gave it to them. Then their eyes were opened, and they recognised him; and he vanished from their sight. They said to each other, 'Were not our hearts burning within us while he was talking to us on the road, while he was opening the scriptures to us?' That same hour they got up and returned to Jerusalem; and they found the eleven and their companions gathered together. They were saying, 'The Lord has risen indeed, and he has appeared to Simon!' Then they told what had happened on the road, and how he had been made known to them in the breaking of the bread.

- 'The Lord has risen indeed, and he has appeared to Simon!' This is the kernel of the Good News, the basic message preached by the apostles, and although seemingly incredible, it convinced many to embrace this new faith in the Risen Jesus. Sometimes we seem to present Christianity in a way that relegates the resurrection to a marginal place in our faith. I pray the Church will never cease to preach this truth, in season and out of season.

Thursday 21 April
Luke 24:35–48

Then they told what had happened on the road, and how he had been made known to them in the breaking of the bread.

While they were talking about this, Jesus himself stood among them and said to them, 'Peace be with you.' They were startled and terrified, and thought that they were seeing a ghost. He said to them, 'Why are you frightened, and why do doubts arise in your hearts? Look at my hands and my feet; see that it is I myself. Touch me and see; for a ghost does not have flesh and bones as you see that I have.' And when he had said this, he showed them his hands and his feet. While in their joy they were disbelieving and still wondering, he said to them, 'Have you anything here to eat?' They gave him a piece of broiled fish, and he took it and ate in their presence.

Then he said to them, 'These are my words that I spoke to you while I was still with you – that everything written about me in the law of Moses, the prophets, and the psalms must be fulfilled.' Then he opened their minds to understand the scriptures, and he said to them, 'Thus it is written, that the Messiah is to suffer and to rise from the dead on the third day, and that repentance and forgiveness of sins is to be proclaimed in his name to all nations, beginning from Jerusalem. You are witnesses of these things.'

• When we share in the Eucharist we meet the crucified and risen Lord just as these disciples did. We are caught up into the life of the resurrection. If we realised what is going on we too would be 'speechless with joy'. We can ask for the gift of allowing ourselves to be surprised at the goodness of the God who never deserts us.

Friday 22 April
John 21:1–14

After these things Jesus showed himself again to the disciples by the Sea of Tiberias; and he showed himself in this way. Gathered there together were Simon Peter, Thomas called the Twin, Nathanael of Cana in Galilee, the sons of Zebedee, and two others of his disciples. Simon Peter said to them, 'I am going fishing.' They said to him, 'We will go with you.' They went out and got into the boat, but that night they caught nothing.

Just after daybreak, Jesus stood on the beach; but the disciples did not know that it was Jesus. Jesus said to them, 'Children, you have no fish, have you?' They answered him, 'No.' He said to them, 'Cast the net to the right side of the boat, and you will find some.' So they cast it, and now they were not able to haul it in because there were so many fish. That disciple whom Jesus loved said to Peter, 'It is the Lord!' When Simon Peter heard that it was the Lord, he put on some clothes, for he was naked, and jumped into the lake. But the other disciples came in the boat, dragging the net full of fish, for they were not far from the land, only about a hundred yards off.

When they had gone ashore, they saw a charcoal fire there, with fish on it, and bread. Jesus said to them, 'Bring some of the fish that you have just caught.' So Simon Peter went aboard and hauled the net ashore, full of large fish, a hundred and fifty-three of them; and though there were so many, the net was not torn. Jesus said to them, 'Come and have breakfast.' Now none of the disciples dared to ask him, 'Who are you?' because they knew it was the Lord. Jesus came and took the bread and gave it to them, and did the same with the fish. This was now the third time that Jesus appeared to the disciples after he was raised from the dead.

- Peter is lost, floundering. He feels that he is a failure at what he usually does well. Can I identify with him sometimes? But Peter is open to another voice which he dimly recognises, but not quite. He does what is suggested to him, and wonderful results follow.

- So it can be for me, if I am open to being surprised. Lord, let me accept you today as a God of good surprises.

Saturday 23 April
Mark 16:9–15

Now after he rose early on the first day of the week, he appeared first to Mary Magdalene, from whom he had cast out seven demons. She went out and told those who had been with him, while they were mourning and weeping. But when they heard that he was alive and had been seen by her, they would not believe it.

After this he appeared in another form to two of them, as they were walking into the country. And they went back and told the rest, but they did not believe them.

Later he appeared to the eleven themselves as they were sitting at the table; and he upbraided them for their lack of faith and stubbornness, because they had not believed those who saw him after he had risen. And he said to them, 'Go into all the world and proclaim the good news to the whole creation.'

- Mary of Magdala is the first person in the world to carry the message of the resurrection of Jesus. But the disciples do not believe her, which leads Jesus to reproach them for their incredulity and obstinacy. How little has changed over 2,000 years! Women are still excluded from the decision-making processes of the Church, and the Church, like a wounded bird flapping around on one wing, will be unable to fly until women are accorded the equality which is their due. Since, however, Jesus does not despair of the Church, neither must we: we must instead pray for it.

The Second Week of Easter
24–30 April 2022

Something to think and pray about each day this week:

Our inner and outer senses play an important role in living a full human existence. Babies in their first months of life largely 'learn' through their senses. Adults have a tendency to rely overly on their intellect when searching for truth. As a consequence we fail to draw on the enrichment that a keen awareness of the senses offers. For some the latter can be missing yet not missed. Living life to the full is more likely when one is fully rooted in the everyday world that we find ourselves in, while using both rational and sensory abilities. If we desire to live at greater depth then attention to our senses is essential. In other words, we need to create moments when we consciously just 'stand and stare, listen and feel, smell and taste'.

Incidents in our lives are often lived automatically as opposed to consciously. In certain activities and circumstances that has to be so. For example, when driving the car we cannot be conscious of every move we make with the brake or steering wheel. However, we do need moments, hopefully several daily, when we deliberately allow ourselves to relish, delight in and wonder at the concrete reality we actually live in. Examples could be the following: noting the sounds around one in a busy street, the view from an office window, the texture and/or flavour of the food we are eating, the inner beauty of the person I am conversing with as well as acknowledging the beauty of who I am. In summary, we need to allow our inner- and outer-sensing worlds to nourish us through the ordinary moments as well as the more extraordinary. Hidden moments can prove to be the gems that make life worthwhile, maybe even 'wonder-filled'.

Catherine McCann,
Spirituality and the Senses: Living Life to the Full

The Presence of God

'I am standing at the door, knocking', says the Lord. What a wonderful privilege that the Lord of all creation desires to come to me. I welcome his presence.

Freedom

I will ask God's help
to be free from my own preoccupations,
to be open to God in this time of prayer,
to come to know, love and serve God more.

Consciousness

In God's loving presence I unwind the past day,
starting from now and looking back, moment by moment.
I gather in all the goodness and light, in gratitude.
I attend to the shadows and what they say to me,
seeking healing, courage, forgiveness.

The Word

Now I turn to the Scripture set out for me this day. I read slowly over the words and see if any sentence or sentiment appeals to me.

(Please turn to the Scripture on the following pages. Inspiration points are there, should you need them. When you are ready, return here to continue.)

Conversation

Sometimes I wonder what I might say if I were to meet you in person, Lord. I think I might say, 'Thank you', because you are always there for me.

Conclusion

I thank God for these moments we have spent together and for any insights I have been given concerning the text.

Sunday 24 April
Second Sunday of Easter (Divine Mercy Sunday)
John 20:19–31

When it was evening on that day, the first day of the week, and the doors of the house where the disciples had met were locked for fear of the Jews, Jesus came and stood among them and said, 'Peace be with you.' After he said this, he showed them his hands and his side. Then the disciples rejoiced when they saw the Lord. Jesus said to them again, 'Peace be with you. As the Father has sent me, so I send you.' When he had said this, he breathed on them and said to them, 'Receive the Holy Spirit. If you forgive the sins of any, they are forgiven them; if you retain the sins of any, they are retained.'

But Thomas (who was called the Twin), one of the twelve, was not with them when Jesus came. So the other disciples told him, 'We have seen the Lord.' But he said to them, 'Unless I see the mark of the nails in his hands, and put my finger in the mark of the nails and my hand in his side, I will not believe.'

A week later his disciples were again in the house, and Thomas was with them. Although the doors were shut, Jesus came and stood among them and said, 'Peace be with you.' Then he said to Thomas, 'Put your finger here and see my hands. Reach out your hand and put it in my side. Do not doubt but believe.' Thomas answered him, 'My Lord and my God!' Jesus said to him, 'Have you believed because you have seen me? Blessed are those who have not seen and yet have come to believe.'

Now Jesus did many other signs in the presence of his disciples, which are not written in this book. But these are written so that you may come to believe that Jesus is the Messiah, the Son of God, and that through believing you may have life in his name.

- Here we are shown twice how Jesus breaks into the lives of his friends. Can he break in on me? Where am I in these scenes? Am I hesitant like Thomas? Am I looking for some sign before committing myself to the fact that I am living in a new world, the world of the resurrection?

Monday 25 April
Saint Mark, Evangelist
Mark 16:15–20

And he said to them, 'Go into all the world and proclaim the good news to the whole creation. The one who believes and is baptised will be saved; but the one who does not believe will be condemned. And these signs will accompany those who believe: by using my name they will cast out demons; they will speak in new tongues; they will pick up snakes in their hands, and if they drink any deadly thing, it will not hurt them; they will lay their hands on the sick, and they will recover.'

So then the Lord Jesus, after he had spoken to them, was taken up into heaven and sat down at the right hand of God. And they went out and proclaimed the good news everywhere, while the Lord worked with them and confirmed the message by the signs that accompanied it.

• Each of us is called into the ministry of Jesus in some way. We are called to be 'other Christs', to be people who wish to make known and spread the love of God and his care for his people in the world. We may never know how much we have done this; it is sufficient that we do what we can. God has some work to do that can be done only through each person. In a time of prayer we ask that we use our gifts and talents as best we can in God's service.

Tuesday 26 April
John 3:7–15

'Do not be astonished that I said to you, "You must be born from above." The wind blows where it chooses, and you hear the sound of it, but you do not know where it comes from or where it goes. So it is with everyone who is born of the Spirit.' Nicodemus said to him, 'How can these things be?' Jesus answered him, 'Are you a teacher of Israel, and yet you do not understand these things?

'Very truly, I tell you, we speak of what we know and testify to what we have seen; yet you do not receive our testimony. If I have told you about earthly things and you do not believe, how can you believe if I tell you about heavenly things? No one has ascended into heaven except the one who descended from heaven, the Son of Man. And just as Moses lifted up the serpent in the wilderness, so must the Son of Man be lifted up, that whoever believes in him may have eternal life.

- Nicodemus was a Pharisee, a Jewish leader, who knew the law but lacked a certain wisdom. Used to citing authorities, he was unable to recognise the authority of Jesus who spoke of what he knew.

- Before God, I recognise my habits, my preferences and my inclinations; I ask God to give me the freedom I need to be touched by Jesus' word, to awaken to his imagination, to want for myself the freedom that he desires for me.

Wednesday 27 April

John 3:16–21

'For God so loved the world that he gave his only Son, so that everyone who believes in him may not perish but may have eternal life.

'Indeed, God did not send the Son into the world to condemn the world, but in order that the world might be saved through him. Those who believe in him are not condemned; but those who do not believe are condemned already, because they have not believed in the name of the only Son of God. And this is the judgement, that the light has come into the world, and people loved darkness rather than light because their deeds were evil. For all who do evil hate the light and do not come to the light, so that their deeds may not be exposed. But those who do what is true come to the light, so that it may be clearly seen that their deeds have been done in God.'

- It has been said that if all the Gospels had been lost early on except the first sentence above, that would be enough for us. Once we know that God 'loves the world to bits' we have hope. God is hard at work to save us – from evil and failure and ruin and darkness. God's plan is to bring us all into eternal life. Pope Francis puts it daringly: 'When everything is said and done, we are infinitely loved' (*The Joy of the Gospel*, 6). That can be my mantra for today and every day. Relationships are transformed when I catch on to the fact that the other person is 'infinitely loved'.

Thursday 28 April
John 3:31–36

The one who comes from above is above all; the one who is of the earth belongs to the earth and speaks about earthly things. The one who comes from heaven is above all. He testifies to what he has seen and heard, yet no one accepts his testimony. Whoever has accepted his testimony has certified this, that God is true. He whom God has sent speaks the words of God, for he gives the Spirit without measure. The Father loves the Son and has placed all things in his hands. Whoever believes in the Son has eternal life; whoever disobeys the Son will not see life, but must endure God's wrath.

- God's Word is spoken unceasingly in my soul. There is never an instant when he is not within me. With him, I make my own soul every day of my earthly life. I need have no fear of birth or rebirth, change or life or death. Instead, I see them for what they are – as thrilling stages along a transcendent journey home.

Friday 29 April
Saint Catherine of Siena, Virgin and Doctor of the Church
John 6: 1–15

After this Jesus went to the other side of the Sea of Galilee, also called the Sea of Tiberias. A large crowd kept following him, because they saw the signs that he was doing for the sick. Jesus went up the mountain and sat down there with his disciples. Now the Passover, the festival of the Jews, was near. When he looked up and saw a large crowd coming towards him, Jesus said to Philip, 'Where are we to buy bread for these people to eat?' He said this to test him, for he himself knew what he was going to do. Philip answered him, 'Six months' wages would not buy enough bread for each of them to get a little.' One of his disciples, Andrew, Simon Peter's brother, said to him, 'There is a boy here who has five barley loaves and two fish. But what are they among so many people?' Jesus said, 'Make the people sit down.' Now there was a great deal of grass in the place; so they sat down, about five thousand in all. Then Jesus took the loaves, and when he had given thanks, he distributed them to those who were seated; so also the fish, as much as they wanted. When they were satisfied, he told his disciples, 'Gather up the fragments left over, so that nothing may be lost.' So they gathered them up, and from the fragments of the five barley loaves, left by those who had eaten, they filled twelve baskets. When the people saw the sign that he had done, they began to say, 'This is indeed the prophet who is to come into the world.'

When Jesus realised that they were about to come and take him by force to make him king, he withdrew again to the mountain by himself.

• Jesus was able to live in a community of ritual and tradition; he accepted it but called people to see more deeply. As Passover approached he moved the people he met on the hillside to appreciate its meaning in a profoundly new way, one that would connect them, not just with the past, but with their neighbours and with a broader community. For some, the miracle was for that moment and they demanded that Jesus be made king. For Jesus, it was a threshold to prayer, an invitation to spend time with God.

Saturday 30 April
John 6:16–21

When evening came, his disciples went down to the lake, got into a boat, and started across the lake to Capernaum. It was now dark, and Jesus had not yet come to them. The lake became rough because a strong wind was blowing. When they had rowed about three or four miles, they saw Jesus walking on the lake and coming near the boat, and they were terrified. But he said to them, 'It is I; do not be afraid.' Then they wanted to take him into the boat, and immediately the boat reached the land towards which they were going.

• The disciples knew they were in difficulty and had work to do. They would have been keenly aware of Jesus' absence. Now, seeing him approach them, they had to ask what they meant to him. I consider how I sometimes struggle 'against the wind' and am slow to recognise the help that Jesus offers to me.

• I pray for all people who are in trouble or in need, that they might recognise the approach of Jesus in experiencing some care from others. May they not be afraid, but be embraced by the one who approaches those who know their need.

1–7 May 2022

Something to think and pray about each day this week:

Limerick-born author Tom Stack, in his book on the Irish poet Patrick Kavanagh, well known to countless numbers of Irish secondary-school students, remarks that Kavanagh 'had a special gift for investing the natural world with spiritual significance' (*No Earthly Estate*, Columba Press, 1994). This is as good a definition of 'finding God in all things' as any other.

Stack continues in the same vein, saying that Kavanagh 'could turn apparently inconsequential items of every day into an experience of hope and delight … he was graced with what might be called a sacramentalising talent.' He explains what's meant by sacrament when he says: 'In sacrament we divine God's presence in particular material entities, in events and relationships . . . It is a sign from creation already existing.' Finding God in all things is the gift of a mindset that facilitates a mystical view of the world, seeing beyond appearances, giving the sense that we're on sacred ground, continually being breathed into life by a Presence whose love has the intensity of a blazing fire.

Jim Maher SJ,
Pathways to a Decision with Ignatius of Loyola

The Presence of God

'Be still, and know that I am God!' Lord, your words lead us to the calmness and greatness of your presence.

Freedom

If God were trying to tell me something, would I know?
If God were reassuring me or challenging me, would I notice?
I ask for the grace to be free of my own preoccupations
and open to what God may be saying to me.

Consciousness

In the presence of my loving Creator, I look honestly at my feelings over the past day: the highs, the lows and the level ground. Can I see where the Lord has been present?

The Word

In this expectant state of mind, please turn to the text for the day with confidence. Believe that the Holy Spirit is present and may reveal whatever the passage has to say to you. Read reflectively, listening with a third ear to what may be going on in your heart.

(Please turn to the Scripture on the following pages. Inspiration points are there, should you need them. When you are ready, return here to continue.)

Conversation

Remembering that I am still in God's presence,
I imagine Jesus standing or sitting beside me,
and I say whatever is on my mind, whatever is in my heart,
speaking as one friend to another.

Conclusion

Glory be to the Father, and to the Son and to the Holy Spirit,
As it was in the beginning, is now and ever shall be,
World without end. Amen.

Sunday 1 May
Third Sunday of Easter

John 21:1–14

After these things Jesus showed himself again to the disciples by the Sea of Tiberias; and he showed himself in this way. Gathered there together were Simon Peter, Thomas called the Twin, Nathanael of Cana in Galilee, the sons of Zebedee, and two others of his disciples. Simon Peter said to them, 'I am going fishing.' They said to him, 'We will go with you.' They went out and got into the boat, but that night they caught nothing.

Just after daybreak, Jesus stood on the beach; but the disciples did not know that it was Jesus. Jesus said to them, 'Children, you have no fish, have you?' They answered him, 'No.' He said to them, 'Cast the net to the right side of the boat, and you will find some.' So they cast it, and now they were not able to haul it in because there were so many fish. That disciple whom Jesus loved said to Peter, 'It is the Lord!' When Simon Peter heard that it was the Lord, he put on some clothes, for he was naked, and jumped into the lake. But the other disciples came in the boat, dragging the net full of fish, for they were not far from the land, only about a hundred yards off.

When they had gone ashore, they saw a charcoal fire there, with fish on it, and bread. Jesus said to them, 'Bring some of the fish that you have just caught.' So Simon Peter went aboard and hauled the net ashore, full of large fish, a hundred and fifty-three of them; and though there were so many, the net was not torn. Jesus said to them, 'Come and have breakfast.' Now none of the disciples dared to ask him, 'Who are you?' because they knew it was the Lord. Jesus came and took the bread and gave it to them, and did the same with the fish. This was now the third time that Jesus appeared to the disciples after he was raised from the dead.

- Aren't there moments in times of need when help seems to come from an unexpected source and we sense the presence of the Lord. The unexpected catch of fish was such a moment for the disciples. Pray for light to recognise such a moment in the recent past.

Monday 2 May
John 6:22–29

The next day the crowd that had stayed on the other side of the lake saw that there had been only one boat there. They also saw that Jesus had not got into the boat with his disciples, but that his disciples had gone away alone. Then some boats from Tiberias came near the place where they had eaten the bread after the Lord had given thanks. So when the crowd saw that neither Jesus nor his disciples were there, they themselves got into the boats and went to Capernaum looking for Jesus.

When they found him on the other side of the lake, they said to him, 'Rabbi, when did you come here?' Jesus answered them, 'Very truly, I tell you, you are looking for me, not because you saw signs, but because you ate your fill of the loaves. Do not work for the food that perishes, but for the food that endures for eternal life, which the Son of Man will give you. For it is on him that God the Father has set his seal.' Then they said to him, 'What must we do to perform the works of God?' Jesus answered them, 'This is the work of God, that you believe in him whom he has sent.'

- Jesus chastises the crowd for seeking him for the wrong reasons: they had tried to make him king, now they were following him because he was some kind of celebrity, able to feed thousands with a few loaves of bread. Our world is too easily impressed by the cult of all sorts of celebrities, and I ask for the wisdom to be aware of the motivation of my decisions. Am I really seeking what lasts in my relationships, or am I only after what is frivolous and will soon perish?

Tuesday 3 May
Saints Philip and James, Apostles
John 14:6–14

Jesus said to him, 'I am the way, and the truth, and the life. No one comes to the Father except through me. If you know me, you will know my Father also. From now on you do know him and have seen him.'

Philip said to him, 'Lord, show us the Father, and we will be satisfied.' Jesus said to him, 'Have I been with you all this time, Philip, and you still do not know me? Whoever has seen me has seen the Father. How can you say, "Show us the Father"? Do you not believe that I am in the Father and the Father is in me? The words that I say to you I do not speak on my own; but the Father who dwells in me does his works. Believe me that I am in the Father and the Father is in me; but if you do not, then believe me because of the works themselves. Very truly, I tell you, the one who believes in me will also do the works that I do and, in fact, will do greater works than these, because I am going to the Father. I will do whatever you ask in my name, so that the Father may be glorified in the Son. If in my name you ask me for anything, I will do it.'

- Philip is captivated by Jesus. But now he starts to wonder what the Father is like. We too can think that the Father must be very different from the Son. But in fact the Son is the presence of the Father in visible form. The words and deeds of Jesus are the words and deeds of God. I ask to be brought ever more deeply into the mystery of who Jesus really is.

Wednesday 4 May
John 6:35–40

Jesus said to them, 'I am the bread of life. Whoever comes to me will never be hungry, and whoever believes in me will never be thirsty. But I said to you that you have seen me and yet do not believe. Everything that the Father gives me will come to me, and anyone who comes to me I will never drive away; for I have come down from heaven, not to do my own will, but the will of him who sent me. And this is the will of him who sent me, that I should lose nothing of all that he has given me, but raise it up on the last day. This is indeed the will of my Father, that all who see the Son and believe in him may have eternal life; and I will raise them up on the last day.'

- On this day I may choose to bring before the Lord some person or persons who have already passed away, and pray for them. In gratitude for all I have received from them, or asking for pardon for my mistakes in dealing with them, or asking for God's mercy on them. I find special consolation in Jesus' words in today's Gospel: 'Anyone who comes to me I will never drive away.'

Thursday 5 May
John 6:44–51

'No one can come to me unless drawn by the Father who sent me; and I will raise that person up on the last day. It is written in the prophets, "And they shall all be taught by God." Everyone who has heard and learned from the Father comes to me. Not that anyone has seen the Father except the one who is from God; he has seen the Father. Very truly, I tell you, whoever believes has eternal life. I am the bread of life. Your ancestors ate the manna in the wilderness, and they died. This is the bread that comes down from heaven, so that one may eat of it and not die. I am the living bread that came down from heaven. Whoever eats of this bread will live for ever; and the bread that I will give for the life of the world is my flesh.'

- All our practices of prayer – our liturgies, disciplines and habits – are like school buses; they bring us to where a special kind of learning happens. We need to be present, ready, eager to go to receive truth. Jesus tells us that God wants to be the teacher of each person, desires to speak heart to heart.

- Our prayer is not our own initiative, but is itself a response to God who draws us; we're invited to leave home so that we might learn and be drawn more fully into life.

Friday 6 May
John 6:52–59

The Jews then disputed among themselves, saying, 'How can this man give us his flesh to eat?' So Jesus said to them, 'Very truly, I tell you, unless you eat the flesh of the Son of Man and drink his blood, you have no life in you. Those who eat my flesh and drink my blood have eternal life, and I will raise them up on the last day; for my flesh is true food and my blood is true drink. Those who eat my flesh and drink my blood abide in me, and I in them. Just as the living Father sent me, and I live because of the Father, so whoever eats me will live because of me. This is the bread that came down from heaven, not like that which your ancestors ate, and they died. But the one who eats this bread will live for ever.' He said these things while he was teaching in the synagogue at Capernaum.

- Jesus states that the bread that he will give is his flesh for the life of the world. He gives his flesh in the sacrifice of the cross, an idea those listening could not grasp, and they would comprehend even less the giving of his flesh as food.

- Jesus did not want the people simply to agree with him, to assent to his ideas. He wanted them to be drawn fully into the life of God, just as he was. He invites us to be consumed by God, to let go of our reservations and hesitations and to trust in the one who gives life.

Saturday 7 May
John 6:60–69

When many of his disciples heard it, they said, 'This teaching is difficult; who can accept it?' But Jesus, being aware that his disciples were complaining about it, said to them, 'Does this offend you? Then what if you were to see the Son of Man ascending to where he was before? It is the spirit that gives life; the flesh is useless. The words that I have spoken to you are spirit and life. But among you there are some who do not believe.' For Jesus knew from the first who were the ones that did not believe, and who was the one that would betray him. And he said, 'For this reason I have told you that no one can come to me unless it is granted by the Father.'

Because of this many of his disciples turned back and no longer went about with him. So Jesus asked the twelve, 'Do you also wish to go away?' Simon Peter answered him, 'Lord, to whom can we go? You have the words of eternal life. We have come to believe and know that you are the Holy One of God.'

- Saint Irenaeus said, 'The glory of God is the human person fully alive'. I know that I'm only half-alive at best, so here and now I ask you to work on me so that I become more like you. You are fully alive as a human being, and this is because you are totally open to God.

- Make that happen to me, whatever it takes! Take me by the hand, hold me tight and bring me along with you, so I shall become like you.

The Fourth Week of Easter
8–14 May 2022

Something to think and pray about each day this week:

Mary saw a slender but sure sign of hope as she stood praying at the foot of the cross. Just when it appeared that all was going to end in complete failure, the suffering and prayer of Jesus brought about the conversion of one of the thieves hanging next to him. 'Then he said, "Jesus, remember me when you come into your kingdom." Jesus answered him, "Truly I tell you, today you will be with me in paradise."' (Luke 23:42–43). One act of genuine love and one act of perfect sorrow were enough to wipe out this man's shameful past.

Thomas Casey SJ,
Smile of Joy: Mary of Nazareth

The Presence of God
As I sit here, the beating of my heart,
the ebb and flow of my breathing, the movements of my mind
are all signs of God's ongoing creation of me.
I pause for a moment and become aware
of this presence of God within me.

Freedom
It is so easy to get caught up with the trappings of wealth in this life.
Grant, O Lord, that I may be free from greed and selfishness.
Remind me that the best things in life are free:
Love, laughter, caring and sharing.

Consciousness
Knowing that God loves me unconditionally, I can afford to be honest
about how I am. How has the day been, and how do I feel now? I share
my feelings openly with the Lord.

The Word
Lord Jesus, you became human to communicate with me.
You walked and worked on this earth.
You endured the heat and struggled with the cold.
All your time on this earth was spent in caring for humanity.
You healed the sick, you raised the dead.
Most important of all, you saved me from death.
(Please turn to the Scripture on the following pages. Inspiration points are there, should you need them. When you are ready, return here to continue.)

Conversation
Sometimes I wonder what I might say if I were to meet you in person,
Lord. I think I might say, 'Thank you', because you are always there for
me.

Conclusion
I thank God for these moments we have spent together and for any insights I have been given concerning the text.

Sunday 8 May
Fourth Sunday of Easter
John 10:27–30

'My sheep hear my voice. I know them, and they follow me. I give them eternal life, and they will never perish. No one will snatch them out of my hand. What my Father has given me is greater than all else, and no one can snatch it out of the Father's hand. The Father and I are one.'

- Once again, Lord, your words ease our aching hearts. You know us; you give us your best gift, which is eternal life; you will defend us from anyone who tries to snatch us away from you. What more can we ask?

- On my side is the invitation to follow you. But do I think of myself as your follower? My daily prayer helps me to keep you always in view, to listen to your voice and to deepen the relationship that exists between us. Thank you for this graced time.

Monday 9 May
John 10:1–10

'Very truly, I tell you, anyone who does not enter the sheepfold by the gate but climbs in by another way is a thief and a bandit. The one who enters by the gate is the shepherd of the sheep. The gatekeeper opens the gate for him, and the sheep hear his voice. He calls his own sheep by name and leads them out. When he has brought out all his own, he goes ahead of them, and the sheep follow him because they know his voice. They will not follow a stranger, but they will run from him because they do not know the voice of strangers.' Jesus used this figure of speech with them, but they did not understand what he was saying to them.

So again Jesus said to them, 'Very truly, I tell you, I am the gate for the sheep. All who came before me are thieves and bandits; but the sheep did not listen to them. I am the gate. Whoever enters by me will be saved, and will come in and go out and find pasture. The thief comes only to steal and kill and destroy. I came that they may have life, and have it abundantly.'

- Jesus uses rich images from daily life to illustrate the depth of his desired relationship with us. On the one side, he speaks of shepherd and sheep, gatekeeper and gate, pasture and life, recognition and salvation.

The contrasting words are: strangers, thieves and bandits, killing and stealing, running away in fear instead of following, climbing in rather than walking through the open gate.

• Lord, let me hear your voice, so that I may open the gate of my heart for you. Draw me to the pathways of life. May others then see me as a safe gateway leading to abundant life.

Tuesday 10 May
John 10:22–30

At that time the festival of the Dedication took place in Jerusalem. It was winter, and Jesus was walking in the temple, in the portico of Solomon. So the Jews gathered around him and said to him, 'How long will you keep us in suspense? If you are the Messiah, tell us plainly.' Jesus answered, 'I have told you, and you do not believe. The works that I do in my Father's name testify to me; but you do not believe, because you do not belong to my sheep. My sheep hear my voice. I know them, and they follow me. I give them eternal life, and they will never perish. No one will snatch them out of my hand. What my Father has given me is greater than all else, and no one can snatch it out of the Father's hand. The Father and I are one.'

• As the sheep recognises the voice of its shepherd, I look over these past days, listening for the word of God spoken to me through those around me, through my observations and experiences.

Wednesday 11 May
John 12:44–50

Then Jesus cried aloud: 'Whoever believes in me believes not in me but in him who sent me. And whoever sees me sees him who sent me. I have come as light into the world, so that everyone who believes in me should not remain in the darkness. I do not judge anyone who hears my words and does not keep them, for I came not to judge the world, but to save the world. The one who rejects me and does not receive my word has a judge; on the last day the word that I have spoken will serve as judge, for I have not spoken on my own, but the Father who sent me has himself given me a commandment about what to say and what to speak. And I know that his commandment is eternal life. What I speak, therefore, I speak just as the Father has told me.'

- This passage is a summary statement which comes at the end of Jesus' public ministry. It sums up everything Jesus has been doing and saying in public. It speaks therefore of listening to the words of Jesus and acting upon them. His words are important, because they are first of all the Father's words. Jesus is so closely connected to his message that he is referred to in this Gospel as the Word.

Thursday 12 May

John 13:16–20

'Very truly, I tell you, servants are not greater than their master, nor are messengers greater than the one who sent them. If you know these things, you are blessed if you do them. I am not speaking of all of you; I know whom I have chosen. But it is to fulfil the scripture, "The one who ate my bread has lifted his heel against me." I tell you this now, before it occurs, so that when it does occur, you may believe that I am he. Very truly, I tell you, whoever receives one whom I send receives me; and whoever receives me receives him who sent me.'

- Followers of Jesus are called to serve. He is himself the model of service. He chooses his followers, but some of those who have enjoyed intimacy with him prove capable of betrayal.

- Saint Ignatius reminds us that love is shown more in deeds than in words. I ask God for the help that I need to allow the words in my mind and heart to become evident in my feet and my hands, that I might recognise where God wants me to be and do what God wants me to do.

Friday 13 May

John 14:1–6

'Do not let your hearts be troubled. Believe in God, believe also in me. In my Father's house there are many dwelling-places. If it were not so, would I have told you that I go to prepare a place for you? And if I go and prepare a place for you, I will come again and will take you to myself, so that where I am, there you may be also. And you know the way to the place where I am going.' Thomas said to him, 'Lord, we do not know where you are going. How can we know the way?' Jesus said to him, 'I am the way, and the truth, and the life. No one comes to the Father except through me.'

- There is something almost homely about the image of the rooms 'in my Father's house', with Jesus getting our accommodation ready and then coming back to escort us to the house. Note that he is still performing the role of servant, looking after important guests.
- The words of Jesus are a source of consolation at funerals. They speak powerfully to our fear of death, 'the undiscovered country', where we are all in the dark. Jesus, the Light, guides us on the most fearful and unknown journey of all.

Saturday 14 May
Saint Matthias, Apostle
John 15:9–17

'As the Father has loved me, so I have loved you; abide in my love. If you keep my commandments, you will abide in my love, just as I have kept my Father's commandments and abide in his love. I have said these things to you so that my joy may be in you, and that your joy may be complete.

'This is my commandment, that you love one another as I have loved you. No one has greater love than this, to lay down one's life for one's friends. You are my friends if you do what I command you. I do not call you servants any longer, because the servant does not know what the master is doing; but I have called you friends, because I have made known to you everything that I have heard from my Father. You did not choose me but I chose you. And I appointed you to go and bear fruit, fruit that will last, so that the Father will give you whatever you ask him in my name. I am giving you these commands so that you may love one another.'

- My love for others must not be conditioned by how they respond. Jesus loves me totally, whether I am good or bad or indifferent. My love must have that quality too. This is costly love – it could demand my very life!
- This costly love will bear rich fruit, whether I see it or not. Just so, Jesus' love bears fruit only after his death. I must not be discouraged when my love seems to be wasted. True love never comes to an end (1 Corinthians 13:8). Loving actions are the building blocks of eternal life.

The Fifth Week of Easter
15–21 May 2022

Something to think and pray about each day this week:

Most people are searching for happiness, but if happiness becomes the sole goal of our search it is often missed. Jesus suggests that happiness comes to those who seek something else. Happiness comes to those who seek to serve others, or, as Jesus declares, it is in giving that we receive. The action of Jesus in washing the feet of his disciples suggests that our service of others is not to be dependent on how they relate to us. At the Last Supper, Jesus washed the feet of all his disciples, including Judas. Jesus washed the feet of the one who rebelled against him. As Jesus declares in Luke's Gospel, 'If you love those who love you, what credit is that to you?' Jesus gives expression to a much more self-emptying kind of love. He calls us to live in the same way and gives us the Holy Spirit to help us to love as he loves.

Martin Hogan,
The Word of God Is Living and Active

The Presence of God
At any time of the day or night we can call on Jesus.
He is always waiting, listening for our call.
What a wonderful blessing.
No phone needed, no emails, just a whisper.

Freedom
Lord, grant me the grace to have freedom of the spirit. Cleanse my heart and soul so that I may live joyously in your love.

Consciousness
Knowing that God loves me unconditionally, I look honestly over the past day, its events and my feelings. Do I have something to be grateful for? Then I give thanks. Is there something I am sorry for? Then I ask forgiveness.

The Word
The word of God comes down to us through the Scriptures.
May the Holy Spirit enlighten my mind and my heart
to respond to the Gospel teachings:
to love my neighbour as myself,
to care for my sisters and brothers in Christ.
(Please turn to the Scripture on the following pages. Inspiration points are there, should you need them. When you are ready, return here to continue.)

Conversation
I know with certainty that there were times when you carried me, Lord. There were times when it was through your strength that I got through the dark times in my life.

Conclusion
Glory be to the Father, and to the Son, and to the Holy Spirit,
As it was in the beginning, is now and ever shall be,
World without end. Amen.

Sunday 15 May
Fifth Sunday of Easter
John 13:31–35

When he had gone out, Jesus said, 'Now the Son of Man has been glorified, and God has been glorified in him. If God has been glorified in him, God will also glorify him in himself and will glorify him at once. Little children, I am with you only a little longer. You will look for me; and as I said to the Jews so now I say to you, "Where I am going, you cannot come." I give you a new commandment, that you love one another. Just as I have loved you, you also should love one another. By this everyone will know that you are my disciples, if you have love for one another.'

- It is moving to look back on this incident during our Easter celebrations of fire and light. It is as if we are looking back on the struggle, when darkness looked as if it would extinguish the light. We are in bright morning, looking back with gratitude that an anxious, sleepless night is over.

- It is at this moment of betrayal, of Jesus' anguish that one of his chosen companions has turned away from him, that we are given a 'new commandment'. We might wonder about the tensions and the divisions within the community of the Fourth Gospel. Why do they need to be told and reminded – repeatedly! – to 'love one another'?

Monday 16 May
John 14:21–26

'They who have my commandments and keep them are those who love me; and those who love me will be loved by my Father, and I will love them and reveal myself to them.' Judas (not Iscariot) said to him, 'Lord, how is it that you will reveal yourself to us, and not to the world?' Jesus answered him, 'Those who love me will keep my word, and my Father will love them, and we will come to them and make our home with them. Whoever does not love me does not keep my words; and the word that you hear is not mine, but is from the Father who sent me.

'I have said these things to you while I am still with you. But the Advocate, the Holy Spirit, whom the Father will send in my name, will teach you everything, and remind you of all that I have said to you.'

- What a lovely question from Judas: 'Lord, what is all this about?' He is mystified, perhaps exasperated, because the words of the Lord are not making sense. Several times in John's Gospel we hear of people being put off by Jesus' words; they are too obscure.

- It is hardly surprising that this invitation to share God's life and work is hard to grasp, for Judas and for us. Learning and understanding take time. But Jesus also promises that we will not be left in a state of frustrating perplexity. The Advocate, the Holy Spirit, will be sent to us, to teach us and to remind us of what is important.

Tuesday 17 May
John 14:27–31

'Peace I leave with you; my peace I give to you. I do not give to you as the world gives. Do not let your hearts be troubled, and do not let them be afraid. You heard me say to you, "I am going away, and I am coming to you." If you loved me, you would rejoice that I am going to the Father, because the Father is greater than I. And now I have told you this before it occurs, so that when it does occur, you may believe. I will no longer talk much with you, for the ruler of this world is coming. He has no power over me; but I do as the Father has commanded me, so that the world may know that I love the Father. Rise, let us be on our way.'

- Jesus speaks from the depths of his heart to his dearest friends. He is facing into his Passion. He wants his friends to know that he is with them, his father is with them. Jesus' farewell wish is 'Peace!' His gift of peace is not a state, but a relationship. It is the fruit of deeply abiding in him. This relationship will never fail. It will enable the disciples to endure suffering and rejection.

- The peace that Jesus gives is available to me; I have to do nothing to receive it. But maybe that's the problem – I want to do something to earn what Jesus offers as a free gift. Lord, help me to do nothing in this time of prayer but to be ready to receive what you offer.

Wednesday 18 May
John 15:1–8

'I am the true vine, and my Father is the vine-grower. He removes every branch in me that bears no fruit. Every branch that bears fruit he prunes to make it bear more fruit. You have already been cleansed by the word that I have spoken to you. Abide in me as I abide in you. Just as the branch cannot bear fruit by itself unless it abides in the vine, neither can you unless you abide in me. I am the vine, you are the branches. Those who abide in me and I in them bear much fruit, because apart from me you can do nothing. Whoever does not abide in me is thrown away like a branch and withers; such branches are gathered, thrown into the fire, and burned. If you abide in me, and my words abide in you, ask for whatever you wish, and it will be done for you. My Father is glorified by this, that you bear much fruit and become my disciples.'

- Today I am invited to recognise my close relationship with Jesus, which he compares to the relationship between a vine and the branches that grow on it. What does it mean for my life that the life of Jesus flows into me? What does it mean for me personally to know that I am as much a part of Jesus as the branch is a part of the vine? Are there things in my life that would be different if I consciously realised this? What are they? I reflect on these things, I talk to Jesus about them and I ask the Holy Spirit to guide and enlighten me.

Thursday 19 May

John 15:9–11

As the Father has loved me, so I have loved you; abide in my love. If you keep my commandments, you will abide in my love, just as I have kept my Father's commandments and abide in his love. I have said these things to you so that my joy may be in you, and that your joy may be complete.

- Saint Ignatius would have us begin our prayer by considering how God sees us. There is no better place to begin, and no better place to end! Each of us can say, 'You see me as your well-beloved'. Much of our prayer time can be taken up in simply savouring this delightful truth about ourselves.

- If we pray like this, the joy of God will fill our hearts. In the Gospels, joy is always linked with closeness to the Lord. So Mary and Elizabeth pour out their joy in the visitation scene and the shepherds and the Magi are full of joy when they find the Lord. Joy is the best indicator that a person is living close to Jesus.

Friday 20 May
John 15:12–17

'This is my commandment, that you love one another as I have loved you. No one has greater love than this, to lay down one's life for one's friends. You are my friends if you do what I command you. I do not call you servants any longer, because the servant does not know what the master is doing; but I have called you friends, because I have made known to you everything that I have heard from my Father. You did not choose me but I chose you. And I appointed you to go and bear fruit, fruit that will last, so that the Father will give you whatever you ask him in my name. I am giving you these commands so that you may love one another.'

- 'I have called you friends.' I too am called the friend of Jesus. I am highly favoured; I am unique and very special. Jesus wants me to know what is most important to him, what is closest to his heart. I take time to hear Jesus address me as friend.

- Jesus reminds me that it is he who has chosen me. Lord, you are inviting me, choosing me, to be your intimate friend, to go out in your name into the world in which I live, and bear lasting fruit.

Saturday 21 May
John 15:18–21

'If the world hates you, be aware that it hated me before it hated you. If you belonged to the world, the world would love you as its own. Because you do not belong to the world, but I have chosen you out of the world – therefore the world hates you. Remember the word that I said to you, "Servants are not greater than their master." If they persecuted me, they will persecute you; if they kept my word, they will keep yours also. But they will do all these things to you on account of my name, because they do not know him who sent me.'

- Not everyone accepts Jesus, which was his experience from the start. Opposition to him took him to death, and love took him from death to resurrection. Persecution and similar opposition is the experience of many of his followers. Goodness sometimes offends people; evil can seem for a while to be stronger than love, but the message of Jesus is that love conquers all.

- I bring any aspect of my life in which I feel rejected or unappreciated before the Lord, considering whether my treatment was because of my being a disciple. I stand beside Jesus, who knows how I feel.

The Sixth Week of Easter
22–28 May 2022

Something to think and pray about each day this week:

Before God created the world, he did what he has always done and will do: he loved. After all, God is love. Everything God does or does not do has to do with love. People like to ask the question about the before and the after. As far as God is concerned, this question is somewhat problematic. Before God created the world there was no time, and if there is no time, there can be no before and after. Only eternity. Time has only come through creation. From then on the sequence of events began: past, present and future. So time itself was also created by God.

It is part of God's being that God creates, because true love reaches beyond itself. God has no choice but to create with love that is overflowing. That is why God's creation is not something one-off. Something from long ago. No, God creates constantly. If God would cease to create for just one moment, everything that is would immediately stop existing. The whole creation exists and continues to exist thanks to God's creative power of love.

Nikolaas Sintobin SJ,
Did Jesus Really Exist? And 51 Other Questions

The Presence of God

Dear Jesus, as I call on you today, I realise that often I come asking for favours. Today I'd like just to be in your presence. Draw my heart in response to your love.

Freedom

God, my creator, you gave me life and the gift of freedom. Through your love I exist in this world. May I never take the gift of life for granted. May I always respect others' right to life.

Consciousness

Dear Lord, help me to remember that you gave me life. Teach me to slow down, to be still and enjoy the pleasures created for me. To be aware of the beauty that surrounds me: the marvel of mountains, the calmness of lakes, the fragility of a flower petal. I need to remember that all these things come from you.

The Word

The word of God comes down to us through the Scriptures. May the Holy Spirit enlighten my mind and my heart to respond to the Gospel teachings.

(Please turn to the Scripture on the following pages. Inspiration points are there, should you need them. When you are ready, return here to continue.)

Conversation

What feelings are rising in me as I pray and reflect on God's word? I imagine Jesus himself sitting or standing near me, and I open my heart to him.

Conclusion

I thank God for these moments we have spent together and for any insights I have been given concerning the text.

Sunday 22 May
Sixth Sunday of Easter
John 17:20–26

'I ask not only on behalf of these, but also on behalf of those who will be-lieve in me through their word, that they may all be one. As you, Father, are in me and I am in you, may they also be in us, so that the world may believe that you have sent me. The glory that you have given me I have given them, so that they may be one, as we are one, I in them and you in me, that they may become completely one, so that the world may know that you have sent me and have loved them even as you have loved me. Father, I desire that those also, whom you have given me, may be with me where I am, to see my glory, which you have given me because you loved me before the foundation of the world.

'Righteous Father, the world does not know you, but I know you; and these know that you have sent me. I made your name known to them, and I will make it known, so that the love with which you have loved me may be in them, and I in them.'

- Jesus prayed for the apostles and for all who would believe. That is us! Can you imagine Jesus praying somewhere, maybe on the hillside where he went to pray, or among his followers? He is praying for you. What might you think he would be asking his Father for, for you? Can you make this prayer for yourself? He prays because he loves each of us. How do I pray for people I love? He prays for everyone I know. I can join my prayer with his today.

Monday 23 May
John 15:26–16:4a

'When the Advocate comes, whom I will send to you from the Father, the Spirit of truth who comes from the Father, he will testify on my behalf. You also are to testify because you have been with me from the beginning.

'I have said these things to you to keep you from stumbling. They will put you out of the synagogues. Indeed, an hour is coming when those who kill you will think that by doing so they are offering worship to God. And they will do this because they have not known the Father or me. But I have said these things to you so that when their hour comes you may remember that I told you about them.'

- Jesus taught his disciples with his word, and prepared them for a life when he would no longer be with them. He knew that there would be opposition to them and danger to their lives because of their following him.

- Jesus reassures us that the Holy Spirit, the Comforter, who comes from the Father, will support us in giving witness to the Good News, despite challenges from those who persecute the Christian faith. He tells us that they do this out of ignorance of him and the Father. 'Jesus said, "Father, forgive them; for they do not know what they are doing"' (Luke 23:34).

- I ask to 'know' Jesus more closely so that I might testify to his presence in my life through my daily choices, words and deeds; and ask the Holy Spirit for the help I need.

Tuesday 24 May

John 16:5–11

'But now I am going to him who sent me; yet none of you asks me, "Where are you going?" But because I have said these things to you, sorrow has filled your hearts. Nevertheless, I tell you the truth: it is to your advantage that I go away, for if I do not go away, the Advocate will not come to you; but if I go, I will send him to you. And when he comes, he will prove the world wrong about sin and righteousness and judgement: about sin, because they do not believe in me; about righteousness, because I am going to the Father and you will see me no longer; about judgement, because the ruler of this world has been condemned.'

- It is hard for us to lose someone we love, and so the disciples grieve. Would I miss Jesus much if he were no longer in my life?

- The gift of the Holy Spirit means we don't have to rely on our own resources to reach God. Our call is to become better attuned to the wavelength of the Spirit, so that our lives are shaped by the Spirit.

Wednesday 25 May
John 16:12–15

'I still have many things to say to you, but you cannot bear them now. When the Spirit of truth comes, he will guide you into all the truth; for he will not speak on his own, but will speak whatever he hears, and he will declare to you the things that are to come. He will glorify me, because he will take what is mine and declare it to you. All that the Father has is mine. For this reason I said that he will take what is mine and declare it to you.'

- In the words of a well-known prayer to the Holy Trinity, we pray: 'O Everlasting and Triune God, I consecrate myself wholly to you today. Let all my days offer you ceaseless praise, my hands move to the rhythm of your impulses, my feet be swift in your service, my voice sing constantly of you, my lips proclaim your message, my eyes perceive you everywhere, and my ears be attuned to your inspirations. May my intellect be filled with your wisdom, my will be moved by your beauty, my heart be enraptured with your love, and my soul be flooded with your grace. Grant that every action of mine be done for your greater glory and the advancement of my salvation. Amen.'

Thursday 26 May
John 16:16–20

'A little while, and you will no longer see me, and again a little while, and you will see me.' Then some of his disciples said to one another, 'What does he mean by saying to us, "A little while, and you will no longer see me, and again a little while, and you will see me"; and "Because I am going to the Father"?' They said, 'What does he mean by this "a little while"? We do not know what he is talking about.' Jesus knew that they wanted to ask him, so he said to them, 'Are you discussing among yourselves what I meant when I said, "A little while, and you will no longer see me, and again a little while, and you will see me"? Very truly, I tell you, you will weep and mourn, but the world will rejoice; you will have pain, but your pain will turn into joy.'

- What Jesus said was not always understood by the disciples, and sometimes their talking to each other seemed only to give rise to more questions. There are times when I need to turn Jesus' words over in my heart rather than seek the answer outside in discussion or inspiration points. Perhaps I can recognise where Jesus has, at times, been hidden from me and, at other times, revealed.

- To be a follower of Jesus is to have feelings that seem to be at odds with the world. Jesus does not promise removal of mourning immediately. I pray for the patience that I may need; and for wisdom.

Friday 27 May
John 16:20–23

'Very truly, I tell you, you will weep and mourn, but the world will rejoice; you will have pain, but your pain will turn into joy. When a woman is in labour, she has pain, because her hour has come. But when her child is born, she no longer remembers the anguish because of the joy of having brought a human being into the world. So you have pain now; but I will see you again, and your hearts will rejoice, and no one will take your joy from you. On that day you will ask nothing of me. Very truly, I tell you, if you ask anything of the Father in my name, he will give it to you.'

- Childbirth was a traditional biblical metaphor for the sufferings that were to herald the age of the Messiah. Giving birth to a renewed world will always entail suffering.

- Jesus, I ask you now to help me to remain with you always, to be close to you with a passionate heart, and to accept patiently whatever you want of me. And make me a joyous person!

Saturday 28 May
John 16:23–28

'On that day you will ask nothing of me. Very truly, I tell you, if you ask anything of the Father in my name, he will give it to you. Until now you have not asked for anything in my name. Ask and you will receive, so that your joy may be complete.

'I have said these things to you in figures of speech. The hour is coming when I will no longer speak to you in figures, but will tell you plainly of the Father. On that day you will ask in my name. I do not say to you that I will ask the Father on your behalf; for the Father himself loves you, because you have loved me and have believed that I came from God. I came from the Father and have come into the world; again, I am leaving the world and am going to the Father.'

- In this passage, I might be inclined to focus on the promise of Jesus that I will be given anything I ask for in his name, and I might feel discouraged. I have often experienced praying hard for something and not getting it. But today, instead, I focus on the central truth that Jesus shares with me, which is this: the Father loves me. I sit quietly and allow this thought to enter into my heart. The Father loves me.

Something to think and pray about each day this week:

In the famous crucifix of San Damiano, the Lord ascends with a smile on his face. It is over, his mission is accomplished, and he has conquered death, and is now with us all days to the end of time.

His earthly mission is accomplished, but not his mission of love for his people. He is with us now.

Jesus often talks of joy, often the joy of God in forgiving a sinner. The big joy of God seems to be mercy, and even in the memory of his own death Jesus finds joy.

While we think today of the loss of Jesus, we are invited to rejoice as he leaves one way of being with us on earth, to another way of being with us from heaven. He both awaits us there and helps us get there, the mystery of the divine son who is one of us. The mystery goes further; in that we are invited and called into sharing this life of his on earth, for in each of us is the life of Jesus, who makes his home in us.

Donal Neary SJ,
Gospel Reflections for Sundays of Year C: Luke

The Presence of God
Dear Jesus, I come to you today longing for your presence. I desire to love you as you love me. May nothing ever separate me from you.

Freedom
Lord, grant me the grace to be free from the excesses of this life. Let me not get caught up with the desire for wealth. Keep my heart and mind free to love and serve you.

Consciousness
Where do I sense hope, encouragement and growth in my life? By looking back over the past few months, I may be able to see which activities and occasions have produced rich fruit. If I do notice such areas, I will determine to give those areas both time and space in the future.

The Word
God speaks to each of us individually. I listen attentively, to hear what he is saying to me. Read the text a few times, then listen.
(Please turn to the Scripture on the following pages. Inspiration points are there should you need them. When you are ready, return here to continue.)

Conversation
What is stirring in me as I pray? Am I consoled, troubled, left cold? I imagine Jesus standing or sitting at my side, and I share my feelings with him.

Conclusion
Glory be to the Father, and to the Son, and to the Holy Spirit,
As it was in the beginning, is now and ever shall be,
World without end. Amen.

Sunday 29 May
The Ascension of the Lord
Luke 24:46–53

And he said to them, 'Thus it is written, that the Messiah is to suffer and to rise from the dead on the third day, and that repentance and forgiveness of sins is to be proclaimed in his name to all nations, beginning from Jerusalem. You are witnesses of these things. And see, I am sending upon you what my Father promised; so stay here in the city until you have been clothed with power from on high.'

Then he led them out as far as Bethany, and, lifting up his hands, he blessed them. While he was blessing them, he withdrew from them and was carried up into heaven. And they worshipped him, and returned to Jerusalem with great joy; and they were continually in the temple blessing God.

- Even as he leaves the disciples and sends them as witnesses, Jesus reminds them that he had to suffer, die and rise. As I face the world into which Jesus sends me I acknowledge that the marks of his suffering will identify me as his disciple.

- I stay before Jesus who lifts his hands in blessing over me. I accept his trust in me as he sends me in his name.

- Jesus promises that his disciples will be clothed with power from on high. I think of those gifts of the Spirit that are necessary for me in my life. I pray for them and prepare to receive them.

Monday 30 May
John 16:29–33

His disciples said, 'Yes, now you are speaking plainly, not in any figure of speech! Now we know that you know all things, and do not need to have anyone question you; by this we believe that you came from God.' Jesus answered them, 'Do you now believe? The hour is coming, indeed it has come, when you will be scattered, each one to his home, and you will leave me alone. Yet I am not alone because the Father is with me. I have said this to you, so that in me you may have peace. In the world you face persecution. But take courage; I have conquered the world!'

- How easy it is to identify with the apostles! Fired by enthusiasm, they profess unwavering faith. Jesus knows them better than they know themselves. He warns them that the fervour will quickly wear off and that they will disappear quickly when the storm begins to gather around him. I have so often vowed to turn aside from things that separate me from God, only to fall at the first hurdle.

- Lord, let me take comfort from your patience with your disciples. You looked past their present failures to see what they would become – bearing steadfast witness to you as they faced torture and death. Grant me the grace to be for ever beginning, for ever becoming – untrammelled by my past failures, always open to growth and change.

Tuesday 31 May
The Visitation of the Blessed Virgin Mary
Luke 1:39–56

In those days Mary set out and went with haste to a Judean town in the hill country, where she entered the house of Zechariah and greeted Elizabeth. When Elizabeth heard Mary's greeting, the child leapt in her womb. And Elizabeth was filled with the Holy Spirit and exclaimed with a loud cry, 'Blessed are you among women, and blessed is the fruit of your womb. And why has this happened to me, that the mother of my Lord comes to me? For as soon as I heard the sound of your greeting, the child in my womb leapt for joy. And blessed is she who believed that there would be a fulfilment of what was spoken to her by the Lord.'

And Mary said,

'My soul magnifies the Lord,

and my spirit rejoices in God my Saviour,
for he has looked with favour on the lowliness of his servant.
Surely, from now on all generations will call me blessed;
for the Mighty One has done great things for me,
and holy is his name.
His mercy is for those who fear him
from generation to generation.
He has shown strength with his arm;
he has scattered the proud in the thoughts of their hearts.
He has brought down the powerful from their thrones,

and lifted up the lowly;
he has filled the hungry with good things,
and sent the rich away empty.
He has helped his servant Israel,
in remembrance of his mercy,
according to the promise he made to our ancestors,
to Abraham and to his descendants for ever.'

And Mary remained with her for about three months and then returned to her home.

- Two pregnant women take centre stage here, and you are privileged to listen in on their conversation. They chat about the mysterious workings of God, to which their own lives bear eloquent witness. Allow them to invite you to participate. Perhaps one of them asks you what you are doing to bear witness to the values of God which run counter to those of your culture.

Wednesday 1 June
John 17:11–19

'And now I am no longer in the world, but they are in the world, and I am coming to you. Holy Father, protect them in your name that you have given me, so that they may be one, as we are one. While I was with them, I protected them in your name that you have given me. I guarded them, and not one of them was lost except the one destined to be lost, so that the scripture might be fulfilled. But now I am coming to you, and I speak these things in the world so that they may have my joy made complete in themselves. I have given them your word, and the world has hated them because they do not belong to the world, just as I do not belong to the world. I am not asking you to take them out of the world, but I ask you to protect them from the evil one. They do not belong to the world, just as I do not belong to the world. Sanctify them in the truth; your word is truth. As you have sent me into the world, so I have sent them into the world. And for their sakes I sanctify myself, so that they also may be sanctified in truth.'

- The earth may belong to us, but we must not belong to it: we must not be possessed by worldly cares. With Pope Francis, we pray that Jesus 'may free us from being Christians without hope, who live as if the Lord were not risen, as if our problems were the centre of our lives'.

Thursday 2 June
John 17:20–26

'I ask not only on behalf of these, but also on behalf of those who will believe in me through their word, that they may all be one. As you, Father, are in me and I am in you, may they also be in us, so that the world may believe that you have sent me. The glory that you have given me I have given them, so that they may be one, as we are one, I in them and you in me, that they may become completely one, so that the world may know that you have sent me and have loved them even as you have loved me. Father, I desire that those also, whom you have given me, may be with me where I am, to see my glory, which you have given me because you loved me before the foundation of the world.

'Righteous Father, the world does not know you, but I know you; and these know that you have sent me. I made your name known to them, and I will make it known, so that the love with which you have loved me may be in them, and I in them.'

- What thoughts and feelings arise in me as I listen to Jesus' prayer for me? I share them now with Jesus.

Friday 3 June
John 21:15–19

When they had finished breakfast, Jesus said to Simon Peter, 'Simon son of John, do you love me more than these?' He said to him, 'Yes, Lord; you know that I love you.' Jesus said to him, 'Feed my lambs.' A second time he said to him, 'Simon son of John, do you love me?' He said to him, 'Yes, Lord; you know that I love you.' Jesus said to him, 'Tend my sheep.' He said to him the third time, 'Simon son of John, do you love me?' Peter felt hurt because he said to him the third time, 'Do you love me?' And he said to him, 'Lord, you know everything; you know that I love you.' Jesus said to him, 'Feed my sheep. Very truly, I tell you, when you were younger, you used to fasten your own belt and to go wherever you wished. But when you grow old, you will stretch out your hands, and someone else will fasten a belt around you and take you where you do not wish to go.' (He said this to indicate the kind of death by which he would glorify God.) After this he said to him, 'Follow me.'

- Peter, despite his failings, is chosen to continue the ministry of Jesus by humble service to others. Jesus gives me a ministry of service also. Am I aware of it? Do I carry it out even if it means pain?
- What answer do I give when, like Peter, I am questioned regarding the extent of my love for Jesus? Can I at least say, 'You know that I try to love you.'

Saturday 4 June
John 21:20–25

Peter turned and saw the disciple whom Jesus loved following them; he was the one who had reclined next to Jesus at the supper and had said, 'Lord, who is it that is going to betray you?' When Peter saw him, he said to Jesus, 'Lord, what about him?' Jesus said to him, 'If it is my will that he remain until I come, what is that to you? Follow me!' So the rumour spread in the community that this disciple would not die. Yet Jesus did not say to him that he would not die, but, 'If it is my will that he remain until I come, what is that to you?'

This is the disciple who is testifying to these things and has written them, and we know that his testimony is true. But there are also many other things that Jesus did; if every one of them were written down, I suppose that the world itself could not contain the books that would be written.

- 'The disciple whom Jesus loved'. What a description of any one! Have I ever thought of myself as 'the one Jesus loved', or had an experience that I can recall, when I considered myself especially loved by Jesus?
- To love Jesus and be loved by Jesus is to 'follow' him.
- The beloved disciple is given the task of 'testifying' to what has happened in his life. I am called to 'testify' to the 'great things the Lord has done' in my life. 'For the Mighty One has done great things for me' – Mary's Magnificat (Luke 1:49).

The Tenth Week in Ordinary Time
5–11 June 2022

Something to think and pray about each day this week:

The four marks of our Christian belonging are our personal journey, our community belonging, our practical discipleship and our adult integration of faith and life. None of us 'inhabits' all four dimensions fully, all of the time, and yet all four dimensions should in principle be there. The good news of Pentecost is that the Spirit, poured into our hearts, enables all four aspects of our faith to live: the Spirit helps us in our prayer; the body of Christ is animated by the gifts of the Spirit; our service of others gets its energy from the Spirit and the Spirit 'reminds us' of all that Jesus taught. Today, we therefore celebrate our being disciples within the community of faith.

> *Living God, breathe on us your Holy Breath that the Spirit,*
> *who raised Jesus from the dead, may bring us new life,*
> *vision and energy in the service of your Son, our Lord Jesus Christ,*
> *who lives and reigns for ever and ever. Amen.*

Kieran J. O'Mahony OSA,
Hearers of the Word: Easter & Pentecost, Year A

The Presence of God

'Be still, and know that I am God.' Lord, your words lead us to the calmness and greatness of your presence.

Freedom

I am free. When I look at these words in writing, they seem to create in me a feeling of awe. Yes, a wonderful feeling of freedom. Thank you, God.

Consciousness

At this moment, Lord, I turn my thoughts to you.
I will leave aside my chores and preoccupations.
I will take rest and refreshment in your presence, Lord.

The Word

The word of God comes down to us through the Scriptures. May the Holy Spirit enlighten my mind and my heart to respond to the Gospel teachings.

(Please turn to the Scripture on the following pages. Inspiration points are there, should you need them. When you are ready, return here to continue.)

Conversation

Begin to talk with Jesus about the Scripture you have just read. What part of it strikes a chord in you? Perhaps the words of a friend – or some story you have heard recently – will slowly rise to the surface of your consciousness. If so, does the story throw light on what the Scripture passage may be trying to say to you?

Conclusion

Glory be to the Father, and to the Son, and to the Holy Spirit,
As it was in the beginning, is now and ever shall be,
World without end. Amen.

Sunday 5 June
Pentecost Sunday
John 14:15–16.23b–26

'If you love me, you will keep my commandments. And I will ask the Father, and he will give you another Advocate, to be with you for ever.' ... 'Those who love me will keep my word, and my Father will love them, and we will come to them and make our home with them. Whoever does not love me does not keep my words; and the word that you hear is not mine, but is from the Father who sent me.

'I have said these things to you while I am still with you. But the Advocate, the Holy Spirit, whom the Father will send in my name, will teach you everything, and remind you of all that I have said to you.'

- When I recall the words of Jesus and am reminded of what he said, the Holy Spirit is at work. I pray that I may be more aware of the quiet working of God's Spirit in my life. I pray that my thoughts, inspirations and desires be open to the prompting of the Advocate.

- I might think of myself as a Temple of the Holy Spirit or I might consider Jesus' more domestic image as he says that God is 'at home' with me. I rest with this thought – that God is comfortable and available in my being.

Monday 6 June
John 19:25–34

Meanwhile, standing near the cross of Jesus were his mother, and his mother's sister, Mary the wife of Clopas, and Mary Magdalene. When Jesus saw his mother and the disciple whom he loved standing beside her, he said to his mother, 'Woman, here is your son.' Then he said to the disciple, 'Here is your mother.' And from that hour the disciple took her into his own home.

After this, when Jesus knew that all was now finished, he said (in order to fulfil the scripture), 'I am thirsty.' A jar full of sour wine was standing there. So they put a sponge full of the wine on a branch of hyssop and held it to his mouth. When Jesus had received the wine, he said, 'It is finished.' Then he bowed his head and gave up his spirit.

Since it was the day of Preparation, the Jews did not want the bodies left on the cross during the sabbath, especially because that sabbath was

a day of great solemnity. So they asked Pilate to have the legs of the crucified men broken and the bodies removed. Then the soldiers came and
broke the legs of the first and of the other who had been crucified with
him. But when they came to Jesus and saw that he was already dead, they
did not break his legs. Instead, one of the soldiers pierced his side with a
spear, and at once blood and water came out.

- As I look back over my life, can I recall times when I have been called
  to 'give' myself in love and been able to do so? Any times when I have
  not been able to give myself in love? And what was that like? And what
  was the fallout from it?

- Can I *be* there with Jesus in loving presence with him?

Tuesday 7 June
Matthew 5:13–16

'You are the salt of the earth; but if salt has lost its taste, how can its saltiness be restored? It is no longer good for anything, but is thrown out and
trampled under foot.

'You are the light of the world. A city built on a hill cannot be hidden. No one after lighting a lamp puts it under the bushel basket, but on
the lampstand, and it gives light to all in the house. In the same way, let
your light shine before others, so that they may see your good works and
give glory to your Father in heaven.'

- Let me forget the bad press that salt has received from dietitians, and
  remember why it has always been prized. It gives flavour to what is
  bland, and lifts the everyday to something interesting. In the same
  way a new baby brings a family together. A visit from an old friend
  banishes my boredom and restores my zest for living. A leader gives
  a sense of purpose to a whole community. Yet I can lose my saltiness
  by self-indulgence or sin or centreing totally on myself. Lord, may I
  always have other people with whom I can engage.

Wednesday 8 June
Matthew 5:17–19

'Do not think that I have come to abolish the law or the prophets; I have
come not to abolish but to fulfil. For truly I tell you, until heaven and
earth pass away, not one letter, not one stroke of a letter, will pass from the

law until all is accomplished. Therefore, whoever breaks one of the least of these commandments, and teaches others to do the same, will be called least in the kingdom of heaven; but whoever does them and teaches them will be called great in the kingdom of heaven.'

- Jesus is no destroyer of people's devotions and faith. He does not abolish the faith practice of a people or a person. All the goodness of our religion and our faith is precious to him. His grace is given to each personally; each of us prays differently, or with a variety of times, places and moods. 'Pray as you can, not as you can't', is one of the oldest and wisest recommendations for prayer. Prayer is entering and relaxing into the mystery of God's love, each in our own way.

Thursday 9 June
Matthew 5:20–26

'For I tell you, unless your righteousness exceeds that of the scribes and Pharisees, you will never enter the kingdom of heaven.

'You have heard that it was said to those of ancient times, "You shall not murder"; and "whoever murders shall be liable to judgement." But I say to you that if you are angry with a brother or sister, you will be liable to judgement; and if you insult a brother or sister, you will be liable to the council; and if you say, "You fool", you will be liable to the hell of fire. So when you are offering your gift at the altar, if you remember that your brother or sister has something against you, leave your gift there before the altar and go; first be reconciled to your brother or sister, and then come and offer your gift. Come to terms quickly with your accuser while you are on the way to court with him, or your accuser may hand you over to the judge, and the judge to the guard, and you will be thrown into prison. Truly I tell you, you will never get out until you have paid the last penny.'

- How challenging the Gospel is! I am called not only to do love but to think love! Can I invite Jesus into my heart to create that sort of loving, respectful heart for me?

- The Spirit is calling me to be changed, to become a more loving, kinder, more merciful and more just person, to be transformed. Do I notice the difference in me when I am loving and when I am unloving? Talk to Jesus about this.

Friday 10 June
Matthew 5:27–32

'You have heard that it was said, "You shall not commit adultery." But I say to you that everyone who looks at a woman with lust has already committed adultery with her in his heart. If your right eye causes you to sin, tear it out and throw it away; it is better for you to lose one of your members than for your whole body to be thrown into hell. And if your right hand causes you to sin, cut it off and throw it away; it is better for you to lose one of your members than for your whole body to go into hell.

'It was also said, "Whoever divorces his wife, let him give her a certificate of divorce." But I say to you that anyone who divorces his wife, except on the ground of unchastity, causes her to commit adultery; and whoever marries a divorced woman commits adultery.'

- Bad intentions can weaken our moral character even if we do not follow them through into action. I can ask God to help me banish temptations to do things that would harm someone.

- The self-mutilation proposed here is a type of exaggerated speech more common in the East. But a good conscience is a pearl of great price. Radical choices need to be made to keep it so.

Saturday 11 June
Saint Barnabas, Apostle
Matthew 5:33–37

'Again, you have heard that it was said to those of ancient times, "You shall not swear falsely, but carry out the vows you have made to the Lord." But I say to you, Do not swear at all, either by heaven, for it is the throne of God, or by the earth, for it is his footstool, or by Jerusalem, for it is the city of the great King. And do not swear by your head, for you cannot make one hair white or black. Let your word be "Yes, Yes" or "No, No"; anything more than this comes from the evil one.'

- We confess sins of 'thought, word and deed'. Do I give less attention to 'word' than I should? Can I build people up by kind words, rather than pulling them down with criticism or backbiting?

- Do I talk honestly to God in my prayer? Perhaps I could try to do that today.

The Eleventh Week in Ordinary Time
12–18 June 2022

Something to think and pray about each day this week:

An old teacher used to say, '*Talk to the grass, children!*' So consider a simple leaf: gaze on it and admire it. Learn about it: its arteries and veins – complex pipelines that transport water, carbon and nutrients to where they are needed; note its capacity to transform sunlight and water into food and energy for its parent plant. Learn how twig and leaf enrich each other.

Now with a touch of imagination take a step further: just as people talk to their pets and plants, invite the leaf to tell its history. After all, what makes childhood books like *The Wind in the Willows* so captivating is the personalising of Rat and Mole: they are not portrayed as objects but as having histories and emotions like ourselves. The Psalmist tells the hills to sing for joy and clap their hands, and Pope Francis speaks of each creature singing the hymn of its existence. God, he says, is trying to teach us even through a leaf. To contemplate is to hear a message, it is to listen to a silent voice (*Laudato Si'*, 85).

Brian Grogan SJ,
Creation Walk: The Amazing Story of a Blue Planet

The Presence of God

'Come to me, all you who are weary and are carrying heavy burdens, and I will give you rest.' Here I am, Lord. I come to seek your presence. I long for your healing power.

Freedom

'In these days, God taught me as a schoolteacher teaches a pupil' (Saint Ignatius).

I remind myself that there are things God has to teach me yet, and I ask for the grace to hear those things and let them change me.

Consciousness

Help me, Lord, to be more conscious of your presence. Teach me to recognise your presence in others.

Fill my heart with gratitude for the times your love has been shown to me through the care of others.

The Word

God speaks to each of us individually. I listen attentively to hear what he is saying to me. Read the text a few times, then listen.

(Please turn to the Scripture on the following pages. Inspiration points are there, should you need them. When you are ready, return here to continue.)

Conversation

Conversation requires talking and listening.

As I talk to Jesus, may I also learn to be still and listen.

I picture the gentleness in his eyes and the smile full of love as he gazes on me. I can be totally honest with Jesus as I tell him of my worries and my cares. I will open my heart to him as I tell him of my fears and my doubts. I will ask him to help me place myself fully in his care and to abandon myself to him, knowing that he always wants what is best for me.

Conclusion

I thank God for these moments we have spent together and for any insights I have been given concerning the text.

Sunday 12 June
The Most Holy Trinity
John 16:12–15

'I still have many things to say to you, but you cannot bear them now. When the Spirit of truth comes, he will guide you into all the truth; for he will not speak on his own, but will speak whatever he hears, and he will declare to you the things that are to come. He will glorify me, because he will take what is mine and declare it to you. All that the Father has is mine. For this reason I said that he will take what is mine and declare it to you.'

- The mystery of the Trinity is at the heart of this passage. Pope Francis reminds us that 'everything, in Christian life, revolves around the mystery of the Trinity and is fulfilled in this infinite mystery. Let us look, therefore, to keep high the "tone" of our life, reminding ourselves to what end, for what glory we exist, work, struggle, suffer; and to which immense prize we are called.'

- Saint Augustine summed up the heart of the Church's belief in the mystery of the Father, Son and Holy Spirit by stating simply, 'If you see charity, you see the Trinity.'

Monday 13 June
Matthew 5:38–42

'You have heard that it was said, "An eye for an eye and a tooth for a tooth." But I say to you, Do not resist an evildoer. But if anyone strikes you on the right cheek, turn the other also; and if anyone wants to sue you and take your coat, give your cloak as well; and if anyone forces you to go one mile, go also the second mile. Give to everyone who begs from you, and do not refuse anyone who wants to borrow from you.'

- The law and duty will provide basic guidelines but won't be enough for a disciple and certainly not enough for one who wants to be a friend of Jesus. Where do I need more generosity or freedom to respond to the vision that Jesus puts before me?

- To answer violence with violence or unreasonable demands with resistance is to do the expected thing. Jesus calls me to imagine my life differently and thus prompt others to see themselves anew.

- Do I use laws and rules to protect my security or to promote justice for others?

Tuesday 14 June
Matthew 5:43–48

'You have heard that it was said, "You shall love your neighbour and hate your enemy." But I say to you, Love your enemies and pray for those who persecute you, so that you may be children of your Father in heaven; for he makes his sun rise on the evil and on the good, and sends rain on the righteous and on the unrighteous. For if you love those who love you, what reward do you have? Do not even the tax-collectors do the same? And if you greet only your brothers and sisters, what more are you doing than others? Do not even the Gentiles do the same? Be perfect, therefore, as your heavenly Father is perfect.'

- There are times, Lord, when you lift us beyond what we thought possible. Here you ask me to be perfect: meaning that in my heart I should bless even those who hate me and wrong me. The love of God can be poured out in our hearts through the Holy Spirit who is given to us. Even when I feel far from blessed myself, even when old age makes me feel there is little I can do for others, I can still give my approval and blessing to those I meet; that will lift them.

- As I think of those whose love I return, I thank God for them and for the blessings we share.

- As I pray for those who bring blessings to me, I pray that I may include others in a widening circle of compassion.

Wednesday 15 June
Matthew 6:1–6.16–18

'Beware of practising your piety before others in order to be seen by them; for then you have no reward from your Father in heaven.

'So whenever you give alms, do not sound a trumpet before you, as the hypocrites do in the synagogues and in the streets, so that they may be praised by others. Truly I tell you, they have received their reward. But when you give alms, do not let your left hand know what your right hand is doing, so that your alms may be done in secret; and your Father who sees in secret will reward you. . . .

'And whenever you pray, do not be like the hypocrites; for they love to stand and pray in the synagogues and at the street corners, so that they may be seen by others. Truly I tell you, they have received their reward. But whenever you pray, go into your room and shut the door and pray to your Father who is in secret; and your Father who sees in secret will reward you.

'And whenever you fast, do not look dismal, like the hypocrites, for they disfigure their faces so as to show others that they are fasting. Truly I tell you, they have received their reward. But when you fast, put oil on your head and wash your face, so that your fasting may be seen not by others but by your Father who is in secret; and your Father who sees in secret will reward you.'

- The main point is that fasting and other works of piety are directed towards God, not other human beings. I wonder if I could do a good turn for somebody without anyone knowing about it?

- What does this passage tell me about myself? I will pray for light.

Thursday 16 June
Matthew 6:7–15

'When you are praying, do not heap up empty phrases as the Gentiles do; for they think that they will be heard because of their many words. Do not be like them, for your Father knows what you need before you ask him.

'Pray then in this way:
Our Father in heaven,
hallowed be your name.
Your kingdom come.
Your will be done,
on earth as it is in heaven.
Give us this day our daily bread.
And forgive us our debts,
as we also have forgiven our debtors.
And do not bring us to the time of trial,
but rescue us from the evil one.
'For if you forgive others their trespasses, your heavenly Father will
    also forgive you; but if you do not forgive others, neither will
    your Father forgive your trespasses.'

- I pray that I may receive from God what I need and that I may be generous and free in my giving to others. I see that everything I give comes from God.

- As I pray for forgiveness, I dispose myself to be forgiving. I make my-self ready for healing by not harbouring resentment.

Friday 17 June
Matthew 6:19–23

'Do not store up for yourselves treasures on earth, where moth and rust consume and where thieves break in and steal; but store up for your-selves treasures in heaven, where neither moth nor rust consumes and where thieves do not break in and steal. For where your treasure is, there your heart will be also.

'The eye is the lamp of the body. So, if your eye is healthy, your whole body will be full of light; but if your eye is unhealthy, your whole body will be full of darkness. If then the light in you is darkness, how great is the darkness!'

- Everybody desires security. If possessions are our god, then we try to find security behind closed gates or in safe deposit boxes locked in vaults. What Jesus desires for us is far different. He wants to hold our hearts and be our treasure. That is not threatened by moths, rust or thieves. Where is your security? What is your treasure?

Saturday 18 June
Matthew 6:24–34

'No one can serve two masters; for a slave will either hate the one and love the other, or be devoted to the one and despise the other. You cannot serve God and wealth.

'Therefore I tell you, do not worry about your life, what you will eat or what you will drink, or about your body, what you will wear. Is not life more than food, and the body more than clothing? Look at the birds of the air; they neither sow nor reap nor gather into barns, and yet your heavenly Father feeds them. Are you not of more value than they? And can any of you by worrying add a single hour to your span of life? And why do you worry about clothing? Consider the lilies of the field, how they grow; they neither toil nor spin, yet I tell you, even Solomon in all his glory was not clothed like one of these. But if God so clothes the grass of the field, which is alive today and tomorrow is thrown into the oven, will he not much more clothe you – you of little faith? Therefore do not worry, saying, "What will we eat?" or "What will we drink?" or "What will we wear?" For it is the Gentiles who strive for all these things; and indeed your heavenly Father knows that you need all these things. But strive first for the kingdom of God and his righteousness, and all these things will be given to you as well.

'So do not worry about tomorrow, for tomorrow will bring worries of its own. Today's trouble is enough for today.'

- As a consumer, I may allow my values to be set by others. I review my wants and desires and ask God's help to be happy with the good things that I enjoy, to resist being wistful about what I am told I lack.

The Twelfth Week in Ordinary Time
19–25 June 2022

Something to think and pray about each day this week:

We look for the fullness of life in money, food, sex, travel, security, reputation – none last. Only the simplest joys of life really satisfy in the end, like the joy of love, the thrill of friendship, the caring in family and the ways we enjoy the goodness of creation.

A man in the hospice at the end of his life was asked – 'what is happiness?' 'Find happiness now' was his answer – 'be satisfied, be grateful, for what you have, for what you have received, for what God has given you.' There is a fullness of life in being happy with who I am, what I have … and asking God for what he knows I need.

No matter what our age, we can do good for others, we can share the graces of life and the soul can grow. That's what I hope can happen for me as life goes on. In any group of people, some look happy and some look miserable. The happiest are not always the ones who had or are having the easiest life. They are the ones who have found peace with themselves, others and God.

Donal Neary SJ,
Gospel Reflections for Sundays of Year C: Luke

The Presence of God

'I am standing at the door, knocking,' says the Lord. What a wonderful privilege that the Lord of all creation desires to come to me. I welcome his presence.

Freedom

Leave me here freely all alone. / In cell where never sunlight shone. / Should no one ever speak to me. / This golden silence makes me free!
—Part of a poem by Bl. Titus Brandsma, written while he was a prisoner at Dachau concentration camp

Consciousness

How am I really feeling? Lighthearted? Heavyhearted? I may be very much at peace, happy to be here. Equally, I may be frustrated, worried, or angry.
I acknowledge how I really am. It is the real me whom the Lord loves.

The Word

I take my time to read the word of God slowly, a few times, allowing myself to dwell on anything that strikes me.
(Please turn to the Scripture on the following pages. Inspiration points are there, should you need them. When you are ready, return here to continue.)

Conversation

Do I notice myself reacting as I pray with the word of God? Do I feel challenged, comforted, angry? Imagining Jesus sitting or standing by me, I speak out my feelings, as one trusted friend to another.

Conclusion

Glory be to the Father, and to the Son, and to the Holy Spirit,
As it was in the beginning, is now and ever shall be,
World without end. Amen.

Sunday 19 June
The Most Holy Body and Blood of Christ
Luke 9:11–17

When the crowds found out about it, they followed him; and he welcomed them, and spoke to them about the kingdom of God, and healed those who needed to be cured.

The day was drawing to a close, and the twelve came to him and said, 'Send the crowd away, so that they may go into the surrounding villages and countryside, to lodge and get provisions; for we are here in a deserted place.' But he said to them, 'You give them something to eat.' They said, 'We have no more than five loaves and two fish – unless we are to go and buy food for all these people.' For there were about five thousand men. And he said to his disciples, 'Make them sit down in groups of about fifty each.' They did so and made them all sit down. And taking the five loaves and the two fish, he looked up to heaven, and blessed and broke them, and gave them to the disciples to set before the crowd. And all ate and were filled. What was left over was gathered up, twelve baskets of broken pieces.

• Mother Teresa said about Jesus, 'He uses us to be his love and compassion in the world in spite of our weaknesses and frailties.' In this miracle Jesus does not produce food out of nowhere. He takes the little that the apostles have, and he multiplies it a thousandfold. No matter how little I think I have to give, once I freely place my gifts in Jesus' service they become limitless.

Monday 20 June
Matthew 7:1–5

'Do not judge, so that you may not be judged. For with the judgement you make you will be judged, and the measure you give will be the measure you get. Why do you see the speck in your neighbour's eye, but do not notice the log in your own eye? Or how can you say to your neighbour, "Let me take the speck out of your eye", while the log is in your own eye? You hypocrite, first take the log out of your own eye, and then you will see clearly to take the speck out of your neighbour's eye.'

• I can ask God to judge me favourably, and God does this. But in turn God wants me to look lovingly on others and to judge them favourably!

- We are to act toward others as God acts toward us. We are to enhance the dignity of others and never despise or rubbish them. It is said that we judge ourselves by our intentions but judge others only by their actions!

Tuesday 21 June
Matthew 7:6.12–14

'Do not give what is holy to dogs; and do not throw your pearls before swine, or they will trample them under foot and turn and maul you. . . .

'In everything do to others as you would have them do to you; for this is the law and the prophets.

'Enter through the narrow gate; for the gate is wide and the road is easy that leads to destruction, and there are many who take it. For the gate is narrow and the road is hard that leads to life, and there are few who find it.'

- 'In everything do to others as you would have them do to you.' The golden rule is so challenging because it is so simple; in fact, 'this is the law and the prophets'. We never seem able to live it fully, even though it is so eminently reasonable. Yet it is not a juridical standard, but one of true love: a little earlier in Matthew's Gospel Jesus calls us to love others as we love ourselves.

- It is the road that leads to life, yet we need to pass through the narrow door of denying ourselves and carrying our cross every day. I pray for the grace to do this gladly, with inner peace, following in the footsteps of Jesus my brother.

Wednesday 22 June
Matthew 7:15–20

'Beware of false prophets, who come to you in sheep's clothing but inwardly are ravenous wolves. You will know them by their fruits. Are grapes gathered from thorns, or figs from thistles? In the same way, every good tree bears good fruit, but the bad tree bears bad fruit. A good tree cannot bear bad fruit, nor can a bad tree bear good fruit. Every tree that does not bear good fruit is cut down and thrown into the fire. Thus you will know them by their fruits.'

- Popular messages appeal though they may not be true to the Gospel. Some predict doom and gloom, while others present a more liberal agenda. Genuine prophets teach the authentic way of Christ, but many false teachers in the human story proclaim their own message. We are reminded to be alert and attentive so that we can reflect and discern what is true.

Thursday 23 June
The Nativity of John the Baptist
Luke 1:57–66.80

Now the time came for Elizabeth to give birth, and she bore a son. Her neighbours and relatives heard that the Lord had shown his great mercy to her, and they rejoiced with her.

On the eighth day they came to circumcise the child, and they were going to name him Zechariah after his father. But his mother said, 'No; he is to be called John.' They said to her, 'None of your relatives has this name.' Then they began motioning to his father to find out what name he wanted to give him. He asked for a writing-tablet and wrote, 'His name is John.' And all of them were amazed. Immediately his mouth was opened and his tongue freed, and he began to speak, praising God. Fear came over all their neighbours, and all these things were talked about throughout the entire hill country of Judea. All who heard them pondered them and said, 'What then will this child become?' For, indeed, the hand of the Lord was with him. . . .

The child grew and became strong in spirit, and he was in the wilderness until the day he appeared publicly to Israel.

- Today we celebrate the birth of John the Baptist, a rare distinction he shares with Jesus and Our Lady. Like many Old Testament figures who played an important role in the history of our salvation, John is born to a sterile woman in her old age. Our salvation is all God's work. Our world is too self-sufficient to admit we need a saviour, but the present situation, with so much violence and pain in relationships, may perhaps move more of us to ask God to save us. Although he does not save us without our collaboration, it is his will that the world be saved, have a happy ending.

Friday 24 June
The Most Sacred Heart of Jesus
Luke 15:3–7

So he told them this parable: 'Which one of you, having a hundred sheep and losing one of them, does not leave the ninety-nine in the wilderness and go after the one that is lost until he finds it? When he has found it, he lays it on his shoulders and rejoices. And when he comes home, he calls together his friends and neighbours, saying to them, "Rejoice with me, for I have found my sheep that was lost." Just so, I tell you, there will be more joy in heaven over one sinner who repents than over ninety-nine righteous people who need no repentance.'

- I know what it feels like to be lost in the wilderness but then found! Do I believe that my return is truly an important ingredient in divine happiness?

- What paths have led me towards the wilderness, and how did God rescue me? I ponder, and then give thanks to my rescuer.

Saturday 25 June
Luke 2:41–51

Now every year his parents went to Jerusalem for the festival of the Passover. And when he was twelve years old, they went up as usual for the festival. When the festival was ended and they started to return, the boy Jesus stayed behind in Jerusalem, but his parents did not know it. Assuming that he was in the group of travellers, they went a day's journey. Then they started to look for him among their relatives and friends. When they did not find him, they returned to Jerusalem to search for him. After three days they found him in the temple, sitting among the teachers, listening to them and asking them questions. And all who heard him were amazed at his understanding and his answers. When his parents saw him they were astonished; and his mother said to him, 'Child, why have you treated us like this? Look, your father and I have been searching for you in great anxiety.' He said to them, 'Why were you searching for me? Did you not know that I must be in my Father's house?' But they did not understand what he said to them. Then he went down with them and came to Nazareth, and was obedient to them. His mother treasured all these things in her heart.

- The parents of Jesus were observant Jews. This vignette is the last we will hear of Jesus' early years. Jesus is coming of age. He is entering his teens. We see already the gradual, slow but steady growing into his sense of identity and mission.

- Lord, today I remember all the children of our world missing through slavery, bonded labour and trafficking. I pray for their distraught parents who frantically seek for the child entrusted to them.

The Thirteenth Week in Ordinary Time
26 June–2 July 2022

Something to think and pray about each day this week:

Saying 'yes' is a vital part of our relationship with God, it is our freedom to say 'no'. So many times in my life I look back on now and see clearly that I said 'no' (even if I didn't understand it as saying 'no' to God at the time). Thank God, I can recall some times of saying 'yes' too. Saying 'yes' to God enables us to be a living presence of love, joy and mercy in this world. Our 'yes' always draws us to love and value ourselves, others and the world around us.

In Christian history and tradition, there are numerous people who said 'yes': Mary, Jeremiah, Moses and Peter, for example. Their yesses mattered. They may not have known exactly what they were saying 'yes' to, but they had the wisdom to know that God was asking and that they should say 'yes'.

If you're faced with a difficult yes, remember you're in good company with those above. Know this too: those who say 'yes' are gifted for that yes (so we see Peter, the uneducated fisherman, become a learned scholar and leader of a new movement – a saint). You too will be gifted for your 'yes'.

Jim Deeds & Brendan McManus SJ,
Finding God in the Mess

The Presence of God

'Be still, and know that I am God!' Lord, may your spirit guide me to seek your loving presence more and more for it is there I find rest and refreshment from this busy world.

Freedom

By God's grace I was born to live in freedom. Free to enjoy the pleasures he created for me. Dear Lord, grant that I may live as you intended, with complete confidence in your loving care.

Consciousness

How am I today?

Where am I with God? With others?

Do I have something to be grateful for? Then I give thanks.

Is there something I am sorry for? Then I ask forgiveness.

The Word

God speaks to each of us individually. I need to listen, to hear what he is saying to me. Read the text a few times, then listen.

(Please turn to the Scripture on the following pages. Inspiration points are there, should you need them. When you are ready, return here to continue.)

Conversation

How has God's word moved me? Has it left me cold?

Has it consoled me or moved me to act in a new way?

I imagine Jesus standing or sitting beside me.

I turn and share my feelings with him.

Conclusion

I thank God for these moments we have spent together and for any insights I have been given concerning the text.

Sunday 26 June
Thirteenth Sunday in Ordinary Time
Luke 9:51–62

When the days drew near for him to be taken up, he set his face to go to Jerusalem. And he sent messengers ahead of him. On their way they entered a village of the Samaritans to make ready for him; but they did not receive him, because his face was set towards Jerusalem. When his disciples James and John saw it, they said, 'Lord, do you want us to command fire to come down from heaven and consume them?' But he turned and rebuked them. Then they went on to another village.

As they were going along the road, someone said to him, 'I will follow you wherever you go.' And Jesus said to him, 'Foxes have holes, and birds of the air have nests; but the Son of Man has nowhere to lay his head.' To another he said, 'Follow me.' But he said, 'Lord, first let me go and bury my father.' But Jesus said to him, 'Let the dead bury their own dead; but as for you, go and proclaim the kingdom of God.' Another said, 'I will follow you, Lord; but let me first say farewell to those at my home.' Jesus said to him, 'No one who puts a hand to the plough and looks back is fit for the kingdom of God.'

- Jesus asks for commitment – real commitment. The time for it is now. On our own road today we must proclaim the kingdom of God. If we keep waiting for the right moment, the sands of time will run quickly through our fingers.

Monday 27 June
Matthew 8:18–22

Now when Jesus saw great crowds around him, he gave orders to go over to the other side. A scribe then approached and said, 'Teacher, I will follow you wherever you go.' And Jesus said to him, 'Foxes have holes, and birds of the air have nests; but the Son of Man has nowhere to lay his head.' Another of his disciples said to him, 'Lord, first let me go and bury my father.' But Jesus said to him, 'Follow me, and let the dead bury their own dead.'

- In this reading Jesus challenges us with the seriousness of our decision to follow him. Notice too that the love that lasts is what matters in his commitment to you as it does in yours to him. He does not hide the implications of your decision to follow him and that your commitment to him must go beyond a short-term emotional one.

- If you wish to dwell with this reading in Jesus' presence, notice how you feel about Jesus laying it on the line for you in this way. Speak to him about how this challenge makes you feel. For example, a part of you might feel threatened by what he says and another part might feel energised by his honesty.

Tuesday 28 June
Matthew 8:23–27

And when he got into the boat, his disciples followed him. A gale arose on the lake, so great that the boat was being swamped by the waves; but he was asleep. And they went and woke him up, saying, 'Lord, save us! We are perishing!' And he said to them, 'Why are you afraid, you of little faith?' Then he got up and rebuked the winds and the sea; and there was a dead calm. They were amazed, saying, 'What sort of man is this, that even the winds and the sea obey him?'

- 'Lord, save us! We are perishing!' As with so many other prayers we find in the Gospel, I may find that today this simple prayer resonates in my heart as I look at my family, my community, my country, our world. I stay with these words, pleading for Jesus' help.

- 'And he said to them, "Why are you afraid, you of little faith?" ' I acknowledge my weak faith, my fear that Jesus is asleep while the gale threatens to overwhelm me. I ask for simple trust, and share in the apostles' wonder at the power present in the person of Jesus.

Wednesday 29 June
Saints Peter and Paul, Apostles
Matthew 16:13–19

Now when Jesus came into the district of Caesarea Philippi, he asked his disciples, 'Who do people say that the Son of Man is?' And they said, 'Some say John the Baptist, but others Elijah, and still others Jeremiah or one of the prophets.' He said to them, 'But who do you say that I am?' Simon Peter answered, 'You are the Messiah, the Son of the living God.' And Jesus answered him, 'Blessed are you, Simon son of Jonah! For flesh and blood has not revealed this to you, but my Father in heaven. And

I tell you, you are Peter, and on this rock I will build my church, and the gates of Hades will not prevail against it. I will give you the keys of the kingdom of heaven, and whatever you bind on earth will be bound in heaven, and whatever you loose on earth will be loosed in heaven.'

- Peter does well here: he has caught on to who Jesus is and Jesus blesses him. But this is not the end of the journey, because when under pressure in the Passion he denies that he even knows Jesus. Peter, however, enters into a new depth of relationship with Jesus when he admits his weakness: he knows he can no longer trust himself but must depend totally on Jesus. And this is enough for him to be told, 'Feed my lambs and sheep' (John 21:15–17).

- At an ordination ceremony the bishop asked: 'Is this man weak enough to be a priest?' He meant that only if he was aware of his frailty would he become a man of prayer and live out his ministry in trust and dependence on God.

Thursday 30 June
Matthew 9:1–8

And after getting into a boat he crossed the water and came to his own town.

And just then some people were carrying a paralysed man lying on a bed. When Jesus saw their faith, he said to the paralytic, 'Take heart, son; your sins are forgiven.' Then some of the scribes said to themselves, 'This man is blaspheming.' But Jesus, perceiving their thoughts, said, 'Why do you think evil in your hearts? For which is easier, to say, "Your sins are forgiven", or to say, "Stand up and walk"? But so that you may know that the Son of Man has authority on earth to forgive sins' – he then said to the paralytic – 'Stand up, take your bed and go to your home.' And he stood up and went to his home. When the crowds saw it, they were filled with awe, and they glorified God, who had given such authority to human beings.

- Here are two things that sometimes bother me, Lord: a conscience that accuses me, and a paralytic weariness that keeps me from doing what I should. When you saw the paralytic laid before you, you looked first to his peace of soul. So much joy is hidden in those words: 'Take heart, your sins are forgiven.' You told him that he enjoyed God's approval and love, and the healing started there. When I know I am OK with God, I find the energy and strength to get on my feet and walk. Touch me in the same way, Lord.

Friday 1 July
Matthew 9:9–13

As Jesus was walking along, he saw a man called Matthew sitting at the tax booth; and he said to him, 'Follow me.' And he got up and followed him.

And as he sat at dinner in the house, many tax-collectors and sinners came and were sitting with him and his disciples. When the Pharisees saw this, they said to his disciples, 'Why does your teacher eat with tax-collectors and sinners?' But when he heard this, he said, 'Those who are well have no need of a physician, but those who are sick. Go and learn what this means, "I desire mercy, not sacrifice." For I have come to call not the righteous but sinners.'

- Tax-collectors were unpopular people, collaborators with the occupying Roman forces. The call of Matthew is therefore shocking to those who think they know God and how God should act. Their exclusive world is further disrupted when they see who is sharing table fellowship with Jesus. Jesus' mission is unequivocal: he, the divine physician, comes to heal and save not the righteous, but those who are sick.

- Lord, your call to Matthew comes right in the midst of the ordinariness of his life. He does not hesitate or delay in order to balance the books, but gets up and follows you. As I move through this day, keep me alert to the many ways your grace seeks entry into my life. May I respond generously and without delay to your calls.

Saturday 2 July
Matthew 9:14–17

Then the disciples of John came to him, saying, 'Why do we and the Pharisees fast often, but your disciples do not fast?' And Jesus said to them, 'The wedding-guests cannot mourn as long as the bridegroom is with them, can they? The days will come when the bridegroom is taken away from them, and then they will fast. No one sews a piece of unshrunk cloth on an old cloak, for the patch pulls away from the cloak, and a worse tear is made. Neither is new wine put into old wineskins; otherwise, the skins burst, and the wine is spilled, and the skins are destroyed; but new wine is put into fresh wineskins, and so both are preserved.'

- New wine in new wineskins: we live in times of deep and radical change, and I am not always sure how to identify what is really new, and what is no longer new and needs to be thrown away. I ask for the wisdom to know how to distinguish what is new and what is not, and to be able to renew myself all the time.

- New wine in new wineskins: what new things did Jesus bring us, what novelty do his words and his actions convey? He tells me that I can possess this novelty only if I have a new heart, one that resembles his own: meek, compassionate, trustful, open to God and to others.

The Fourteenth Week in Ordinary Time
3–9 July 2022

Something to think and pray about each day this week:

On 11 September 2001, two hijacked airplanes carrying many hundreds of people were crashed deliberately into the World Trade Center. The fire department of New York instantly responded, sending out many hundreds of brave men and women to save the people trapped in the wreckage. They knew the risks; they had seen many of their friends and colleagues killed and injured in other fires. This was the biggest challenge they had ever encountered but they still took it on.

Among those firefighters was their chaplain, Fr Mychal Judge. When the call came, he was on duty and went with them into the burning North Tower. Fr Judge was killed when the South Tower collapsed and the North Tower was struck by its debris. It happened that his was the first body brought out of the wreckage and he was the first certified fatality of 9/11. He died as he lived, doing his duty before God and the people with whom he worked. He stayed awake listening for the Lord's call, and when it came he was ready.

None of us knows the future. None of us knows when we will meet a certain darkness in our lives. None of us knows the moment when the most essential thing will be that the lamps of faith be well supplied with oil, so that we can show the light of Christ to those around us and to those who love us. To be able to do that is not a matter of a moment's impulsive courage. It is a matter of a person's lifelong character. It is the outcome of a life well lived in love and in prayer.

Paul O'Reilly SJ,
Hope in All Things

The Presence of God

As I sit here, the beating of my heart,
the ebb and flow of my breathing, the movements of my mind
are all signs of God's ongoing creation of me.
I pause for a moment and become aware
of this presence of God within me.

Freedom

Everything has the potential to draw from me a fuller love and life.
Yet my desires are often fixed, caught, on illusions of fulfilment.
I ask that God, through my freedom, may orchestrate my desires in a vibrant loving melody rich in harmony.

Consciousness

I ask, how am I within myself today? Am I particularly tired, stressed, or off-form? If any of these characteristics apply, can I try to let go of the concerns that disturb me?

The Word

I read the word of God slowly, a few times over, and I listen to what God is saying to me.

(Please turn to the Scripture on the following pages. Inspiration points are there, should you need them. When you are ready, return here to continue.)

Conversation

I begin to talk with Jesus about the Scripture I have just read. What part of it strikes a chord in me? Perhaps the words of a friend or a story I have heard recently will slowly rise to the surface of my consciousness. If so, does the story throw light on what the Scripture passage may be trying to say to me?

Conclusion

Glory be to the Father, and to the Son and to the Holy Spirit,
As it was in the beginning, is now and ever shall be,
World without end. Amen.

Sunday 3 July
Fourteenth Sunday in Ordinary Time
Luke 10:1–12.17–20

After this the Lord appointed seventy others and sent them on ahead of him in pairs to every town and place where he himself intended to go. He said to them, 'The harvest is plentiful, but the labourers are few; therefore ask the Lord of the harvest to send out labourers into his harvest. Go on your way. See, I am sending you out like lambs into the midst of wolves. Carry no purse, no bag, no sandals; and greet no one on the road. Whatever house you enter, first say, "Peace to this house!" And if anyone is there who shares in peace, your peace will rest on that person; but if not, it will return to you. Remain in the same house, eating and drinking whatever they provide, for the labourer deserves to be paid. Do not move about from house to house. Whenever you enter a town and its people welcome you, eat what is set before you; cure the sick who are there, and say to them, "The kingdom of God has come near to you." But whenever you enter a town and they do not welcome you, go out into its streets and say, "Even the dust of your town that clings to our feet, we wipe off in protest against you. Yet know this: the kingdom of God has come near." I tell you, on that day it will be more tolerable for Sodom than for that town. . . .

The seventy returned with joy, saying, 'Lord, in your name even the demons submit to us!' He said to them, 'I watched Satan fall from heaven like a flash of lightning. See, I have given you authority to tread on snakes and scorpions, and over all the power of the enemy; and nothing will hurt you. Nevertheless, do not rejoice at this, that the spirits submit to you, but rejoice that your names are written in heaven.'

- Jesus is preparing his disciples for mission. He leaves them in no doubt about the challenges, obstacles and dangers that will await them. They will succeed, however, because the power of God is working with them. Accordingly, 'the seventy return with joy'. Do I experience that joy when I do what the Lord wants?

Monday 4 July
Matthew 9:18–26

While he was saying these things to them, suddenly a leader of the synagogue came in and knelt before him, saying, 'My daughter has just died; but come and lay your hand on her, and she will live.' And Jesus got up and followed him, with his disciples. Then suddenly a woman who had been suffering from haemorrhages for twelve years came up behind him and touched the fringe of his cloak, for she said to herself, 'If I only touch his cloak, I will be made well.' Jesus turned, and seeing her he said, 'Take heart, daughter; your faith has made you well.' And instantly the woman was made well. When Jesus came to the leader's house and saw the flute-players and the crowd making a commotion, he said, 'Go away; for the girl is not dead but sleeping.' And they laughed at him. But when the crowd had been put outside, he went in and took her by the hand, and the girl got up. And the report of this spread throughout that district.

- Jesus is open to the needs of a child, to the prayer of a humble woman. It may be that sometimes my great needs get in the way and attract my attention. I let myself lower my eyes and become more humble to see if I might see what Jesus sees. Help me, Lord, not to seek many great things but to pay attention to what is really important.

Tuesday 5 July
Matthew 9:32–38

After they had gone away, a demoniac who was mute was brought to him. And when the demon had been cast out, the one who had been mute spoke; and the crowds were amazed and said, 'Never has anything like this been seen in Israel.' But the Pharisees said, 'By the ruler of the demons he casts out the demons.'

Then Jesus went about all the cities and villages, teaching in their synagogues, and proclaiming the good news of the kingdom, and curing every disease and every sickness. When he saw the crowds, he had compassion for them, because they were harassed and helpless, like sheep without a shepherd. Then he said to his disciples, 'The harvest is plentiful, but the labourers are few; therefore ask the Lord of the harvest to send out labourers into his harvest.'

- The crowds were amazed after the demon was expelled, but the Pharisees said, 'By the ruler of the demons he casts out the demons'. How hard the human heart can be even in religious circles. I pray for peace and deep mutual respect in my Church and among all religious people.

Wednesday 6 July
Matthew 10:1–7

Then Jesus summoned his twelve disciples and gave them authority over unclean spirits, to cast them out, and to cure every disease and every sickness. These are the names of the twelve apostles: first, Simon, also known as Peter, and his brother Andrew; James son of Zebedee, and his brother John; Philip and Bartholomew; Thomas and Matthew the tax-collector; James son of Alphaeus, and Thaddaeus; Simon the Cananaean, and Judas Iscariot, the one who betrayed him.

These twelve Jesus sent out with the following instructions: 'Go nowhere among the Gentiles, and enter no town of the Samaritans, but go rather to the lost sheep of the house of Israel. As you go, proclaim the good news, "The kingdom of heaven has come near." '

- I look in wonder at the Twelve Jesus seems to have chosen so carefully. He even calls them by name. I find myself asking whether he could have chosen better: they seem so far from what an apostle should be, always bickering and finding it very difficult to understand what Jesus was saying.

- Yet he trusted them so much that he sent them even at the beginning of his ministry, and gave them great power. He shared his own mission with them! I realise that Jesus calls me too by name, in spite of all my failings and limitations, and sends me to join him in combatting evil, healing hurts and proclaiming the kingdom. I thank Jesus for his trust in me and ask for the grace to be able to hear his call sending me to others.

Thursday 7 July
Matthew 10:7–15

'As you go, proclaim the good news, "The kingdom of heaven has come near." Cure the sick, raise the dead, cleanse the lepers, cast out demons. You received without payment; give without payment. Take no gold, or silver, or copper in your belts, no bag for your journey, or two tunics, or sandals, or a staff; for labourers deserve their food. Whatever town or village you enter, find out who in it is worthy, and stay there until you leave. As you enter the house, greet it. If the house is worthy, let your peace come upon it; but if it is not worthy, let your peace return to you. If anyone will not welcome you or listen to your words, shake off the dust from your feet as you leave that house or town. Truly I tell you, it will be more tolerable for the land of Sodom and Gomorrah on the day of judgement than for that town.'

- Jesus wants discipleship to be free of calculation and of measurement. He invites me to see myself as someone who gives freely of the good I have received. I offer to others what I received from God, knowing that it has cost me nothing, remembering that I and others may benefit in the giving.

- I take this time to allow God to give me what I need so that I may give, not of my own resources, but of what I have freely received.

Friday 8 July
Matthew 10:16–23

'See, I am sending you out like sheep into the midst of wolves; so be wise as serpents and innocent as doves. Beware of them, for they will hand you over to councils and flog you in their synagogues; and you will be dragged before governors and kings because of me, as a testimony to them and the Gentiles. When they hand you over, do not worry about how you are to speak or what you are to say; for what you are to say will be given to you at that time; for it is not you who speak, but the Spirit of your Father speaking through you. Brother will betray brother to death, and a father his child, and children will rise against parents and have them put to death; and you will be hated by all because of my name. But the one who endures to the end will be saved. When they persecute you in one town, flee to the next; for truly I tell you, you will not have gone through all the towns of Israel before the Son of Man comes.'

- Often we struggle with the opposition we face when we try to live an honest Christian life, and with the increasing duplicity that seems to surround us. So we do well to listen to Jesus' words about sheep among wolves, and the need to know how to be both wise and transparent.

Jesus knows all this, yet he still sends us to take the Gospel to this difficult world. But he also promises us his assistance: he asks us not to worry!

Saturday 9 July
Matthew 10:24–33

'A disciple is not above the teacher, nor a slave above the master; it is enough for the disciple to be like the teacher, and the slave like the master. If they have called the master of the house Beelzebul, how much more will they malign those of his household!

'So have no fear of them; for nothing is covered up that will not be uncovered, and nothing secret that will not become known. What I say to you in the dark, tell in the light; and what you hear whispered, proclaim from the housetops. Do not fear those who kill the body but cannot kill the soul; rather fear him who can destroy both soul and body in hell. Are not two sparrows sold for a penny? Yet not one of them will fall to the ground unperceived by your Father. And even the hairs of your head are all counted. So do not be afraid; you are of more value than many sparrows.

'Everyone therefore who acknowledges me before others, I also will acknowledge before my Father in heaven; but whoever denies me before others, I also will deny before my Father in heaven.'

• Faith in Jesus Christ is a total human experience, not something to practise only on Sundays. Faith without action is dead. I pray therefore that mine may be a living faith and that I may accept God's direction for my life's journey.

The Fifteenth Week in Ordinary Time
10–16 July 2022

Something to think and pray about each day this week:

An older Jesuit friend once said to me, 'I don't know any more what's going on between me and God: either I'm praying all the time or I'm not praying at all!' Lord, that honesty is helpful to me as I age. My prayer used to be more structured; I'd try to become still, ask for the grace I wanted, read the Gospel of the day, imagine myself in the scene, ask Jesus what he was trying to teach me. After thirty minutes I'd wrap my prayer package up neatly with an Our Father and go off contented to breakfast!

Now my prayer is a bit of a shambles: dull, unfocused, distracted. Sometimes I don't pray: instead I do 'something useful' like helping someone, or even writing pages like this! Yet, I'm aware that I'm missing something when I don't give even a little daily quality time to you. It may seem as if it's an empty waiting, as when I'm flicking through the magazines in the surgery when the doctor is delayed. It's empty time, perhaps, but it's not wasted! Just to sit for a bit, with my icon and my lighted candle, shows that I want you more than anything else. Perhaps my distracted mind and empty heart are the best symbols of generosity that I can muster up. You work well in barrenness, as Scripture shows: so where there are no obstructions perhaps your grace can work in me at depths I know little of.

Perhaps too my life mirrors my prayer – no great order in it: bits and bobs, kindnesses, interruptions, glad surprises. But like a tired pilgrim, so long as I am walking the road that is leading to my goal, which is you, perhaps all my plodding time is not wasted but quality time.

Brian Grogan SJ,
I Am Infinitely Loved

The Presence of God

Dear Jesus, I come to you today longing for your presence. I desire to love you as you love me. May nothing ever separate me from you.

Freedom

Lord, grant me the grace to be free from the excesses of this life. Let me not get caught up with the desire for wealth. Keep my heart and mind free to love and serve you.

Consciousness

Where do I sense hope, encouragement and growth in my life? By looking back over the past few months, I may be able to see which activities and occasions have produced rich fruit. If I do notice such areas, I will determine to give those areas both time and space in the future.

The Word

God speaks to each of us individually. I listen attentively to hear what he is saying to me. Read the text a few times, then listen.

(Please turn to the Scripture on the following pages. Inspiration points are there, should you need them. When you are ready, return here to continue.)

Conversation

What is stirring in me as I pray? Am I consoled, troubled, left cold? I imagine Jesus standing or sitting at my side, and I share my feelings with him.

Conclusion

Glory be to the Father, and to the Son, and to the Holy Spirit,
As it was in the beginning, is now and ever shall be,
World without end. Amen.

Sunday 10 July
Fifteenth Sunday in Ordinary Time
Luke 10:25–37

Just then a lawyer stood up to test Jesus. 'Teacher,' he said, 'what must I do to inherit eternal life?' He said to him, 'What is written in the law? What do you read there?' He answered, 'You shall love the Lord your God with all your heart, and with all your soul, and with all your strength, and with all your mind; and your neighbour as yourself.' And he said to him, 'You have given the right answer; do this, and you will live.'

But wanting to justify himself, he asked Jesus, 'And who is my neighbour?' Jesus replied, 'A man was going down from Jerusalem to Jericho, and fell into the hands of robbers, who stripped him, beat him, and went away, leaving him half dead. Now by chance a priest was going down that road; and when he saw him, he passed by on the other side. So likewise a Levite, when he came to the place and saw him, passed by on the other side. But a Samaritan while travelling came near him; and when he saw him, he was moved with pity. He went to him and bandaged his wounds, having poured oil and wine on them. Then he put him on his own animal, brought him to an inn, and took care of him. The next day he took out two denarii, gave them to the innkeeper, and said, "Take care of him; and when I come back, I will repay you whatever more you spend." Which of these three, do you think, was a neighbour to the man who fell into the hands of the robbers?' He said, 'The one who showed him mercy.' Jesus said to him, 'Go and do likewise.'

- Does this story touch me? Could I spend some time reflecting on this parable as if it were addressed personally to me? I may love the Lord with all my heart and all my soul, but who in my life is my neighbour? And to whom am I a good neighbour?

Monday 11 July
Matthew 10:34–11:1

'Do not think that I have come to bring peace to the earth; I have
    not come to bring peace, but a sword.
For I have come to set a man against his father,
and a daughter against her mother,

and a daughter-in-law against her mother-in-law;
and one's foes will be members of one's own household.

Whoever loves father or mother more than me is not worthy of me; and whoever loves son or daughter more than me is not worthy of me; and whoever does not take up the cross and follow me is not worthy of me. Those who find their life will lose it, and those who lose their life for my sake will find it.

'Whoever welcomes you welcomes me, and whoever welcomes me welcomes the one who sent me. Whoever welcomes a prophet in the name of a prophet will receive a prophet's reward; and whoever welcomes a righteous person in the name of a righteous person will receive the reward of the righteous; and whoever gives even a cup of cold water to one of these little ones in the name of a disciple – truly I tell you, none of these will lose their reward.'

Now when Jesus had finished instructing his twelve disciples, he went on from there to teach and proclaim his message in their cities.

- Do I want to save my life or to lose it? Am I ready to lose it, or do I cling on for fear of losing it? This is perhaps the basic condition for discipleship, and no moralistic or perfect obedience to any law or system of rules can replace it. I ask insistently for the grace of real interior freedom and for courage to be true to myself and to my calling.

Tuesday 12 July

Matthew 11:20–24

Then he began to reproach the cities in which most of his deeds of power had been done, because they did not repent. 'Woe to you, Chorazin! Woe to you, Bethsaida! For if the deeds of power done in you had been done in Tyre and Sidon, they would have repented long ago in sackcloth and ashes. But I tell you, on the day of judgement it will be more tolerable for Tyre and Sidon than for you. And you, Capernaum, will you be exalted to heaven? No, you will be brought down to Hades. For if the deeds of power done in you had been done in Sodom, it would have remained until this day. But I tell you that on the day of judgement it will be more tolerable for the land of Sodom than for you.'

- These verses hint at the mass of unrecorded history that the Gospels omit: the deeds of power performed by Jesus in the towns at the northern end of the Sea of Tiberias. Here were communities that listened to Jesus, and saw his miracles, but shrugged their shoulders and sent him on his way.

- Lord, open my eyes and my heart to the signs of your grace around me. Help me to hear your message, even if it upsets my habits.

Wednesday 13 July
Matthew 11:25–27

At that time Jesus said, 'I thank you, Father, Lord of heaven and earth, because you have hidden these things from the wise and the intelligent and have revealed them to infants; yes, Father, for such was your gracious will. All things have been handed over to me by my Father; and no one knows the Son except the Father, and no one knows the Father except the Son and anyone to whom the Son chooses to reveal him.

- The ordinary people would have considered the learned doctors of the Law to be on a higher level than themselves. But the people are now invited or elevated to a dignity that is nothing less than super-human: they are to be adopted sisters and brothers of God's Son – to be adopted royalty of the kingdom of heaven.

Thursday 14 July
Matthew 11:28–30

'Come to me, all you that are weary and are carrying heavy burdens, and I will give you rest. Take my yoke upon you, and learn from me; for I am gentle and humble in heart, and you will find rest for your souls. For my yoke is easy, and my burden is light.'

- Here we see Jesus as the epitome of the Beatitudes for he presents himself as 'gentle and humble in heart'. We see this in the way that throughout the Gospels Jesus is comfortable with our limitations as human beings, and also in the way he invites us to face the greatness he shares with us.

- Be with Jesus for some time as he invites you to rest with these two sides of yourself which he wants you to live happily with. In doing this Jesus promises that you will find 'rest for your soul'.

Friday 15 July
Matthew 12:1–8

At that time Jesus went through the cornfields on the sabbath; his disciples were hungry, and they began to pluck heads of grain and to eat. When the Pharisees saw it, they said to him, 'Look, your disciples are doing what is not lawful to do on the sabbath.' He said to them, 'Have you not read what David did when he and his companions were hungry? He entered the house of God and ate the bread of the Presence, which it was not lawful for him or his companions to eat, but only for the priests. Or have you not read in the law that on the sabbath the priests in the temple break the sabbath and yet are guiltless? I tell you, something greater than the temple is here. But if you had known what this means, "I desire mercy and not sacrifice", you would not have condemned the guiltless. For the Son of Man is lord of the sabbath.'

- The sabbath was modelled on God's rest day after the days of Creation. It was meant more as a relief for people than as a set of religious exactions. 'God did not institute the Sabbath to add burdens to an already over-burdened humanity. The Sabbath is a moment for God's people to pause and take time out to come to know better the God whose delight is to be with them.'

Saturday 16 July
Matthew 12:14–21

But the Pharisees went out and conspired against him, how to destroy him.

When Jesus became aware of this, he departed. Many crowds followed him, and he cured all of them, and he ordered them not to make him known. This was to fulfil what had been spoken through the prophet Isaiah:

'Here is my servant, whom I have chosen,
my beloved, with whom my soul is well pleased.
I will put my Spirit upon him,
and he will proclaim justice to the Gentiles.
He will not wrangle or cry aloud,
nor will anyone hear his voice in the streets.

He will not break a bruised reed
or quench a smouldering wick
until he brings justice to victory.
And in his name the Gentiles will hope.'

- 'The Pharisees went out and conspired against Jesus, how to destroy him.' Chilling words, indeed, even more so when their only reason was that they found Jesus' integrity and powerful message of love a real threat to their power. Yet the crowds, the simple people, followed him. So many good people are destroyed because they pose a threat to the corrupt and deceitful, sometimes even in the Church itself. I ask God to have mercy on us and on our world, and to purify my heart.

The Sixteenth Week in Ordinary Time
17–23 July 2022

Something to think and pray about each day this week:

Christians believe that God has become a human person. In other words: God does not live at a safe distance from evil. Jesus did not escape from evil. God has chosen to expose himself to evil. In this way, the suffering of ordinary people has also become the suffering of God. Indeed, Jesus, the Son of God, has suffered in the most horrible way the destructive effects of evil. He was even killed by it.

At first sight, therefore, it seems that evil has destroyed Jesus, but those who know the whole story know that Jesus has overcome evil through the love with which he answered it. Jesus' resurrection from the dead is the confirmation of this.

Is this an answer to the question 'does God want evil'? It shows that, in the confrontation with evil, God does not abandon people. Together with them God takes up the fight. However strong the evil may be, Christians believe that God's love has overcome evil.

Nikolaas Sintobin SJ,
Did Jesus Really Exist? And 51 Other Questions

The Presence of God
'I am standing at the door, knocking,' says the Lord. What a wonderful privilege that the Lord of all creation desires to come to me. I welcome his presence.

Freedom
I will ask God's help
to be free from my own preoccupations,
to be open to God in this time of prayer,
to come to know, love and serve God more.

Consciousness
In God's loving presence I unwind the past day,
starting from now and looking back, moment by moment.
I gather in all the goodness and light, in gratitude.
I attend to the shadows and what they say to me,
seeking healing, courage, forgiveness.

The Word
Now I turn to the Scripture set out for me this day. I read slowly over the words and see if any sentence or sentiment appeals to me.
(Please turn to the Scripture on the following pages. Inspiration points are there, should you need them. When you are ready, return here to continue.)

Conversation
Sometimes I wonder what I might say if I were to meet you in person, Lord. I think I might say, 'Thank you', because you are always there for me.

Conclusion
I thank God for these moments we have spent together and for any insights I have been given concerning the text.

Sunday 17 July
Sixteenth Sunday in Ordinary Time
Luke 10:38–42

Now as they went on their way, he entered a certain village, where a woman named Martha welcomed him into her home. She had a sister named Mary, who sat at the Lord's feet and listened to what he was saying. But Martha was distracted by her many tasks; so she came to him and asked, 'Lord, do you not care that my sister has left me to do all the work by myself? Tell her then to help me.' But the Lord answered her, 'Martha, Martha, you are worried and distracted by many things; there is need of only one thing. Mary has chosen the better part, which will not be taken away from her.'

- Most significant in this story is the attitude taken by Mary, sitting attentively at the feet of Jesus, listening to what he was saying. As a true disciple, Mary recognises that Jesus has far more to offer her in terms of spiritual nourishment than she or Martha can offer him. Each of us has to find the balance between service of the Kingdom and moments of serious attentiveness to God. Both the active and contemplative dimensions of Christian life are necessary.

Monday 18 July
Matthew 12:38–42

Then some of the scribes and Pharisees said to him, 'Teacher, we wish to see a sign from you.' But he answered them, 'An evil and adulterous generation asks for a sign, but no sign will be given to it except the sign of the prophet Jonah. For just as Jonah was for three days and three nights in the belly of the sea monster, so for three days and three nights the Son of Man will be in the heart of the earth. The people of Nineveh will rise up at the judgement with this generation and condemn it, because they repented at the proclamation of Jonah, and see, something greater than Jonah is here! The queen of the South will rise up at the judgement with this generation and condemn it, because she came from the ends of the earth to listen to the wisdom of Solomon, and see, something greater than Solomon is here!'

- Jesus compares himself to Jonah, the prophet who preached conversion. Moreover, he claims he is even greater than Jonah, than the wise

Solomon, so that our resistance to conversion will be our condemnation. Elsewhere, Jesus says that he will sit in judgement on the nations at the end. I ask not to be deaf to his call to change what I need to change, so that I will not be deserving of condemnation.

Tuesday 19 July
Matthew 12:46–50

While he was still speaking to the crowds, his mother and his brothers were standing outside, wanting to speak to him. Someone told him, 'Look, your mother and your brothers are standing outside, wanting to speak to you.' But to the one who had told him this, Jesus replied, 'Who is my mother, and who are my brothers?' And pointing to his disciples, he said, 'Here are my mother and my brothers! For whoever does the will of my Father in heaven is my brother and sister and mother.'

- This text can give rise to criticism of Jesus for being disrespectful to his mother and brothers. However, we should read it in the light of how he wishes to extend his family, so that we are all members of the one family where God is our father. Families who have adopted sons and daughters can understand this when all are treated equally as belonging to the one family. We are reminded that we are to love God and love our neighbour with one and the self-same love.

Wednesday 20 July
Matthew 13:1–9

That same day Jesus went out of the house and sat beside the lake. Such great crowds gathered around him that he got into a boat and sat there, while the whole crowd stood on the beach. And he told them many things in parables, saying: 'Listen! A sower went out to sow. And as he sowed, some seeds fell on the path, and the birds came and ate them up. Other seeds fell on rocky ground, where they did not have much soil, and they sprang up quickly, since they had no depth of soil. But when the sun rose, they were scorched; and since they had no root, they withered away. Other seeds fell among thorns, and the thorns grew up and choked them. Other seeds fell on good soil and brought forth grain, some a hundredfold, some sixty, some thirty. Let anyone with ears listen!'

- Many biblical commentators see this parable as the basic metaphor of the whole Gospel. The seed is the Word, and the sower is God, whose will can never be stopped. The seed falls on different types of ground, but the great majority certainly falls on good ground, and its fruit more than makes up for the seeds that fall on more difficult ground. It is the parable of optimism, something that is often lacking in followers of the Gospel.

- If I am a normal person, my heart contains all four sorts of ground, being more or less open to the Gospel message. I ask for light to see where the hardness and the insecurity lie, and ask the Sower that my life may bear abundant fruit.

Thursday 21 July

Matthew 13:10–17

Then the disciples came and asked him, 'Why do you speak to them in parables?' He answered, 'To you it has been given to know the secrets of the kingdom of heaven, but to them it has not been given. For to those who have, more will be given, and they will have an abundance; but from those who have nothing, even what they have will be taken away. The reason I speak to them in parables is that "seeing they do not perceive, and hearing they do not listen, nor do they understand." With them indeed is fulfilled the prophecy of Isaiah that says:

"You will indeed listen, but never understand,
and you will indeed look, but never perceive.
For this people's heart has grown dull,
and their ears are hard of hearing,
and they have shut their eyes;
so that they might not look with their eyes,
and listen with their ears,
and understand with their heart and turn –
and I would heal them."
'But blessed are your eyes, for they see, and your ears, for they
hear. Truly I tell you, many prophets and righteous people
longed to see what you see, but did not see it, and to hear what
you hear, but did not hear it.'

- Am I one of those who look without seeing, or hear without understanding? Jesus speaks in parables to challenge us out of our laziness, seeking the deeper meaning of things. How easy to be distracted, especially nowadays when we feel overwhelmed by too much information and images without any insight.

Friday 22 July
John 20:1–2.11–18

Early on the first day of the week, while it was still dark, Mary Magdalene came to the tomb and saw that the stone had been removed from the tomb. So she ran and went to Simon Peter and the other disciple, the one whom Jesus loved, and said to them, 'They have taken the Lord out of the tomb, and we do not know where they have laid him.' . . .

But Mary stood weeping outside the tomb. As she wept, she bent over to look into the tomb; and she saw two angels in white, sitting where the body of Jesus had been lying, one at the head and the other at the feet. They said to her, 'Woman, why are you weeping?' She said to them, 'They have taken away my Lord, and I do not know where they have laid him.' When she had said this, she turned round and saw Jesus standing there, but she did not know that it was Jesus. Jesus said to her, 'Woman, why are you weeping? For whom are you looking?' Supposing him to be the gardener, she said to him, 'Sir, if you have carried him away, tell me where you have laid him, and I will take him away.' Jesus said to her, 'Mary!' She turned and said to him in Hebrew, 'Rabbouni!' (which means Teacher). Jesus said to her, 'Do not hold on to me, because I have not yet ascended to the Father. But go to my brothers and say to them, "I am ascending to my Father and your Father, to my God and your God."' Mary Magdalene went and announced to the disciples, 'I have seen the Lord'; and she told them that he had said these things to her.

- Through the resurrection of Jesus we celebrate the joy of his victory over sin and death. It is the basic tenet of the Christian faith. How does the grace of the resurrection affect me? I pray that I may welcome with joy the message of the risen Jesus, believing in the power of his presence in my life.

Saturday 23 July
Matthew 13:24–30

He put before them another parable: 'The kingdom of heaven may be compared to someone who sowed good seed in his field; but while everybody was asleep, an enemy came and sowed weeds among the wheat, and then went away. So when the plants came up and bore grain, then the weeds appeared as well. And the slaves of the householder came and said to him, "Master, did you not sow good seed in your field? Where, then, did these weeds come from?" He answered, "An enemy has done this." The slaves said to him, "Then do you want us to go and gather them?" But he replied, "No; for in gathering the weeds you would uproot the wheat along with them. Let both of them grow together until the harvest; and at harvest time I will tell the reapers, Collect the weeds first and bind them in bundles to be burned, but gather the wheat into my barn."'

- We are frustrated and baffled by the presence of evil in our midst; it is one of our biggest questions. In this parable Jesus tells us that this is the work of the enemy: the struggle between good and evil is to the death, but we can rest assured that God will have the last word. It is never easy to believe this, for often the evidence points in the other direction, so I ask for the grace to believe that God is the just and powerful judge.

The Seventeenth Week in Ordinary Time
24–30 July 2022

Something to think and pray about each day this week:

We hear Jesus himself saying, 'I am not alone. He who sent me is with me' (John 16:32). This simple phrase 'with me' is enough to indicate all that is going on: Jesus has been commissioned by his Father for a particular task, but he can feel inadequate to it, as the agony in Gethsemane makes clear (Mark 14:32–36). Nonetheless, as John tells us, God will be 'with' him to support him, as the angel did in Gethsemane (Luke 22:43), and his Father will not forsake him in spite of his feeling of dereliction (Matthew 27:46).

We should keep an eye and an ear open in the liturgy and in our reading of the Bible to pick up the many references to God being 'with' us and his other chosen servants, so that we can appreciate their full theological significance. This should encourage us to appreciate the depth and all the implications of the apparently simple universal greeting with which we Christians are so familiar that it glides off our minds regularly without our appreciating it: 'The Lord be with you'. Hearing this from the priest at Mass should stop us regularly in our tracks: it is not just a blessing; it is always also a challenge. As we see throughout the Bible, it implies a previous particular commission that we have personally received from God. It should remind us that God promises to be always 'with' us, as the risen Jesus promised his disciples (Matthew 28:20), regardless of – even because of – our inadequacies, so that God can bring about through us what he is asking of us at this moment in our lives. That's the point.

Jack Mahoney SJ,
Glimpses of the Gospels

The Presence of God

At any time of the day or night we can call on Jesus.
He is always waiting, listening for our call.
What a wonderful blessing.
No phone needed, no emails, just a whisper.

Freedom

If God were trying to tell me something, would I know?
If God were reassuring me or challenging me, would I notice?
I ask for the grace to be free of my own preoccupations
and open to what God may be saying to me.

Consciousness

Help me, Lord, become more conscious of your presence. Teach me to recognise your presence in others. Fill my heart with gratitude for the times your love has been shown to me through the care of others.

The Word

In this expectant state of mind, please turn to the text for the day with confidence. Believe that the Holy Spirit is present and may reveal whatever the passage has to say to you. Read reflectively, listening with a third ear to what may be going on in your heart.

(Please turn to the Scripture on the following pages. Inspiration points are there, should you need them. When you are ready, return here to continue.)

Conversation

Conversation requires talking and listening.
As I talk to Jesus, may I also learn to pause and listen.
I picture the gentleness in his eyes and the love in his smile.
I can be totally honest with Jesus as I tell him my worries and cares.
I will open my heart to Jesus as I tell him my fears and doubts.
I will ask him to help me place myself fully in his care, knowing that he always desires good for me.

Conclusion

I thank God for these moments we have spent together and for any insights I have been given concerning the text.

Sunday 24 July
Seventeenth Sunday in Ordinary Time
Luke 11:1–13

He was praying in a certain place, and after he had finished, one of his disciples said to him, 'Lord, teach us to pray, as John taught his disciples.' He said to them, 'When you pray, say:

> "Father, hallowed be your name.
> Your kingdom come.
> Give us each day our daily bread.
> And forgive us our sins,
> for we ourselves forgive everyone indebted to us.
> And do not bring us to the time of trial."'

And he said to them, 'Suppose one of you has a friend, and you go to him at midnight and say to him, "Friend, lend me three loaves of bread; for a friend of mine has arrived, and I have nothing to set before him." And he answers from within, "Do not bother me; the door has already been locked, and my children are with me in bed; I cannot get up and give you anything." I tell you, even though he will not get up and give him anything because he is his friend, at least because of his persistence he will get up and give him whatever he needs.

'So I say to you, Ask, and it will be given to you; search, and you will find; knock, and the door will be opened for you. For everyone who asks receives, and everyone who searches finds, and for everyone who knocks, the door will be opened. Is there anyone among you who, if your child asks for a fish, will give a snake instead of a fish? Or if the child asks for an egg, will give a scorpion? If you then, who are evil, know how to give good gifts to your children, how much more will the heavenly Father give the Holy Spirit to those who ask him!'

- Heavenly Father, each day I depend upon you. I confidently ask for daily bread for my family and myself. And you generously keep on giving. I thank you also for your loving forgiveness when I disappoint you. Give me a forgiving heart when others disappoint me.

Monday 25 July
Matthew 20:20–28

Then the mother of the sons of Zebedee came to him with her sons, and kneeling before him, she asked a favour of him. And he said to her, 'What do you want?' She said to him, 'Declare that these two sons of mine will sit, one at your right hand and one at your left, in your kingdom.' But Jesus answered, 'You do not know what you are asking. Are you able to drink the cup that I am about to drink?' They said to him, 'We are able.' He said to them, 'You will indeed drink my cup, but to sit at my right hand and at my left, this is not mine to grant, but it is for those for whom it has been prepared by my Father.'

When the ten heard it, they were angry with the two brothers. But Jesus called them to him and said, 'You know that the rulers of the Gentiles lord it over them, and their great ones are tyrants over them. It will not be so among you; but whoever wishes to be great among you must be your servant, and whoever wishes to be first among you must be your slave; just as the Son of Man came not to be served but to serve, and to give his life a ransom for many.'

• James and John were two of the three apostles who were closest to Jesus. Yet they too seem to have misunderstood his message, and asked to be given the highest posts in the future kingdom. No wonder I too feel so attracted to power and prestige, and that even the Church nowadays seems not to be exempt from power struggles. I ask for a deeper understanding of the Gospel and its radical message of service. I ask Jesus to make me a real disciple of his, able to drink the same cup he drank.

Tuesday 26 July
Matthew 13:36–43

Then he left the crowds and went into the house. And his disciples approached him, saying, 'Explain to us the parable of the weeds of the field.' He answered, 'The one who sows the good seed is the Son of Man; the field is the world, and the good seed are the children of the kingdom; the weeds are the children of the evil one, and the enemy who sowed them is the devil; the harvest is the end of the age, and the reapers are angels. Just as the weeds are collected and burned up with fire, so will it be at the end of the age. The Son of Man will send his angels, and they will collect out of his kingdom all causes of sin and all evildoers, and they will throw them into the furnace of fire, where there will be weeping and gnashing of teeth. Then the righteous will shine like the sun in the kingdom of their Father. Let anyone with ears listen!

- We must live in a world where good and evil are intertwined. Jesus warns that only at the end of time will all be resolved. In the meantime we are not to despair in the face of evil, but to trust that God can bring good out of human evil. I ask that by the end of history all of us may be made righteous and shine together like the sun.

Wednesday 27 July
Matthew 13:44–46

'The kingdom of heaven is like treasure hidden in a field, which someone found and hid; then in his joy he goes and sells all that he has and buys that field.

'Again, the kingdom of heaven is like a merchant in search of fine pearls; on finding one pearl of great value, he went and sold all that he had and bought it.'

- Seekers, who may be unclear about what exactly they are seeking but who pursue their search with sincerity, show by this very fact that God is with them. Their peace will be in the seeking, as it will eventually be in the finding.

- 'Let me seek you in desiring you; let me desire you in seeking you; let me find you in loving you; let me love you in finding you.' (Saint Anselm)

Thursday 28 July
Matthew 13:47–53

'Again, the kingdom of heaven is like a net that was thrown into the sea and caught fish of every kind; when it was full, they drew it ashore, sat down, and put the good into baskets but threw out the bad. So it will be at the end of the age. The angels will come out and separate the evil from the righteous and throw them into the furnace of fire, where there will be weeping and gnashing of teeth.

'Have you understood all this?' They answered, 'Yes.' And he said to them, 'Therefore every scribe who has been trained for the kingdom of heaven is like the master of a household who brings out of his treasure what is new and what is old.' When Jesus had finished these parables, he left that place.

- In this dramatic story about the end of human history Jesus is trying to jolt us into awareness that the decisions we make day by day are important. His overall concern is that we should always love one another: this is what shapes our eternal destiny. It won't do to say, 'I won't bother helping this needy person' or 'I can get away with this: no one will ever know!'

- We are meant always to be growing in love of others, rather than living for ourselves. That's the drama of Christian life. Our joy at the end will be to see how we have helped others to become as God wants them to be.

Friday 29 July

John 11:19–27

And many of the Jews had come to Martha and Mary to console them about their brother. When Martha heard that Jesus was coming, she went and met him, while Mary stayed at home. Martha said to Jesus, 'Lord, if you had been here, my brother would not have died. But even now I know that God will give you whatever you ask of him.' Jesus said to her, 'Your brother will rise again.' Martha said to him, 'I know that he will rise again in the resurrection on the last day.' Jesus said to her, 'I am the resurrection and the life. Those who believe in me, even though they die, will live, and everyone who lives and believes in me will never die. Do you believe this?' She said to him, 'Yes, Lord, I believe that you are the Messiah, the Son of God, the one coming into the world.'

- Martha's faith in Jesus is absolute. She believes that her brother Lazarus will rise again in the resurrection on the last day. She acknowledges Jesus as 'the Messiah, the Son of God'.

- Faith in the resurrection helps us to live with an attitude of hope, sharing in the joy of the victory of the risen Christ over sin and death. It is because of the resurrection that Christ is with me on all of my journeys through life. Can I recognise his presence and open my heart to encounter him more fully?

Saturday 30 July
Matthew 14:1–12

At that time Herod the ruler heard reports about Jesus; and he said to his servants, 'This is John the Baptist; he has been raised from the dead, and for this reason these powers are at work in him.' For Herod had arrested John, bound him, and put him in prison on account of Herodias, his brother Philip's wife, because John had been telling him, 'It is not lawful for you to have her.' Though Herod wanted to put him to death, he feared the crowd, because they regarded him as a prophet. But when Herod's birthday came, the daughter of Herodias danced before the company, and she pleased Herod so much that he promised on oath to grant her whatever she might ask. Prompted by her mother, she said, 'Give me the head of John the Baptist here on a platter.' The king was grieved, yet out of regard for his oaths and for the guests, he commanded it to be given; he sent and had John beheaded in the prison. The head was brought on a platter and given to the girl, who brought it to her mother. His disciples came and took the body and buried it; then they went and told Jesus.

- John is an example to us of integrity. And, like him, we have each one of us been called in our own way to be prophets, to be spokespersons for God's way. It may not always be easy. Take a few moments to reflect on this in prayer.

31 July–6 August 2022

Something to think and pray about each day this week:

In the Book of Deuteronomy (15:4), it is written as part of the social laws that 'there should be no poor among you'. Jesus says, 'the poor you will have always with you' (Mark 14: 7).

German artist Johannes Wickert, who was born in 1954, paints inspiring works of the widespread begging in the city of Aachen, Germany. It could be London, Dublin or any city in the world. His paintings confront you with a tough and stark reality as he wants to rouse people's conscience.

Etty Hillesum (1914–1943), a Dutch Jewish writer and a victim of the Holocaust in Auschwitz, wrote in her diary: 'Time becomes a gift when it has a receiver. When a gift is offered and it is not received it loses its power as gift. The gift may be delivered but the door is closed. Prayer is the practice of opening the door, opening the heart to welcome these gifts' (*Diaries and Letters of Etty Hillesum: An Interrupted Life*).

Election campaigns at home, across Europe and in the US focus on lack of housing, health issues, migrants and the poor. By playing tawdry politics with such issues, we risk anaesthetising and even censuring our hearts, as well as setting the scene for a total eclipse of the values and ideals of the Gospel.

> The meek shall obtain fresh joy in the Lord,
> And the neediest people shall exult in the Holy One of Israel.
> (Isaiah 29:19)

John Cullen,
Alert, Aware, Attentive

The Presence of God
As I sit here, the beating of my heart,
the ebb and flow of my breathing, the movements of my mind
are all signs of God's ongoing creation of me.
I pause for a moment and become aware
of this presence of God within me.

Freedom
It is so easy to get caught up with the trappings of wealth in this life.
Grant, O Lord, that I may be free from greed and selfishness.
Remind me that the best things in life are free:
Love, laughter, caring and sharing.

Consciousness
Knowing that God loves me unconditionally, I can afford to be honest
about how I am. How has the day been, and how do I feel now? I share
my feelings openly with the Lord.

The Word
Lord Jesus, you became human to communicate with me.
You walked and worked on this earth.
You endured the heat and struggled with the cold.
All your time on this earth was spent in caring for humanity.
You healed the sick, you raised the dead.
Most important of all, you saved me from death.
*(Please turn to the Scripture on the following pages. Inspiration points are there,
should you need them. When you are ready, return here to continue.)*

Conversation
Sometimes I wonder what I might say if I were to meet you in person, Lord.
I think I might say, 'Thank you', because you are always there for me.

Conclusion
I thank God for these moments we have spent together and for any insights I have been given concerning the text.

Sunday 31 July
Eighteenth Sunday in Ordinary Time
Luke 12:13–21

Someone in the crowd said to him, 'Teacher, tell my brother to divide the family inheritance with me.' But he said to him, 'Friend, who set me to be a judge or arbitrator over you?' And he said to them, 'Take care! Be on your guard against all kinds of greed; for one's life does not consist in the abundance of possessions.' Then he told them a parable: 'The land of a rich man produced abundantly. And he thought to himself, "What should I do, for I have no place to store my crops?" Then he said, "I will do this: I will pull down my barns and build larger ones, and there I will store all my grain and my goods. And I will say to my soul, Soul, you have ample goods laid up for many years; relax, eat, drink, be merry." But God said to him, "You fool! This very night your life is being demanded of you. And the things you have prepared, whose will they be?" So it is with those who store up treasures for themselves but are not rich towards God.'

- This is certainly a parable for our own times, where seeking money and more money often turns us into fools who prepare our own downfall. Jesus tells us, 'A man's life is not made secure by what he owns, even when he has more than he needs'. I pray that our world may grow in wisdom and choose solidarity and respect for one another and for the earth, our common home.

Monday 1 August
Matthew 14:13–21

Now when Jesus heard this, he withdrew from there in a boat to a deserted place by himself. But when the crowds heard it, they followed him on foot from the towns. When he went ashore, he saw a great crowd; and he had compassion for them and cured their sick. When it was evening, the disciples came to him and said, 'This is a deserted place, and the hour is now late; send the crowds away so that they may go into the villages and buy food for themselves.' Jesus said to them, 'They need not go away; you give them something to eat.' They replied, 'We have nothing here but five loaves and two fish.' And he said, 'Bring them here to me.' Then he ordered the crowds to sit down on the grass. Taking the five loaves and the two fish, he looked up to heaven, and blessed and broke the loaves, and gave them to the disciples, and the disciples gave them to the crowds. And all ate and were filled; and they took up what was left over of the broken pieces, twelve baskets full. And those who ate were about five thousand men, besides women and children.

• This great miracle took place at the most unlikely moment: at the end of the day, when it was time to return home, when the disciples realised they had only five loaves and two fish. Yet Jesus asked his disciples and his hearers to trust him, to 'sit down' on the grass as if they were not in any hurry. Those who trusted got more than they needed. I look back on some moments when I too experienced God's generosity in my life, and I ask to know how to 'sit down' in trust in the moment of crisis.

Tuesday 2 August
Matthew 14:22–36

Immediately he made the disciples get into the boat and go on ahead to the other side, while he dismissed the crowds. And after he had dismissed the crowds, he went up the mountain by himself to pray. When evening came, he was there alone, but by this time the boat, battered by the waves, was far from the land, for the wind was against them. And early in the morning he came walking towards them on the lake. But when the disciples saw him walking on the lake, they were terrified, saying, 'It is a ghost!' And they cried out in fear. But immediately Jesus spoke to them and said, 'Take heart, it is I; do not be afraid.'

Peter answered him, 'Lord, if it is you, command me to come to you on the water.' He said, 'Come.' So Peter got out of the boat, started walking on the water, and came towards Jesus. But when he noticed the strong wind, he became frightened, and beginning to sink, he cried out, 'Lord, save me!' Jesus immediately reached out his hand and caught him, saying to him, 'You of little faith, why did you doubt?' When they got into the boat, the wind ceased. And those in the boat worshipped him, saying, 'Truly you are the Son of God.'

When they had crossed over, they came to land at Gennesaret. After the people of that place recognised him, they sent word throughout the region and brought all who were sick to him, and begged him that they might touch even the fringe of his cloak; and all who touched it were healed.

- The disciples in their later trials would have remembered what happened next on the lake; how Jesus reached out and caught the drowning Peter; how he got into their boat and how somehow his presence made the wind die down. Jesus does the same for you, but less dramatically.

Wednesday 3 August
Matthew 15:21–28

Jesus left that place and went away to the district of Tyre and Sidon. Just then a Canaanite woman from that region came out and started shouting, 'Have mercy on me, Lord, Son of David; my daughter is tormented by a demon.' But he did not answer her at all. And his disciples came and urged him, saying, 'Send her away, for she keeps shouting after us.' He answered, 'I was sent only to the lost sheep of the house of Israel.' But she came and knelt before him, saying, 'Lord, help me.' He answered, 'It is not fair to take the children's food and throw it to the dogs.' She said, 'Yes, Lord, yet even the dogs eat the crumbs that fall from their masters' table.' Then Jesus answered her, 'Woman, great is your faith! Let it be done for you as you wish.' And her daughter was healed instantly.

- In a way this pagan woman can give us a lesson on prayer. We are not always happy with our lot or the lot of others, and we should express our real feelings to Christ, not just our sanitised ones. Jesus hears my prayer.

Thursday 4 August
Matthew 16:13–23

Now when Jesus came into the district of Caesarea Philippi, he asked his disciples, 'Who do people say that the Son of Man is?' And they said, 'Some say John the Baptist, but others Elijah, and still others Jeremiah or one of the prophets.' He said to them, 'But who do you say that I am?' Simon Peter answered, 'You are the Messiah, the Son of the living God.' And Jesus answered him, 'Blessed are you, Simon son of Jonah! For flesh and blood has not revealed this to you, but my Father in heaven. And I tell you, you are Peter, and on this rock I will build my church, and the gates of Hades will not prevail against it. I will give you the keys of the kingdom of heaven, and whatever you bind on earth will be bound in heaven, and whatever you loose on earth will be loosed in heaven.' Then he sternly ordered the disciples not to tell anyone that he was the Messiah.

From that time on, Jesus began to show his disciples that he must go to Jerusalem and undergo great suffering at the hands of the elders and chief priests and scribes, and be killed, and on the third day be raised. And Peter took him aside and began to rebuke him, saying, 'God forbid it, Lord! This must never happen to you.' But he turned and said to Peter, 'Get behind me, Satan! You are a stumbling-block to me; for you are setting your mind not on divine things but on human things.'

- We live in times of turmoil in the Church, of a deep-seated mistrust in all leaders, including those in the Church. I listen to Jesus giving Peter the mission of being the rock upon which he chose to build his Church. Jesus, who here acknowledges he is the Christ, the promised one, made this choice of building his Church on Peter, when he could well have chosen a different way. I pray to be given the faith that was given to Peter, of professing Jesus as the Son of the living God.

Friday 5 August
Matthew 16:24–28

Then Jesus told his disciples, 'If any want to become my followers, let them deny themselves and take up their cross and follow me. For those who want to save their life will lose it, and those who lose their life for my sake will find it. For what will it profit them if they gain the whole world but forfeit their life? Or what will they give in return for their life?

'For the Son of Man is to come with his angels in the glory of his Father, and then he will repay everyone for what has been done. Truly I tell you, there are some standing here who will not taste death before they see the Son of Man coming in his kingdom.'

- Only by uniting our suffering in life to that of Jesus can we carry our crosses. Is there something in my life today or every day that I am struggling under the weight of? Ask for the grace you need from God in this time of prayer.

Saturday 6 August
The Transfiguration of the Lord
Luke 9:28b–36

Jesus took with him Peter and John and James, and went up on the mountain to pray. And while he was praying, the appearance of his face changed, and his clothes became dazzling white. Suddenly they saw two men, Moses and Elijah, talking to him. They appeared in glory and were speaking of his departure, which he was about to accomplish at Jerusalem. Now Peter and his companions were weighed down with sleep; but since they had stayed awake, they saw his glory and the two men who stood with him. Just as they were leaving him, Peter said to Jesus, 'Master, it is good for us to be here; let us make three dwellings, one for you, one for Moses, and one for Elijah' – not knowing what he said. While he was saying this, a cloud came and overshadowed them; and they were terrified as they entered the cloud. Then from the cloud came a voice that said, 'This is my Son, my Chosen; listen to him!' When the voice had spoken, Jesus was found alone. And they kept silent and in those days told no one any of the things they had seen.

- All we do our whole lives long is go from one little piece of holy ground to the next. Lord, give me the strength to keep going in between.

Something to think and pray about each day this week:

Head said: 'I am full of bright ideas.'

Heart said: 'I am full of tenderness and passion.'

Head said: 'I am reason. I am order. I am the lynchpin which holds everything together.'

Heart said: 'I am feeling. I am mystery. I am the creative energy which sparks wonder and authentic life.'

Then Head and Heart began to squabble. Head said: 'You are easily swayed and misled. You live in a world without order.' Heart replied: 'You are dispassionate and detached. You don't live. You just exist.'

So Head and Heart went to God and asked if they could be split up. God laughed at them and said: 'You two belong together. Apart you are worthless. Head, you are the container. Heart, you are the contents. The container without the contents is as useless as an empty vessel, all sham and no substance. The contents without the container will scatter to the ends of the earth, and blow into the empty wind. It's not possible for you to live apart and have productive lives.'

Head and Heart were puzzled: 'But we are total opposites. How can we find harmony?' God said: 'Draw close and embrace like lovers. Protect each other. Look out for each other. Help each other to be equal partners. Then you will join together as one and I promise you something fantastic and wonderful will happen.'

At this Head and Heart asked in unison: 'What?'

God simply smiled and said: 'Wait and see.'

John Scally,
Waiting in Joy

The Presence of God

'Come to me, all you who are weary and are carrying heavy burdens, and I will give you rest.' Here I am, Lord. I come to seek your presence. I long for your healing power.

Freedom

God is not foreign to my freedom. The Spirit breathes life into my most intimate desires, gently nudging me towards all that is good. I ask for the grace to let myself be enfolded by the Spirit.

Consciousness

I remind myself that I am in the presence of the Lord. I will take refuge in his loving heart. He is my strength in times of weakness. He is my comforter in times of sorrow.

The Word

I take my time to read the word of God slowly, a few times, allowing myself to dwell on anything that strikes me.

(Please turn to the Scripture on the following pages. Inspiration points are there, should you need them. When you are ready, return here to continue.)

Conversation

Jesus, you always welcomed little children when you walked on this earth. Teach me to have a childlike trust in you. Teach me to live in the knowledge that you will never abandon me.

Conclusion

Glory be to the Father, and to the Son, and to the Holy Spirit,
As it was in the beginning, is now and ever shall be,
World without end. Amen.

Sunday 7 August
Nineteenth Sunday in Ordinary Time
Luke 12:32–48

'Do not be afraid, little flock, for it is your Father's good pleasure to give you the kingdom. Sell your possessions, and give alms. Make purses for yourselves that do not wear out, an unfailing treasure in heaven, where no thief comes near and no moth destroys. For where your treasure is, there your heart will be also.

'Be dressed for action and have your lamps lit; be like those who are waiting for their master to return from the wedding banquet, so that they may open the door for him as soon as he comes and knocks. Blessed are those slaves whom the master finds alert when he comes; truly I tell you, he will fasten his belt and have them sit down to eat, and he will come and serve them. If he comes during the middle of the night, or near dawn, and finds them so, blessed are those slaves.

'But know this: if the owner of the house had known at what hour the thief was coming, he would not have let his house be broken into. You also must be ready, for the Son of Man is coming at an unexpected hour.'

Peter said, 'Lord, are you telling this parable for us or for everyone?' And the Lord said, 'Who then is the faithful and prudent manager whom his master will put in charge of his slaves, to give them their allowance of food at the proper time? Blessed is that slave whom his master will find at work when he arrives. Truly I tell you, he will put that one in charge of all his possessions. But if that slave says to himself, "My master is delayed in coming", and if he begins to beat the other slaves, men and women, and to eat and drink and get drunk, the master of that slave will come on a day when he does not expect him and at an hour that he does not know, and will cut him in pieces, and put him with the unfaithful. That slave who knew what his master wanted, but did not prepare himself or do what was wanted, will receive a severe beating. But one who did not know and did what deserved a beating will receive a light beating. From everyone to whom much has been given, much will be required; and from one to whom much has been entrusted, even more will be demanded.'

- Once more, Jesus reminds us to be watchful, making sure we are awake when the master comes. I ask for his help not to live a distracted life, so that when Jesus comes into my life, in a way and at a time I do not expect, through events and persons, he finds me ready to welcome him. I look at my day so far, at yesterday, and see how aware I have been of God's coming into my life, in so many ways. I ask for the grace not to be deaf to his call, and always ready to respond to the best of my ability.

Monday 8 August
Matthew 17:22–27

As they were gathering in Galilee, Jesus said to them, 'The Son of Man is going to be betrayed into human hands, and they will kill him, and on the third day he will be raised.' And they were greatly distressed.

When they reached Capernaum, the collectors of the temple tax came to Peter and said, 'Does your teacher not pay the temple tax?' He said, 'Yes, he does.' And when he came home, Jesus spoke of it first, asking, 'What do you think, Simon? From whom do kings of the earth take toll or tribute? From their children or from others?' When Peter said, 'From others', Jesus said to him, 'Then the children are free. However, so that we do not give offence to them, go to the lake and cast a hook; take the first fish that comes up; and when you open its mouth, you will find a coin; take that and give it to them for you and me.'

- Jesus wanted people to be free to live their lives to the full, and that is his desire for you too. In your prayer, ask him to free you from the fixations, irritations and trivialities that distract you from the fundamental task of growing in love and of playing your part in advancing the kingdom of God.

Tuesday 9 August
Matthew 18:1–5.10.12–14

At that time the disciples came to Jesus and asked, 'Who is the greatest in the kingdom of heaven?' He called a child, whom he put among them, and said, 'Truly I tell you, unless you change and become like children, you will never enter the kingdom of heaven. Whoever becomes humble like this child is the greatest in the kingdom of heaven. Whoever welcomes one such child in my name welcomes me. . . .

'Take care that you do not despise one of these little ones; for, I tell you, in heaven their angels continually see the face of my Father in heaven. . . .

What do you think? If a shepherd has a hundred sheep, and one of them has gone astray, does he not leave the ninety-nine on the mountains and go in search of the one that went astray? And if he finds it, truly I tell you, he rejoices over it more than over the ninety-nine that never went astray. So it is not the will of your Father in heaven that one of these little ones should be lost.'

- Jesus here portrays God as watching out for everyone, especially those who are vulnerable and dependent. Jesus did that himself and, as a disciple, so must I! It is a humbling task, but it carries a divine reward, because when I welcome a vulnerable person I am welcoming the Lord himself.

Wednesday 10 August
John 12:24–26

'Very truly, I tell you, unless a grain of wheat falls into the earth and dies, it remains just a single grain; but if it dies, it bears much fruit. Those who love their life lose it, and those who hate their life in this world will keep it for eternal life. Whoever serves me must follow me, and where I am, there will my servant be also. Whoever serves me, the Father will honour.'

- Pope Francis says in *Laudato Si'* that 'God has written a precious book, "whose letters are the multitude of created things present in the universe"' (85). Jesus saw nature in this way: do I? Let's imagine a wheat grain at harvest time. It feels happy and fulfilled in the autumn sunshine. But winter comes and it is ploughed into the damp earth. It loses its beauty and begins to rot. But with the coming of spring it starts to stir. Its stalk pushes up to meet the sun and steadily a whole head of wheat emerges, thirty, sixty, perhaps a hundred grains.

- Can you imagine your life as being like this? 'I know the plans I have for you, says the LORD, plans for your welfare and not for harm' (Jeremiah 29:11). God always works to bring good out of what is less than good in your life. Ask to allow him to work unimpeded in you.

Thursday 11 August
Matthew 18:21–19:1

Then Peter came and said to him, 'Lord, if another member of the church sins against me, how often should I forgive? As many as seven times?' Jesus said to him, 'Not seven times, but, I tell you, seventy-seven times.

'For this reason the kingdom of heaven may be compared to a king who wished to settle accounts with his slaves. When he began the reckoning, one who owed him ten thousand talents was brought to him; and, as he could not pay, his lord ordered him to be sold, together with his wife and children and all his possessions, and payment to be made. So the slave fell on his knees before him, saying, "Have patience with me, and I will pay you everything." And out of pity for him, the lord of that slave released him and forgave him the debt. But that same slave, as he went out, came upon one of his fellow-slaves who owed him a hundred denarii; and seizing him by the throat, he said, "Pay what you owe." Then his fellow-slave fell down and pleaded with him, "Have patience with me, and I will pay you." But he refused; then he went and threw him into prison until he should pay the debt. When his fellow-slaves saw what had happened, they were greatly distressed, and they went and reported to their lord all that had taken place. Then his lord summoned him and said to him, "You wicked slave! I forgave you all that debt because you pleaded with me. Should you not have had mercy on your fellow-slave, as I had mercy on you?" And in anger his lord handed him over to be tortured until he should pay his entire debt. So my heavenly Father will also do to every one of you, if you do not forgive your brother or sister from your heart.'

When Jesus had finished saying these things, he left Galilee and went to the region of Judea beyond the Jordan.

- The world needs me to radiate God's own love and to foster reconciliation and peace. Lord, for my shortcomings in living out the Gospel I ask forgiveness and mercy. Enable me, in turn, to show forgiveness to those who do me wrong. In this way I can be more truly the light of the world.

Friday 12 August
Matthew 19:3–12

Some Pharisees came to him, and to test him they asked, 'Is it lawful for a man to divorce his wife for any cause?' He answered, 'Have you not read that the one who made them at the beginning "made them male and female", and said, "For this reason a man shall leave his father and mother and be joined to his wife, and the two shall become one flesh"? So they are no longer two, but one flesh. Therefore what God has joined together, let no one separate.' They said to him, 'Why then did Moses command us to give a certificate of dismissal and to divorce her?' He said to them, 'It was because you were so hard-hearted that Moses allowed you to divorce your wives, but at the beginning it was not so. And I say to you, whoever divorces his wife, except for unchastity, and marries another commits adultery.'

His disciples said to him, 'If such is the case of a man with his wife, it is better not to marry.' But he said to them, 'Not everyone can accept this teaching, but only those to whom it is given. For there are eunuchs who have been so from birth, and there are eunuchs who have been made eunuchs by others, and there are eunuchs who have made themselves eunuchs for the sake of the kingdom of heaven. Let anyone accept this who can.'

- I pray that I am not 'unteachable', but be given an open heart. A heart that is ready to listen to what God wants of humanity, and a heart that is gentle and kind towards those who do not succeed in following these high ideals. I pray for Pope Francis and for the whole Church as it grapples with the pastoral challenge of marriages that have broken down irretrievably.

Saturday 13 August
Matthew 19:13–15

Then little children were being brought to him in order that he might lay his hands on them and pray. The disciples spoke sternly to those who brought them; but Jesus said, 'Let the little children come to me, and do not stop them; for it is to such as these that the kingdom of heaven belongs.' And he laid his hands on them and went on his way.

- Children are always a challenge to us. Am I one of those who bring children to Jesus, or like the disciples who turn them away, for one reason or another? Do I believe it is good for children to be near Jesus, to know him better and love him as a friend and benefactor? In prayer, I bring some children I know to Jesus, to lay his hands on them and say a prayer.

- I thank Jesus for the children in my life, for they teach me so many things about the kingdom.

The Twentieth Week in Ordinary Time
14–20 August 2022

Something to think and pray about each day this week:

Mary was victorious in the battle between good and evil because she always looked towards God. We, on the other hand, become unsettled when we are tempted. We stop focusing on God, and we start to focus on the temptation and upon ourselves. We try to fight against it.

When we are in a good relationship with God, the evil spirit tries to unsettle us by making us anxious, frustrated, dissatisfied and sad. We shouldn't enter his playing field by engaging with the temptation or arguing with these unhelpful thoughts or promptings. If we do, we'll probably lose the battle. Instead, we should return calmly into God's presence. As the Book of Exodus puts it: 'The LORD will fight for you; you only need to be still' (Exodus 14:14).

Mary's example teaches us that genuine joy comes from being united with the source of all true joy: God. The more we're one with God, the less we are disturbed by anxieties, fears and pains. We don't need to defend ourselves against these incursions, because God's presence itself is our defence. Even while Mary was on earth, it was as though she was already in heaven, because she was fully in God's presence, always adoring the one who filled her with light and with joy. And as her life approached its end, the light that had always shone in her heart became more and more intense. It drew her whole being upwards, as though it wanted to snatch her from the earth and draw her upwards where her spirit already soared, so that she could sing her beautiful Magnificat in gratitude to God for ever and ever.

Thomas Casey SJ,
Smile of Joy: Mary of Nazareth

The Presence of God

What is present to me is what has a hold on my becoming.
I reflect on the presence of God always there in love,
amidst the many things that have a hold on me.
I pause and pray that I may let God
affect my becoming in this precise moment.

Freedom

By God's grace I was born to live in freedom. Free to enjoy the pleasures
he created for me. Dear Lord, grant that I may live as you intended, with
complete confidence in your loving care.

Consciousness

I exist in a web of relationships: links to nature, people, God.
I trace out these links, giving thanks for the life that flows through them.
Some links are twisted or broken; I may feel regret, anger, disappointment.
I pray for the gift of acceptance and forgiveness.

The Word

God speaks to each of us individually. I listen attentively to hear what he
is saying to me. Read the text a few times, then listen.
*(Please turn to the Scripture on the following pages. Inspiration points are there,
should you need them. When you are ready, return here to continue.)*

Conversation

I begin to talk with Jesus about the Scripture I have just read. What part
of it strikes a chord in me? Perhaps the words of a friend – or some story
I have heard recently – will rise to the surface in my consciousness. If so,
does the story throw light on what the Scripture passage may be saying
to me?

Conclusion

Glory be to the Father, and to the Son, and to the Holy Spirit,
As it was in the beginning, is now and ever shall be,
World without end. Amen.

Sunday 14 August
Twentieth Sunday in Ordinary Time
Luke 12:49–53

'I came to bring fire to the earth, and how I wish it were already kindled! I have a baptism with which to be baptised, and what stress I am under until it is completed! Do you think that I have come to bring peace to the earth? No, I tell you, but rather division! From now on, five in one household will be divided, three against two and two against three; they will be divided:

> father against son
> and son against father,
> mother against daughter
> and daughter against mother,
> mother-in-law against her daughter-in-law
> and daughter-in-law against mother-in-law.'

- Jesus shed his blood to reconcile us with God and among ourselves. Yet the radicality of his message leads inevitably to division, between those who accept it and those who resist it. Often these divisions run across families. I pray that I may know how to bear the division that being faithful to Jesus and his message can bring to my life. I pray for my family and friends that Jesus can be for us the source of unity rather than division.

Monday 15 August
The Assumption of the Blessed Virgin Mary
Luke 1:39–56

In those days Mary set out and went with haste to a Judean town in the hill country, where she entered the house of Zechariah and greeted Elizabeth. When Elizabeth heard Mary's greeting, the child leapt in her womb. And Elizabeth was filled with the Holy Spirit and exclaimed with a loud cry, 'Blessed are you among women, and blessed is the fruit of your womb. And why has this happened to me, that the mother of my Lord comes to me? For as soon as I heard the sound of your greeting, the child in my womb leapt for joy. And blessed is she who believed that there would be a fulfilment of what was spoken to her by the Lord.'

And Mary said,
'My soul magnifies the Lord,
and my spirit rejoices in God my Saviour,
for he has looked with favour on the lowliness of his servant.
Surely, from now on all generations will call me blessed;
for the Mighty One has done great things for me,
and holy is his name.
His mercy is for those who fear him
from generation to generation.
He has shown strength with his arm;
he has scattered the proud in the thoughts of their hearts.
He has brought down the powerful from their thrones,
and lifted up the lowly;
he has filled the hungry with good things,
and sent the rich away empty.
He has helped his servant Israel,
in remembrance of his mercy,
according to the promise he made to our ancestors,
to Abraham and to his descendants for ever.'

And Mary remained with her for about three months and then returned to her home.

• I look at my life, at the beauty of God's faithful presence. I remind myself in gratitude that I too share Mary's destiny, and will be raised to live with God and my loved ones for ever, in body and soul. I thank God for the gift of my body, which, in spite of its many limitations, is what makes possible most of what I do, and will be glorified for ever.

Tuesday 16 August
Matthew 19:23–30

Then Jesus said to his disciples, 'Truly I tell you, it will be hard for a rich person to enter the kingdom of heaven. Again I tell you, it is easier for a camel to go through the eye of a needle than for someone who is rich to enter the kingdom of God.' When the disciples heard this, they were greatly astounded and said, 'Then who can be saved?' But Jesus looked at them and said, 'For mortals it is impossible, but for God all things are possible.'

Then Peter said in reply, 'Look, we have left everything and followed you. What then will we have?' Jesus said to them, 'Truly I tell you, at the renewal of all things, when the Son of Man is seated on the throne of his glory, you who have followed me will also sit on twelve thrones, judging the twelve tribes of Israel. And everyone who has left houses or brothers or sisters or father or mother or children or fields, for my name's sake, will receive a hundredfold, and will inherit eternal life. But many who are first will be last, and the last will be first.'

- Sometimes I find myself asking the same questions as Peter in today's reading: 'What about us? We have left everything and followed you. What are we to have, then?' I look back at the times when Jesus' promise of a hundredfold return for anything I gave up came true in my life. I let myself be touched by God's generosity and faithfulness.

Wednesday 17 August
Matthew 20:1–16

'For the kingdom of heaven is like a landowner who went out early in the morning to hire labourers for his vineyard. After agreeing with the labourers for the usual daily wage, he sent them into his vineyard. When he went out about nine o'clock, he saw others standing idle in the market-place; and he said to them, "You also go into the vineyard, and I will pay you whatever is right." So they went. When he went out again about noon and about three o'clock, he did the same. And about five o'clock he went out and found others standing around; and he said to them, "Why are you standing here idle all day?" They said to him, "Because no one has hired us." He said to them, "You also go into the vineyard." When evening came, the owner of the vineyard said to his manager, "Call the labourers and give them their pay, beginning with the last and then going to the first." When those hired about five o'clock came, each of them received the usual daily wage. Now when the first came, they thought they would receive more; but each of them also received the usual daily wage. And when they received it, they grumbled against the landowner, saying, "These last worked only one hour, and you have made them equal to us who have borne the burden of the day and the scorching heat." But he replied to one of them, "Friend, I am doing you no wrong; did you not agree with me for the usual daily wage? Take what belongs to you and go; I choose to give to this last the same as I give to you. Am I not allowed to do what I choose with what belongs to me? Or are you envious because I am generous?" So the last will be first, and the first will be last.'

- God gives his love, all of his love, to every person without exception if they open themselves to this love. It does not matter whether that happens early or late in life as this love can never be earned, only accepted. The fact that the latecomers were only employed at the last hour does not make their needs any less than those who came earlier. How big is my need for God today?

Thursday 18 August
Matthew 22:1–14

Once more Jesus spoke to them in parables, saying: 'The kingdom of heaven may be compared to a king who gave a wedding banquet for his son. He sent his slaves to call those who had been invited to the wedding banquet, but they would not come. Again he sent other slaves, saying, "Tell those who have been invited: Look, I have prepared my dinner, my oxen and my fat calves have been slaughtered, and everything is ready; come to the wedding banquet." But they made light of it and went away, one to his farm, another to his business, while the rest seized his slaves, maltreated them, and killed them. The king was enraged. He sent his troops, destroyed those murderers, and burned their city. Then he said to his slaves, "The wedding is ready, but those invited were not worthy. Go therefore into the main streets, and invite everyone you find to the wedding banquet." Those slaves went out into the streets and gathered all whom they found, both good and bad; so the wedding hall was filled with guests.

'But when the king came in to see the guests, he noticed a man there who was not wearing a wedding robe, and he said to him, "Friend, how did you get in here without a wedding robe?" And he was speechless. Then the king said to the attendants, "Bind him hand and foot, and throw him into the outer darkness, where there will be weeping and gnashing of teeth." For many are called, but few are chosen.'

- This parable tells a very strange story: all those who received the invitation to the king's banquet not only refused to attend but treated the messengers very badly. The king was not to be stopped: he sent his servants to the crossroads and they gathered 'all they could find, good and bad alike'. The hall was full. God's invitation to partake of his great banquet is not restricted to the Jews; his kingdom is now open to all, without any distinction, even to those who seem unworthy. I stand and wonder at God's goodness and mercy towards all. I ask to be like the Father in his mercy and generosity.

Friday 19 August
Matthew 22:34–40

When the Pharisees heard that he had silenced the Sadducees, they gathered together, and one of them, a lawyer, asked him a question to test him. 'Teacher, which commandment in the law is the greatest?' He said to him, '"You shall love the Lord your God with all your heart, and with all your soul, and with all your mind." This is the greatest and first commandment. And a second is like it: "You shall love your neighbour as yourself." On these two commandments hang all the law and the prophets.'

- The Gospel today centres the message of Jesus on love; on two loves united in each of us. Love God, love the neighbour – this is the only commandment of Jesus. Without this, all we say we do for him is really done for ourselves. No detail of religious observance is above this law of love. Jesus said this, and lived it in his life. He never allowed the laws of religion to overtake the need for love. The message of Jesus is all embracing and covers all our relationships, both the close relationships of marriage, family and friendship, as well as the call to love the wider world, particularly where the needs are great.

Saturday 20 August
Matthew 23:1–12

Then Jesus said to the crowds and to his disciples, 'The scribes and the Pharisees sit on Moses' seat; therefore, do whatever they teach you and follow it; but do not do as they do, for they do not practise what they teach. They tie up heavy burdens, hard to bear, and lay them on the shoulders of others; but they themselves are unwilling to lift a finger to move them. They do all their deeds to be seen by others; for they make their phylacteries broad and their fringes long. They love to have the place of honour at banquets and the best seats in the synagogues, and to be greeted with respect in the market-places, and to have people call them rabbi. But you are not to be called rabbi, for you have one teacher, and you are all students. And call no one your father on earth, for you have one Father – the one in heaven. Nor are you to be called instructors, for you have one instructor, the Messiah. The greatest among you will be your servant. All who exalt themselves will be humbled, and all who humble themselves will be exalted.'

- Authority is not for power but for empowering and enabling others. Real authority is a form of service, not a way of control. We are all brothers and sisters. Jesus tells us that the greatest among us is the one who best serves the needs of those around them rather than the one who has the most impressive titles.

- Who can I serve today with love?

The Twenty-first Week in Ordinary Time
21–27 August 2022

Something to think and pray about each day this week:

Few things in life are certain, but one of the certainties of life is this: we will make mistakes. We will make a lot of mistakes. Early in life we often feel guilty and ashamed of our mistakes, perhaps thinking that we are the only ones who make them. As we grow older, however, we see that making mistakes – messing things up and failure – is part of life for everyone. While mistakes are not to be sought out, they are not the end of the story.

Mistakes are to be learned from and grown out of. They are opportunities for us to sheepishly, maybe, and humbly, definitely, turn back to God in search of the forgiveness or strength that will inevitably await us and help us to move on along a better path. One of the best lines in the New Testament dealing with failure comes in the story of the Prodigal Son, or the Forgiving Father, as it is increasingly known. When the wayward son, who has really messed up, comes back to his father seeking forgiveness for his mistakes, we read the following about the father's reaction to the son: 'He fell on his neck and kissed him.'

How wonderful to have a God who falls on our neck and kisses us when we mess up and ask for his forgiveness! And what better way to be his presence in the world than to do the same for others in our lives?

Jim Deeds & Brendan McManus SJ,
Deeper into the Mess

The Presence of God

'Be still, and know that I am God!' Lord, your words lead us to the calmness and greatness of your presence.

Freedom

'In these days, God taught me as a schoolteacher teaches a pupil' (Saint Ignatius). I remind myself that there are things God has to teach me yet, and I ask for the grace to hear them and let them change me.

Consciousness

How am I really feeling? Lighthearted? Heavyhearted? I may be very much at peace, happy to be here.
Equally, I may be frustrated, worried or angry.
I acknowledge how I really am. It is the real me whom the Lord loves.

The Word

God speaks to each of us individually. I listen attentively to hear what he is saying to me. Read the text a few times, then listen.
(Please turn to the Scripture on the following pages. Inspiration points are there, should you need them. When you are ready, return here to continue.)

Conversation

Do I notice myself reacting as I pray with the word of God? Do I feel challenged, comforted, angry? Imagining Jesus sitting or standing by me, I speak out my feelings, as one trusted friend to another.

Conclusion

I thank God for these moments we have spent together and for any insights I have been given concerning the text.

Sunday 21 August
Twenty-first Sunday in Ordinary Time
Luke 13:22–30

Jesus went through one town and village after another, teaching as he made his way to Jerusalem. Someone asked him, 'Lord, will only a few be saved?' He said to them, 'Strive to enter through the narrow door; for many, I tell you, will try to enter and will not be able. When once the owner of the house has got up and shut the door, and you begin to stand outside and to knock at the door, saying, "Lord, open to us", then in reply he will say to you, "I do not know where you come from." Then you will begin to say, "We ate and drank with you, and you taught in our streets." But he will say, "I do not know where you come from; go away from me, all you evildoers!" There will be weeping and gnashing of teeth when you see Abraham and Isaac and Jacob and all the prophets in the kingdom of God, and you yourselves thrown out. Then people will come from east and west, from north and south, and will eat in the kingdom of God. Indeed, some are last who will be first, and some are first who will be last.'

• Unlike Jesus, we seem very often too concerned about numbers, as if that is the most important sign of the presence of the Kingdom and of its power to save the world. Rather than numbers, Jesus asks us to concentrate on entering through the narrow door. This phrase has given rise to all sorts of negative spiritualities, but what Jesus is saying is to take up the cross and follow him every day of our lives. It is the cross that will bring us joy and everlasting life.

Monday 22 August
Matthew 23:13–22

'But woe to you, scribes and Pharisees, hypocrites! For you lock people out of the kingdom of heaven. For you do not go in yourselves, and when others are going in, you stop them. Woe to you, scribes and Pharisees, hypocrites! For you cross sea and land to make a single convert, and you make the new convert twice as much a child of hell as yourselves.

'Woe to you, blind guides, who say, "Whoever swears by the sanctuary is bound by nothing, but whoever swears by the gold of the sanctuary is bound by the oath." You blind fools! For which is greater, the gold or the sanctuary that has made the gold sacred? And you say, "Whoever swears by the altar is bound by nothing, but whoever swears by the gift that is on the altar is bound by the oath." How blind you are! For which is greater, the gift or the altar that makes the gift sacred? So whoever swears by the altar, swears by it and by everything on it; and whoever swears by the sanctuary, swears by it and by the one who dwells in it; and whoever swears by heaven, swears by the throne of God and by the one who is seated upon it.'

• Lord, reveal to me my hidden faults and heal me. Amen.

Tuesday 23 August
Matthew 23:23–26

'Woe to you, scribes and Pharisees, hypocrites! For you tithe mint, dill, and cummin, and have neglected the weightier matters of the law: justice and mercy and faith. It is these you ought to have practised without neglecting the others. You blind guides! You strain out a gnat but swallow a camel!

'Woe to you, scribes and Pharisees, hypocrites! For you clean the outside of the cup and of the plate, but inside they are full of greed and self-indulgence. You blind Pharisee! First clean the inside of the cup, so that the outside also may become clean.'

• Today I pray for the grace of integrity. Jesus accuses the scribes and Pharisees of straining out gnats and swallowing camels! If I am honest I find this tendency in myself too, and I ask that the word of Jesus may challenge and enlighten me, even to the deepest and darkest recesses of my heart.

• Living in times when image is so important, we too are often tempted to give more importance to the outside of the cup than to the inside. In the presence of Jesus, I look at my relationships, in my family and in my work, in my Christian community, and ask for the grace of being ever more transparent, to God, to myself and to others.

Wednesday 24 August
Saint Bartholomew, Apostle

John 1:45–51

Philip found Nathanael and said to him, 'We have found him about whom Moses in the law and also the prophets wrote, Jesus son of Joseph from Nazareth.' Nathanael said to him, 'Can anything good come out of Nazareth?' Philip said to him, 'Come and see.' When Jesus saw Nathanael coming towards him, he said of him, 'Here is truly an Israelite in whom there is no deceit!' Nathanael asked him, 'Where did you come to know me?' Jesus answered, 'I saw you under the fig tree before Philip called you.' Nathanael replied, 'Rabbi, you are the Son of God! You are the King of Israel!' Jesus answered, 'Do you believe because I told you that I saw you under the fig tree? You will see greater things than these.' And he said to him, 'Very truly, I tell you, you will see heaven opened and the angels of God ascending and descending upon the Son of Man.'

- Nathanael, whom some commentators identify with Bartholomew, is promised that as Israel (Jacob) of the Old Testament saw the Glory of God in the vision of the ladder, so he (Nathanael), who is worthy of the name Israel, will see the glory of the Son of Man at the miracle at Cana.

- We could pray today for the grace to see the glory of the Lord in all that is around us.

Thursday 25 August

Matthew 24:42–51

Keep awake therefore, for you do not know on what day your Lord is coming. But understand this: if the owner of the house had known in what part of the night the thief was coming, he would have stayed awake and would not have let his house be broken into. Therefore you also must be ready, for the Son of Man is coming at an unexpected hour.

'Who then is the faithful and wise slave, whom his master has put in charge of his household, to give the other slaves their allowance of food at the proper time? Blessed is that slave whom his master will find at work when he arrives. Truly I tell you, he will put that one in charge of all his possessions. But if that wicked slave says to himself, "My master is delayed", and he begins to beat his fellow-slaves, and eats and drinks with drunkards, the master of that slave will come on a day when he does not expect him and at an hour that he does not know. He will cut him in pieces and put him with the hypocrites, where there will be weeping and gnashing of teeth.'

- We face an ongoing temptation to jog along in the present, as if there were no significant changes to be made in our lifestyles. We can get comfortable about the way things are, or upset and cynical about the poor state of the world, but do we do anything to make it better? Jesus urges us to take the longer view; to believe that God is in charge of human history and wants us to play our part in bringing it to completion. We are to be 'faithful and wise' and live as if the Son of Man were just about to come.

Friday 26 August
Matthew 25:1–13

'Then the kingdom of heaven will be like this. Ten bridesmaids took their lamps and went to meet the bridegroom. Five of them were foolish, and five were wise. When the foolish took their lamps, they took no oil with them; but the wise took flasks of oil with their lamps. As the bridegroom was delayed, all of them became drowsy and slept. But at midnight there was a shout, "Look! Here is the bridegroom! Come out to meet him." Then all those bridesmaids got up and trimmed their lamps. The foolish said to the wise, "Give us some of your oil, for our lamps are going out." But the wise replied, "No! there will not be enough for you and for us; you had better go to the dealers and buy some for yourselves." And while they went to buy it, the bridegroom came, and those who were ready went with him into the wedding banquet; and the door was shut. Later the other bridesmaids came also, saying, "Lord, lord, open to us." But he replied, "Truly I tell you, I do not know you." Keep awake therefore, for you know neither the day nor the hour.'

- This Gospel helps us to focus on the here and now. It helps us to learn to live totally in the present, to seek and find God there. If we can do that, then all the rest will take care of itself. Whether the Groom arrives early or late, it will not matter as he has constantly been part of my everyday life.

- Let us try to renew our commitment to God and to building and growing our relationship with God through regular prayer and reflection.

Saturday 27 August

Matthew 25:14–30

'For it is as if a man, going on a journey, summoned his slaves and entrusted his property to them; to one he gave five talents, to another two,
to another one, to each according to his ability. Then he went away. The
one who had received the five talents went off at once and traded with
them, and made five more talents. In the same way, the one who had the
two talents made two more talents. But the one who had received the one
talent went off and dug a hole in the ground and hid his master's money. After a long time the master of those slaves came and settled accounts
with them. Then the one who had received the five talents came forward,
bringing five more talents, saying, "Master, you handed over to me five
talents; see, I have made five more talents." His master said to him, "Well
done, good and trustworthy slave; you have been trustworthy in a few
things, I will put you in charge of many things; enter into the joy of your
master." And the one with the two talents also came forward, saying,
"Master, you handed over to me two talents; see, I have made two more
talents." His master said to him, "Well done, good and trustworthy slave;
you have been trustworthy in a few things, I will put you in charge of
many things; enter into the joy of your master." Then the one who had received the one talent also came forward, saying, "Master, I knew that you
were a harsh man, reaping where you did not sow, and gathering where
you did not scatter seed; so I was afraid, and I went and hid your talent
in the ground. Here you have what is yours." But his master replied, "You
wicked and lazy slave! You knew, did you, that I reap where I did not sow,
and gather where I did not scatter? Then you ought to have invested my
money with the bankers, and on my return I would have received what
was my own with interest. So take the talent from him, and give it to the
one with the ten talents. For to all those who have, more will be given,
and they will have an abundance; but from those who have nothing, even
what they have will be taken away. As for this worthless slave, throw him
into the outer darkness, where there will be weeping and gnashing of
teeth."'

- As Pope Francis puts it about those who live a 'tomb-psychology' in the Church: 'Let us not allow ourselves to be robbed of the joy of evangelisation! Disillusioned with reality, with the Church and with themselves, they experience a constant temptation to cling to a faint melancholy, lacking in hope, which seizes the heart like "the most precious of the devil's potions". Called to radiate light and communicate life, in the end they are caught up in things that generate only darkness and inner weariness, and slowly consume all zeal for the apostolate. For all this, I repeat: Let us not allow ourselves to be robbed of the joy of evangelisation!'(*EG,* I, 3; II, 83)

28 August–3 September 2022

Something to think and pray about each day this week:

The Jewish-American violinist Itzhak Perlman contracted polio at the age of four. Ever since he has worn metal braces on his legs and walks with crutches, yet he is one of the great virtuosi of our time. A story is told that he once came out on the stage at a concert to play a violin concerto. Laying down his crutches, he placed the violin under his chin and began tuning the instrument when one of the strings broke. The audience saw what happened and thought he would ask for another string or send for another violin. Itzhak signalled to the conductor to begin and he played the entire concerto on three strings. The audience gave him a standing ovation and called on him to speak. What he said, so the story goes, was this: 'Our task is to make music with what remains'. That was a comment on more than a broken violin string. It was also a comment on his paralysis and on all that is broken in life.

John Cullen,
Alert, Aware, Attentive

The Presence of God

I remind myself that, as I sit here now,
God is gazing on me with love and holding me in being.
I pause for a moment and think of this.

Freedom

'There are very few people who realise what God would make of them
if they abandoned themselves into his hands, and let themselves be
formed by his grace' (Saint Ignatius). I ask for the grace to trust myself
totally to God's love.

Consciousness

Where do I sense hope, encouragement and growth in my life? By looking
back over the past few months, I may be able to see which activities and
occasions have produced rich fruit. If I do notice such areas, I will determine to give those areas both time and space in the future.

The Word

Lord Jesus, you became human to communicate with me.
You walked and worked on this earth.
You endured the heat and struggled with the cold.
All your time on this earth was spent in caring for humanity.
You healed the sick, you raised the dead.
Most important of all, you saved me from death.
*(Please turn to the Scripture on the following pages. Inspiration points are there,
should you need them. When you are ready, return here to continue.)*

Conversation

What is stirring in me as I pray? Am I consoled, troubled, left cold? I
imagine Jesus standing or sitting at my side, and I share my feelings
with him.

Conclusion

Glory be to the Father, and to the Son, and to the Holy Spirit,
As it was in the beginning, is now and ever shall be,
World without end. Amen.

Sunday 28 August
Twenty-second Sunday in Ordinary Time
Luke 14:1.7–14

On one occasion when Jesus was going to the house of a leader of the Pharisees to eat a meal on the sabbath, they were watching him closely. . . .

When he noticed how the guests chose the places of honour, he told them a parable. 'When you are invited by someone to a wedding banquet, do not sit down at the place of honour, in case someone more distinguished than you has been invited by your host; and the host who invited both of you may come and say to you, "Give this person your place", and then in disgrace you would start to take the lowest place. But when you are invited, go and sit down at the lowest place, so that when your host comes, he may say to you, "Friend, move up higher"; then you will be honoured in the presence of all who sit at the table with you. For all who exalt themselves will be humbled, and those who humble themselves will be exalted.'

He said also to the one who had invited him, 'When you give a luncheon or a dinner, do not invite your friends or your brothers or your relatives or rich neighbours, in case they may invite you in return, and you would be repaid. But when you give a banquet, invite the poor, the crippled, the lame, and the blind. And you will be blessed, because they cannot repay you, for you will be repaid at the resurrection of the righteous.'

- Saint Ignatius suggests we ask insistently for the grace to be able to make the same choices Jesus made: to ask to be like him in refusing honours, and to choose to be humble and even humiliated as he was. I ask for the freedom to accept humiliations calmly and gracefully when they come.

Monday 29 August
Mark 6:17–29

For Herod himself had sent men who arrested John, bound him, and put him in prison on account of Herodias, his brother Philip's wife, because Herod had married her. For John had been telling Herod, 'It is not lawful for you to have your brother's wife.' And Herodias had a grudge against him, and wanted to kill him. But she could not, for Herod feared John, knowing that he was a righteous and holy man, and he protected him.

When he heard him, he was greatly perplexed; and yet he liked to listen to him. But an opportunity came when Herod on his birthday gave a banquet for his courtiers and officers and for the leaders of Galilee. When his daughter Herodias came in and danced, she pleased Herod and his guests; and the king said to the girl, 'Ask me for whatever you wish, and I will give it.' And he solemnly swore to her, 'Whatever you ask me, I will give you, even half of my kingdom.' She went out and said to her mother, 'What should I ask for?' She replied, 'The head of John the baptiser.' Immediately she rushed back to the king and requested, 'I want you to give me at once the head of John the Baptist on a platter.' The king was deeply grieved; yet out of regard for his oaths and for the guests, he did not want to refuse her. Immediately the king sent a soldier of the guard with orders to bring John's head. He went and beheaded him in the prison, brought his head on a platter, and gave it to the girl. Then the girl gave it to her mother. When his disciples heard about it, they came and took his body, and laid it in a tomb.

- Pray to develop a detestation of sin, symbolised in the story in the Gospel.

Tuesday 30 August
Luke 4:31–37

He went down to Capernaum, a city in Galilee, and was teaching them on the sabbath. They were astounded at his teaching, because he spoke with authority. In the synagogue there was a man who had the spirit of an unclean demon, and he cried out with a loud voice, 'Let us alone! What have you to do with us, Jesus of Nazareth? Have you come to destroy us? I know who you are, the Holy One of God.' But Jesus rebuked him, saying, 'Be silent, and come out of him!' When the demon had thrown him down before them, he came out of him without having done him any harm. They were all amazed and kept saying to one another, 'What kind of utterance is this? For with authority and power he commands the unclean spirits, and out they come!' And a report about him began to reach every place in the region.

- When was the last time somebody made a deep impression on me? What did I do in consequence, how have I grown? I give thanks to

God for those who have spoken or acted with authority, bringing truth or meaning to my life.

- The evil spirit knew its opposite and saw that its time was up; I pray that my presence and values may create a space for good where God's positive Spirit is present and evident.

Wednesday 31 August
Luke 4:38–44

After leaving the synagogue he entered Simon's house. Now Simon's mother-in-law was suffering from a high fever, and they asked him about her. Then he stood over her and rebuked the fever, and it left her. Immediately she got up and began to serve them.

As the sun was setting, all those who had any who were sick with various kinds of diseases brought them to him; and he laid his hands on each of them and cured them. Demons also came out of many, shouting, 'You are the Son of God!' But he rebuked them and would not allow them to speak, because they knew that he was the Messiah.

At daybreak he departed and went into a deserted place. And the crowds were looking for him; and when they reached him, they wanted to prevent him from leaving them. But he said to them, 'I must proclaim the good news of the kingdom of God to the other cities also; for I was sent for this purpose.' So he continued proclaiming the message in the synagogues of Judea.

- The Institution of the Eucharist means that we can in fact always have Jesus as a travelling companion in our journey through life. It's wonderful to realise that the Word of God is at our disposal if only we call on him in faith. 'I believe, help my unbelief' (Mark 9:24).

Thursday 1 September
Luke 5:1–11

Once while Jesus was standing beside the lake of Gennesaret, and the crowd was pressing in on him to hear the word of God, he saw two boats there at the shore of the lake; the fishermen had gone out of them and were washing their nets. He got into one of the boats, the one belonging to Simon, and asked him to put out a little way from the shore. Then he sat down and taught the crowds from the boat. When he had finished speaking, he said to Simon, 'Put out into the deep water and let down your nets for a catch.' Simon answered, 'Master, we have worked all night long but have caught nothing. Yet if you say so, I will let down the nets.' When they had done this, they caught so many fish that their nets were beginning to break. So they signalled to their partners in the other boat to come and help them. And they came and filled both boats, so that they began to sink. But when Simon Peter saw it, he fell down at Jesus' knees, saying, 'Go away from me, Lord, for I am a sinful man!' For he and all who were with him were amazed at the catch of fish that they had taken; and so also were James and John, sons of Zebedee, who were partners with Simon. Then Jesus said to Simon, 'Do not be afraid; from now on you will be catching people.' When they had brought their boats to shore, they left everything and followed him.

- Lord, you tell me, as you told Simon, to 'Put out into the deep water'. You are ready to surprise me with the depths I can find in myself, with the work you can do through me. Save me from complacency, from settling for a routine existence. Open me to recognising your hand in my daily encounters.

Friday 2 September
Luke 5:33–39

Then they said to him, 'John's disciples, like the disciples of the Pharisees, frequently fast and pray, but your disciples eat and drink.' Jesus said to them, 'You cannot make wedding-guests fast while the bridegroom is with them, can you? The days will come when the bridegroom will be taken away from them, and then they will fast in those days.' He also told them a parable: 'No one tears a piece from a new garment and sews it on an old garment; otherwise the new will be torn, and the piece from the new will not match the old. And no one puts new wine into old wineskins; otherwise the new wine will burst the skins and will be spilled, and the skins will be destroyed. But new wine must be put into fresh wineskins. And no one after drinking old wine desires new wine, but says, "The old is good."'

- Sometimes we try to 'patch up' our lives with half efforts when a deeper change is really required. Prayer is wonderful for letting God communicate with you regarding change in your life when it is required.

God can do more in us than we can ask or imagine. Let him direct you – listen to him – he can be trusted.

Saturday 3 September
Luke 6:1–5

One sabbath while Jesus was going through the cornfields, his disciples plucked some heads of grain, rubbed them in their hands, and ate them. But some of the Pharisees said, 'Why are you doing what is not lawful on the sabbath?' Jesus answered, 'Have you not read what David did when he and his companions were hungry? He entered the house of God and took and ate the bread of the Presence, which it is not lawful for any but the priests to eat, and gave some to his companions?' Then he said to them, 'The Son of Man is lord of the sabbath.'

• Jesus invites the Pharisees to recognise that there is more than meets the eye. If I find myself like the Pharisees in judging, I pray that I may be like them too in asking what Jesus thinks.

The Twenty-third Week in Ordinary Time
4–10 September 2022

Something to think and pray about each day this week:

Jealousy kills, envy too, and isn't it great to rejoice in the good fortune of another?

Love is what we bring with us at the end of life. 'We will be judged in the evening of life by love' (Saint John of the Cross). Love for those near and far, for love in the Gospel is more than love for just the family, the friend, the attractive one, the neighbour: it is for all.

There are different calls to Christian love – near and dear daily love, friendship, marriage, relationships. The wider world, like in our job, where we live in a loving way, in justice with all, not using others for personal gain; the wider world, where a universal love makes me want to make a difference in the bigger world. Love carries us into wide seas and waters. It involves us with everyone. It obviously doesn't mean we relate to everyone – nor that we even like everyone. Love is when others' lives become at least as important as our own; and in the deepest loves like marriage, family, and often friendship, others' lives become even more important.

Love changes – we look back and see how the people we loved make the difference. Life is too short to look love in the face and say no. 'We are moulded and remoulded by those who have loved us, and though their love may pass, we are nevertheless their work' (François Mauriac).

Jesus, whose heart is wide enough to love us all, make our hearts like yours.

Donal Neary SJ,
Gospel Reflections for Sundays of Year C: Luke

The Presence of God
I pause for a moment
and reflect on God's life-giving presence
in every part of my body,
in everything around me,
in the whole of my life.

Freedom
Many countries are at this moment suffering the agonies of war. I bow my head in thanksgiving for my freedom. I pray for all prisoners and captives.

Consciousness
Knowing that God loves me unconditionally, I look honestly over the past day, its events, and my feelings. Do I have something to be grateful for? Then I give thanks. Is there something I am sorry for? Then I ask forgiveness.

The Word
Now I turn to the Scripture set out for me this day. I read slowly over the words and see if any sentence or sentiment appeals to me.
(Please turn to the Scripture on the following pages. Inspiration points are there, should you need them. When you are ready, return here to continue.)

Conversation
I know with certainty that there were times when you carried me, Lord. There were times when it was through your strength that I got through the dark times in my life.

Conclusion
Glory be to the Father, and to the Son, and to the Holy Spirit,
As it was in the beginning, is now and ever shall be,
World without end. Amen.

Sunday 4 September
Twenty-third Sunday in Ordinary Time
Luke 14:25–33

Now large crowds were travelling with him; and he turned and said to them, 'Whoever comes to me and does not hate father and mother, wife and children, brothers and sisters, yes, and even life itself, cannot be my disciple. Whoever does not carry the cross and follow me cannot be my disciple. For which of you, intending to build a tower, does not first sit down and estimate the cost, to see whether he has enough to complete it? Otherwise, when he has laid a foundation and is not able to finish, all who see it will begin to ridicule him, saying, "This fellow began to build and was not able to finish." Or what king, going out to wage war against another king, will not sit down first and consider whether he is able with ten thousand to oppose the one who comes against him with twenty thousand? If he cannot, then, while the other is still far away, he sends a delegation and asks for the terms of peace. So therefore, none of you can become my disciple if you do not give up all your possessions.'

- Jesus wants us to know the scale of the task ahead of us; when it seems too much for us, what are we to do? To whom can we turn for help? I ask God to keep me in mind of my own need, that I may have the humility and trust always to seek help.

Monday 5 September
Luke 6:6–11

On another sabbath he entered the synagogue and taught, and there was a man there whose right hand was withered. The scribes and the Pharisees watched him to see whether he would cure on the sabbath, so that they might find an accusation against him. Even though he knew what they were thinking, he said to the man who had the withered hand, 'Come and stand here.' He got up and stood there. Then Jesus said to them, 'I ask you, is it lawful to do good or to do harm on the sabbath, to save life or to destroy it?' After looking around at all of them, he said to him, 'Stretch out your hand.' He did so, and his hand was restored. But they were filled with fury and discussed with one another what they might do to Jesus.

- How are we on our priorities in life – do we sometimes hide behind our duties rather than have compassion? When we ourselves receive an act of kindness, we are so grateful that the giver has the priority of doing a good deed.

- What have we that we have not received?

Tuesday 6 September
Luke 6:12–19

Now during those days he went out to the mountain to pray; and he spent the night in prayer to God. And when day came, he called his disciples and chose twelve of them, whom he also named apostles: Simon, whom he named Peter, and his brother Andrew, and James, and John, and Philip, and Bartholomew, and Matthew, and Thomas, and James son of Alphaeus, and Simon, who was called the Zealot, and Judas son of James, and Judas Iscariot, who became a traitor.

He came down with them and stood on a level place, with a great crowd of his disciples and a great multitude of people from all Judea, Jerusalem, and the coast of Tyre and Sidon. They had come to hear him and to be healed of their diseases; and those who were troubled with unclean spirits were cured. And all in the crowd were trying to touch him, for power came out from him and healed all of them.

- Luke's Gospel highlights the centrality of prayer in the life and mission of Jesus. His decisions and choices emerge from lengthy periods of communion with the one he calls 'Abba'. He chooses twelve very ordinary people, and entrusts to them the task of making his values known to the world.

- Lord, I come to you in this time of prayer to feel your presence. Let me hear again your call to me. Let me sense your power at work in and through me.

Wednesday 7 September
Luke 6:20–26

Then he looked up at his disciples and said:

> 'Blessed are you who are poor,
> for yours is the kingdom of God.

'Blessed are you who are hungry now,
for you will be filled.
'Blessed are you who weep now,
for you will laugh.
'Blessed are you when people hate you, and when they exclude
you, revile you, and defame you on account of the Son of
Man. Rejoice on that day and leap for joy, for surely your
reward is great in heaven; for that is what their ancestors did to
the prophets.
'But woe to you who are rich,
for you have received your consolation.
'Woe to you who are full now,
for you will be hungry.
'Woe to you who are laughing now,
for you will mourn and weep.
'Woe to you when all speak well of you, for that is what their
ancestors did to the false prophets.'

- Each of the Beatitudes describes a human condition from which we would want to move along, yet Jesus proclaims them as states of blessing. I notice what it is in me that causes me to hurry past poverty, hunger or mourning. I ask Jesus to help me to look again that I may see what grace is present despite appearances.

- I pray for all who experience rejection, denunciation or hostility; I pray that I may see in them what Jesus sees and I consider what Jesus wants me to learn from them.

Thursday 8 September
The Nativity of the Blessed Virgin Mary
Matthew 1:1–16.18–23

An account of the genealogy of Jesus the Messiah, the son of David, the son of Abraham.

Abraham was the father of Isaac, and Isaac the father of Jacob, and Jacob the father of Judah and his brothers, and Judah the father of Perez and Zerah by Tamar, and Perez the father of Hezron, and Hezron the father of Aram, and Aram the father of Aminadab, and Aminadab the father of Nahshon, and Nahshon the father of Salmon, and Salmon the father of Boaz by Rahab, and Boaz the father of Obed by Ruth, and Obed the father of Jesse, and Jesse the father of King David.

And David was the father of Solomon by the wife of Uriah, and Solomon the father of Rehoboam, and Rehoboam the father of Abijah, and Abijah the father of Asaph, and Asaph the father of Jehoshaphat, and Jehoshaphat the father of Joram, and Joram the father of Uzziah, and Uzziah the father of Jotham, and Jotham the father of Ahaz, and Ahaz the father of Hezekiah, and Hezekiah the father of Manasseh, and Manasseh the father of Amos, and Amos the father of Josiah, and Josiah the father of Jechoniah and his brothers, at the time of the deportation to Babylon.

And after the deportation to Babylon: Jechoniah was the father of Salathiel, and Salathiel the father of Zerubbabel, and Zerubbabel the father of Abiud, and Abiud the father of Eliakim, and Eliakim the father of Azor, and Azor the father of Zadok, and Zadok the father of Achim, and Achim the father of Eliud, and Eliud the father of Eleazar, and Eleazar the father of Matthan, and Matthan the father of Jacob, and Jacob the father of Joseph the husband of Mary, of whom Jesus was born, who is called the Messiah. . . .

Now the birth of Jesus the Messiah took place in this way. When his mother Mary had been engaged to Joseph, but before they lived together, she was found to be with child from the Holy Spirit. Her husband Joseph, being a righteous man and unwilling to expose her to public disgrace, planned to dismiss her quietly. But just when he had resolved to do this, an angel of the Lord appeared to him in a dream and said, 'Joseph, son of David, do not be afraid to take Mary as your wife, for the child conceived in her is from the Holy Spirit. She will bear a son, and you are to name him Jesus, for he will save his people from their sins.' All this took place to fulfil what had been spoken by the Lord through the prophet:

'Look, the virgin shall conceive and bear a son,
 and they shall name him Emmanuel',
which means, 'God is with us.'

- I suggest that we base our prayer on the words of Saint Ignatius when proposing the contemplation on the Nativity of the Lord, adapting them to suit our purpose thus: I will see the persons, namely Saint

Joachim, Saint Anne, the servant and the Child Mary after her birth. I will be the servant and, as though present, look upon them, contemplate them and serve them in their needs with all possible homage and reverence.

Friday 9 September
Luke 6:39–42

He also told them a parable: 'Can a blind person guide a blind person? Will not both fall into a pit? A disciple is not above the teacher, but everyone who is fully qualified will be like the teacher. Why do you see the speck in your neighbour's eye, but do not notice the log in your own eye? Or how can you say to your neighbour, "Friend, let me take out the speck in your eye", when you yourself do not see the log in your own eye? You hypocrite, first take the log out of your own eye, and then you will see clearly to take the speck out of your neighbour's eye.'

- Jesus doesn't deny that people have failings, but he invites me to look to my own blind spots first. If the just person falls seven times, how often do I fall? Jesus uses humour to make his point. He invites me to imagine how many people I would be hurting if I had a log attached to my eye!

- Lord, make me more aware of my inadequacies, so that I may become gentle in dealing with others.

Saturday 10 September
Luke 6:43–49

'No good tree bears bad fruit, nor again does a bad tree bear good fruit; for each tree is known by its own fruit. Figs are not gathered from thorns, nor are grapes picked from a bramble bush. The good person out of the good treasure of the heart produces good, and the evil person out of evil treasure produces evil; for it is out of the abundance of the heart that the mouth speaks.

'Why do you call me "Lord, Lord", and do not do what I tell you? I will show you what someone is like who comes to me, hears my words, and acts on them. That one is like a man building a house, who dug deeply and laid the foundation on rock; when a flood arose, the river burst against that house but could not shake it, because it had been well built. But the one who hears and does not act is like a man who built a house on the ground without a foundation. When the river burst against it, immediately it fell, and great was the ruin of that house.'

- Lord, mature discipleship is costly! Christians face many storms today. Without firm foundations I am in danger of being swept away. You search me and you know me, so grant me wisdom and strength to listen to your word and to live according to your truth. You are my sure and only foundation in times of distress and upheaval.

The Twenty-fourth Sunday in Ordinary Time
11–17 September 2022

Something to think and pray about each day this week:

When making an acoustic guitar, two of the factors that the craftsperson considers are how long the notes will sustain or last and how well they will be heard (volume or output or impact).

The strength and rigidity of the body governs how long the note lasts (sustains), and volume or impact is governed by the flexibility of the body. Therefore acoustic guitars are not solid but essentially box-like; they have thinly topped shallow bodies that can make imperceptible movements when the string is struck.

There is an essential wisdom in all of this: the constant challenge to find the balance between having sustainability (keeping ourselves strong, safe and well) and output (impacting on the world and those around us) is one that we face daily, both as individuals and as groups of people.

If we focus too much on ourselves and our own sustainability we can become self-obsessed and introspective. We won't let our voices of love, joy and mercy be heard by those who might just need to hear them.

Too much volume and output into the world without taking care of sustainability might mean that we will be prone to burn-out. We might also put people off because our own volume and actions might crowd out the voices or actions of others – we might just miss some of the richness others have to offer.

Jim Deed & Brendan McManus,
Deeper Into the Mess

The Presence of God

I pause for a moment
and reflect on God's life-giving presence
in every part of my body,
in everything around me,
in the whole of my life.

Freedom

Many countries are at this moment suffering the agonies of war. I bow my head in thanksgiving for my freedom. I pray for all prisoners and captives.

Consciousness

Knowing that God loves me unconditionally, I look honestly over the past day, its events and my feelings. Do I have something to be grateful for? Then I give thanks. Is there something I am sorry for? Then I ask forgiveness.

The Word

Now I turn to the Scripture set out for me this day. I read slowly over the words and see if any sentence or sentiment appeals to me.

(Please turn to the Scripture on the following pages. Inspiration points are there, should you need them. When you are ready, return here to continue.)

Conversation

I know with certainty that there were times when you carried me, Lord. There were times when it was through your strength that I got through the dark times in my life.

Conclusion

Glory be to the Father, and to the Son, and to the Holy Spirit,
As it was in the beginning, is now and ever shall be,
World without end. Amen.

Sunday 11 September
Twenty-fourth Sunday in Ordinary Time
Luke 15:1–32

Now all the tax-collectors and sinners were coming near to listen to him. And the Pharisees and the scribes were grumbling and saying, 'This fellow welcomes sinners and eats with them.'

So he told them this parable: 'Which one of you, having a hundred sheep and losing one of them, does not leave the ninety-nine in the wilderness and go after the one that is lost until he finds it? When he has found it, he lays it on his shoulders and rejoices. And when he comes home, he calls together his friends and neighbours, saying to them, "Rejoice with me, for I have found my sheep that was lost." Just so, I tell you, there will be more joy in heaven over one sinner who repents than over ninety-nine righteous people who need no repentance.

'Or what woman having ten silver coins, if she loses one of them, does not light a lamp, sweep the house, and search carefully until she finds it? When she has found it, she calls together her friends and neighbours, saying, "Rejoice with me, for I have found the coin that I had lost." Just so, I tell you, there is joy in the presence of the angels of God over one sinner who repents.'

Then Jesus said, 'There was a man who had two sons. The younger of them said to his father, "Father, give me the share of the property that will belong to me." So he divided his property between them. A few days later the younger son gathered all he had and travelled to a distant country, and there he squandered his property in dissolute living. When he had spent everything, a severe famine took place throughout that country, and he began to be in need. So he went and hired himself out to one of the citizens of that country, who sent him to his fields to feed the pigs. He would gladly have filled himself with the pods that the pigs were eating; and no one gave him anything. But when he came to himself he said, "How many of my father's hired hands have bread enough and to spare, but here I am dying of hunger! I will get up and go to my father, and I will say to him, 'Father, I have sinned against heaven and before you; I am no longer worthy to be called your son; treat me like one of your hired hands.'" So he set off and went to his father. But while he was still far off, his father saw him and was filled with compassion; he ran and put his arms around him and kissed him. Then the son said to him, "Father,

I have sinned against heaven and before you; I am no longer worthy to be called your son." But the father said to his slaves, "Quickly, bring out a robe – the best one – and put it on him; put a ring on his finger and sandals on his feet. And get the fatted calf and kill it, and let us eat and celebrate; for this son of mine was dead and is alive again; he was lost and is found!" And they began to celebrate.

'Now his elder son was in the field; and when he came and approached the house, he heard music and dancing. He called one of the slaves and asked what was going on. He replied, "Your brother has come, and your father has killed the fatted calf, because he has got him back safe and sound." Then he became angry and refused to go in. His father came out and began to plead with him. But he answered his father, "Listen! For all these years I have been working like a slave for you, and I have never disobeyed your command; yet you have never given me even a young goat so that I might celebrate with my friends. But when this son of yours came back, who has devoured your property with prostitutes, you killed the fatted calf for him!" Then the father said to him, "Son, you are always with me, and all that is mine is yours. But we had to celebrate and rejoice, because this brother of yours was dead and has come to life; he was lost and has been found."'

• The son who initially seems selfish was actually the one who saw beyond himself; the self-centred one turns out to be the one who seemed dutiful but who had a false image of himself, his father and his brother. I ask God to let me glimpse and celebrate the good in the hearts of those around me.

Monday 12 September
Luke 7:1–10

After Jesus had finished all his sayings in the hearing of the people, he entered Capernaum. A centurion there had a slave whom he valued highly, and who was ill and close to death. When he heard about Jesus, he sent some Jewish elders to him, asking him to come and heal his slave. When they came to Jesus, they appealed to him earnestly, saying, 'He is worthy of having you do this for him, for he loves our people, and it is he who built our synagogue for us.' And Jesus went with them, but when he was not far from the house, the centurion sent friends to say to him, 'Lord, do not trouble yourself, for I am not worthy to have you come under my roof; therefore I did not presume to come to you. But only speak the word, and let my servant be healed. For I also am a man set under authority, with soldiers under me; and I say to one, "Go", and he goes, and to another, "Come", and he comes, and to my slave, "Do this", and the slave does it.' When Jesus heard this he was amazed at him, and turning to the crowd that followed him, he said, 'I tell you, not even in Israel have I found such faith.' When those who had been sent returned to the house, they found the slave in good health.

- There is something saintly about this centurion. He is a model of compassion, taking great pains on behalf of a slave. The more common attitude would have been to discard a slave once he could no longer work. He is a model of humility. Though an officer of the imperial army, he begs a favour of this travelling rabbi. And he is a model of faith, recognising the authority of Jesus, who marvels at him.

Tuesday 13 September
Luke 7:11–17

Soon afterwards he went to a town called Nain, and his disciples and a large crowd went with him. As he approached the gate of the town, a man who had died was being carried out. He was his mother's only son, and she was a widow; and with her was a large crowd from the town. When the Lord saw her, he had compassion for her and said to her, 'Do not weep.' Then he came forward and touched the bier, and the bearers stood still. And he said, 'Young man, I say to you, rise!' The dead man sat up and began to speak, and Jesus gave him to his mother. Fear seized all of them; and they glorified God, saying, 'A great prophet has risen among us!' and 'God has looked favourably on his people!' This word about him spread throughout Judea and all the surrounding country.

- Are there any moments or events in your life, not necessarily as dramatic as this story, where you have thanked God for a saving grace?

Wednesday 14 September
The Exaltation of the Holy Cross
John 3:13–17

No one has ascended into heaven except the one who descended from heaven, the Son of Man. And just as Moses lifted up the serpent in the wilderness, so must the Son of Man be lifted up, that whoever believes in him may have eternal life.

'For God so loved the world that he gave his only Son, so that everyone who believes in him may not perish but may have eternal life.

'Indeed, God did not send the Son into the world to condemn the world, but in order that the world might be saved through him.'

- In our exaltation of the cross lies the basic paradox of our faith in Jesus Christ. We believe that the suffering of Jesus brought us salvation, and that we are called to express this faith by joining our own suffering with his. I believe that doing this saves my suffering from meaninglessness and furthers the salvation of the world from suffering.

- I gaze in wonder at the depth of God's wisdom and mercy, I adore the crucified Jesus and ask for a deep sense of gratitude in front of this mystery.

Thursday 15 September
Luke 2:33–35

And the child's father and mother were amazed at what was being said about him. Then Simeon blessed them and said to his mother Mary, 'This child is destined for the falling and the rising of many in Israel, and to be a sign that will be opposed so that the inner thoughts of many will be revealed – and a sword will pierce your own soul too.'

- Mary and Joseph were amazed at Simeon's words. They did not just nod their heads and say 'That fits what we expected'. Like all mothers, Mary knew that her precious baby was unique. But she was only gradually discovering what that might mean, in his life and in hers. Savour the scene.

Friday 16 September
Luke 8:1–3

Soon afterwards he went on through cities and villages, proclaiming and bringing the good news of the kingdom of God. The twelve were with him, as well as some women who had been cured of evil spirits and infirmities: Mary, called Magdalene, from whom seven demons had gone out, and Joanna, the wife of Herod's steward Chuza, and Susanna, and many others, who provided for them out of their resources.

- This passage illustrates the call of the women who followed Jesus. It shows how people of means supported the Lord's mission; Jesus and the Christian community depended on the generosity of people to sustain its mission. In what ways do I support the mission of the Church?

Saturday 17 September
Luke 8:4–15

When a great crowd gathered and people from town after town came to him, he said in a parable: 'A sower went out to sow his seed; and as he sowed, some fell on the path and was trampled on, and the birds of the air ate it up. Some fell on the rock; and as it grew up, it withered for lack of moisture. Some fell among thorns, and the thorns grew with it and choked it. Some fell into good soil, and when it grew, it produced a hundredfold.' As he said this, he called out, 'Let anyone with ears to hear listen!'

Then his disciples asked him what this parable meant. He said, 'To you it has been given to know the secrets of the kingdom of God; but to others I speak in parables, so that

'looking they may not perceive,
   and listening they may not understand.'

'Now the parable is this: The seed is the word of God. The ones on the path are those who have heard; then the devil comes and takes away the word from their hearts, so that they may not believe and be saved. The ones on the rock are those who, when they hear the word, receive it with joy. But these have no root; they believe only for a while and in a time of testing fall away. As for what fell among the thorns, these are the ones who hear; but as they go on their way, they are choked by the cares and riches and pleasures of life, and their fruit does not mature. But as for that in the good soil, these are the ones who, when they hear the word, hold it fast in an honest and good heart, and bear fruit with patient endurance.'

- Matthew states that Jesus always spoke to the crowds in parables to expound to them things hidden since the foundation of the world. Let us pause now to thank the Lord for his revelation through the parables.

The Twenty-fifth Week in Ordinary Time
18–24 September 2022

Something to think and pray about each day this week:

Dear God, because you are purest mystery you can't be grasped, and so I must simply let you be and let you speak. Is this how I can come to know you as you are?

What were you trying to get across to Moses when you said 'I am who I am'? Were you saying, 'I am simply myself; I need no explaining'? Is this what it means to be the creator – to be comfortably secure in your own existence? My existence, on the other hand, is not in my hands: it depends totally on you. I'm like a song: if you stop singing me, empty silence would follow. A great physicist surprised his students by saying that the world is made not of matter but of music: the world's continuing existence depends on you!

Small children educate me best about you. For them, everything is a source of wonder – each person, each thing, each moment is unique and special. 'Children's faces, looking up; holding wonder like a cup.' Let me be like them, and so live even now in the kingdom of heaven.

Brian Grogan SJ,
I Am Infinitely Loved

The Presence of God

Dear Jesus, today I call on you, but not to ask for anything. I'd like only to dwell in your presence. May my heart respond to your love.

Freedom

God my creator, you gave me life and the gift of freedom. Through your love I exist in this world. May I never take the gift of life for granted. May I always respect others' right to life.

Consciousness

I ask how I am today. Am I particularly tired, stressed or anxious? If any of these characteristics apply, can I try to let go of the concerns that disturb me?

The Word

The word of God comes down to us through the Scriptures. May the Holy Spirit enlighten my mind and my heart to respond to the Gospel teachings.

(Please turn to the Scripture on the following pages. Inspiration points are there, should you need them. When you are ready, return here to continue.)

Conversation

I begin to talk with Jesus about the Scripture I have just read. What part of it strikes a chord in me? Perhaps the words of a friend – or some story I have heard recently – will rise to the surface in my consciousness. If so, does the story throw light on what the Scripture passage may be saying to me?

Conclusion

Glory be to the Father, and to the Son, and to the Holy Spirit,
As it was in the beginning, is now and ever shall be,
World without end. Amen.

Sunday 18 September
Twenty-fifth Sunday in Ordinary Time

Luke 16:1–13

Then Jesus said to the disciples, 'There was a rich man who had a manager, and charges were brought to him that this man was squandering his property. So he summoned him and said to him, "What is this that I hear about you? Give me an account of your management, because you cannot be my manager any longer." Then the manager said to himself, "What will I do, now that my master is taking the position away from me? I am not strong enough to dig, and I am ashamed to beg. I have decided what to do so that, when I am dismissed as manager, people may welcome me into their homes." So, summoning his master's debtors one by one, he asked the first, "How much do you owe my master?" He answered, "A hundred jugs of olive oil." He said to him, "Take your bill, sit down quickly, and make it fifty." Then he asked another, "And how much do you owe?" He replied, "A hundred containers of wheat." He said to him, "Take your bill and make it eighty." And his master commended the dishonest manager because he had acted shrewdly; for the children of this age are more shrewd in dealing with their own generation than are the children of light. And I tell you, make friends for yourselves by means of dishonest wealth so that when it is gone, they may welcome you into the eternal homes.

'Whoever is faithful in a very little is faithful also in much; and whoever is dishonest in a very little is dishonest also in much. If then you have not been faithful with the dishonest wealth, who will entrust to you the true riches? And if you have not been faithful with what belongs to another, who will give you what is your own? No slave can serve two masters; for a slave will either hate the one and love the other, or be devoted to the one and despise the other. You cannot serve God and wealth.'

- The point of this passage is in the commendation of the dishonest steward, not for the moral quality of his behaviour, but for his worldly prudence in using the things of this life to ensure his future in this life. Believers should behave with prudence to ensure their eternal future. You might reflect on how diligently people work for the goods that pass while neglecting the goods that are eternal. Then reflect on yourself.

Monday 19 September
Luke 8:16–18

'No one after lighting a lamp hides it under a jar, or puts it under a bed, but puts it on a lampstand, so that those who enter may see the light. For nothing is hidden that will not be disclosed, nor is anything secret that will not become known and come to light. Then pay attention to how you listen; for to those who have, more will be given; and from those who do not have, even what they seem to have will be taken away.'

- Commentators have struggled to interpret this short passage. What do you make of it? In what way do you make it part of your prayer? Are you conscious of your call to be a light for others, an inviting light to lead them to Christ? What is your reaction to being given that task? Ask the Lord to help you to see and accept that role.

Tuesday 20 September
Luke 8:19–21

Then his mother and his brothers came to him, but they could not reach him because of the crowd. And he was told, 'Your mother and your brothers are standing outside, wanting to see you.' But he said to them, 'My mother and my brothers are those who hear the word of God and do it.'

- Hearing the word and doing it: for Jesus these two verbs go together. Once he said that those who do so are building their life on rock rather than on sand so that they can be strong in the midst of difficulties.

- Here he goes even further, identifying those who hear the word of God and do it with his own innermost circle, with his own mother and brothers. I thank Jesus for this great compliment, and ask for the grace to be able to put into practice the word of God in my life, not as an obligation but as a privilege.

Wednesday 21 September
Saint Matthew, Apostle and Evangelist
Matthew 9:9–13

As Jesus was walking along, he saw a man called Matthew sitting at the tax booth; and he said to him, 'Follow me.' And he got up and followed him.

And as he sat at dinner in the house, many tax-collectors and sinners came and were sitting with him and his disciples. When the Pharisees saw this, they said to his disciples, 'Why does your teacher eat with tax-collectors and sinners?' But when he heard this, he said, 'Those who are well have no need of a physician, but those who are sick. Go and learn what this means, "I desire mercy, not sacrifice." For I have come to call not the righteous but sinners.'

- There was reason for the unpopularity of tax-collectors. They were disliked for collaborating with the Roman imperial authorities; and also for extorting more tax than was due, in order to inflate their profits. Tax-collectors were despised, along with ass-drivers, tanners and bath attendants. They tended to be social outcasts.

- Lord, maybe I have my own secret list of social outcasts, people I do not like to be mixed up with. You chose your friends differently. You saw need and goodness where others saw only disreputable villainy. I have to do some serious work on my choosiness.

Thursday 22 September
Luke 9:7–9

Now Herod the ruler heard about all that had taken place, and he was perplexed, because it was said by some that John had been raised from the dead, by some that Elijah had appeared, and by others that one of the ancient prophets had arisen. Herod said, 'John I beheaded; but who is this about whom I hear such things?' And he tried to see him.

- Herod's curiosity is aroused by the stories circulating around Jesus. God is knocking at his door. This is his moment of grace. The moment passes and does not return until Jesus is brought before him for trial. Again God knocks on his door and grants his wish. He indeed sees Jesus, and Saint Luke says that he was very glad of this. But he rejects the grace offered him because his wish is too small. He wants Jesus to perform some amusing sign, no more. But Jesus says and does nothing, so Herod has his troops mock him and then sends him back to Pilate. His door is closed.

- Lord, may I recognise you in the moments of grace that come my way. May I be open to you, no matter under what disguise you come to me.

Friday 23 September
Luke 9:18–22

Once when Jesus was praying alone, with only the disciples near him, he asked them, 'Who do the crowds say that I am?' They answered, 'John the Baptist; but others, Elijah; and still others, that one of the ancient prophets has arisen.' He said to them, 'But who do you say that I am?' Peter answered, 'The Messiah of God.'

He sternly ordered and commanded them not to tell anyone, saying, 'The Son of Man must undergo great suffering, and be rejected by the elders, chief priests, and scribes, and be killed, and on the third day be raised.'

- Our life of faith is based on the fact that we ourselves have made this confession of faith in Jesus. The Lord appreciates very much our act of faith in him, especially when we thank him for the depth of the love he has shown through his passion, death and resurrection. This is the space out of which we make our prayer to God – from a place of thanksgiving in our hearts.

Saturday 24 September
Luke 9:43–45

While everyone was amazed at all that he was doing, he said to his disciples, 'Let these words sink into your ears: The Son of Man is going to be betrayed into human hands.' But they did not understand this saying; its meaning was concealed from them, so that they could not perceive it. And they were afraid to ask him about this saying.

- How was the meaning hidden from them? Does it make sense to you? How would you explain the incident to a well-meaning inquirer? Reflect on the fact that everything is under God's providence and so has a purpose. What could be the purpose of hiding the meaning from the disciples? Speak to the Lord about this. When you come across something whose meaning is obscure to you, how do you cope?

The Twenty-sixth Week in Ordinary Time
25 September–1 October 2022

Something to think and pray about each day this week:

Every Christian enjoys a call, paraphrasing St Thérèse of Lisieux, to be holiness at the heart of the Church. This is a 'powerful summons to all of us' (*GE*, 23) that both respects and regards the experience of each person who seeks the inspiration of the Holy Spirit in the interior movements that make up the story of their life. No moment or matter is excluded from this sense of mission. Like the facets of a diamond in the sunlight, the action of the Spirit is to illuminate each aspect of a person's pathway through life, integrating all into a unique pattern of perfection. By fusing mission with mystery in the meaning of a person's vocation to holiness, Pope Francis is reminding all members of the Church that they must see themselves foremost as missionaries. In a final and felicitious note of encouragement Francis says that failures in the course of a particular mission are not fatal, for 'the Lord will bring it to fulfilment despite your mistakes and missteps' (*GE*, 24) as long as a person continues to relate lovingly and remains open to the grace of God which heals, holding out hope for the rest of the journey.

Kevin O'Gorman SMA,
Journeying in Joy and Gladness

The Presence of God

God is with me, but even more astounding, God is within me.
Let me dwell for a moment on God's life-giving presence
in my body, in my mind, in my heart,
as I sit here, right now.

Freedom

Lord, may I never take the gift of freedom for granted. You gave me the great blessing of freedom of spirit. Fill my spirit with your peace and joy.

Consciousness

I remind myself that I am in the presence of God, who is my strength in times of weakness and my comforter in times of sorrow.

The Word

I take my time to read the word of God slowly, a few times, allowing myself to dwell on anything that strikes me.

(Please turn to the Scripture on the following pages. Inspiration points are there, should you need them. When you are ready, return here to continue.)

Conversation

Jesus, you always welcomed little children when you walked on this earth. Teach me to have a childlike trust in you. Teach me to live in the knowledge that you will never abandon me.

Conclusion

Glory be to the Father, and to the Son, and to the Holy Spirit,
As it was in the beginning, is now and ever shall be,
World without end. Amen.

Sunday 25 September
Twenty-sixth Sunday in Ordinary Time
Luke 16:19–31

'There was a rich man who was dressed in purple and fine linen and who feasted sumptuously every day. And at his gate lay a poor man named Lazarus, covered with sores, who longed to satisfy his hunger with what fell from the rich man's table; even the dogs would come and lick his sores. The poor man died and was carried away by the angels to be with Abraham. The rich man also died and was buried. In Hades, where he was being tormented, he looked up and saw Abraham far away with Lazarus by his side. He called out, "Father Abraham, have mercy on me, and send Lazarus to dip the tip of his finger in water and cool my tongue; for I am in agony in these flames." But Abraham said, "Child, remember that during your lifetime you received your good things, and Lazarus in like manner evil things; but now he is comforted here, and you are in agony. Besides all this, between you and us a great chasm has been fixed, so that those who might want to pass from here to you cannot do so, and no one can cross from there to us." He said, "Then, father, I beg you to send him to my father's house – for I have five brothers – that he may warn them, so that they will not also come into this place of torment." Abraham replied, "They have Moses and the prophets; they should listen to them." He said, "No, father Abraham; but if someone goes to them from the dead, they will repent." He said to him, "If they do not listen to Moses and the prophets, neither will they be convinced even if someone rises from the dead."'

- As in so many other parables, Jesus reverses the usual order in telling the story of Lazarus, the poor man – the rich man remaining anonymous. As I bring my life before God, I allow my usual priorities to be changed as God values and cherishes what I may have come to take for granted.

Monday 26 September
Luke 9:46–50

An argument arose among them as to which one of them was the greatest. But Jesus, aware of their inner thoughts, took a little child and put it by his side, and said to them, 'Whoever welcomes this child in my name welcomes me, and whoever welcomes me welcomes the one who sent me; for the least among all of you is the greatest.'

John answered, 'Master, we saw someone casting out demons in your name, and we tried to stop him, because he does not follow with us.' But Jesus said to him, 'Do not stop him; for whoever is not against you is for you.'

- This was a strange argument to have just after the Lord had told his followers that he was going to be betrayed. It shows that his disciples had not grasped his teaching – a fact that would be made perfectly clear at the time of his passion.

- Have there been times when you found yourself entertaining thoughts that were completely contrary to the message of Jesus? How did you cope? Ask the Lord to help you see where this happens and give you the power to reject such thoughts.

Tuesday 27 September
Luke 9:51–56

When the days drew near for him to be taken up, he set his face to go to Jerusalem. And he sent messengers ahead of him. On their way they entered a village of the Samaritans to make ready for him; but they did not receive him, because his face was set towards Jerusalem. When his disciples James and John saw it, they said, 'Lord, do you want us to command fire to come down from heaven and consume them?' But he turned and rebuked them. Then they went on to another village.

- Jesus, you will not be distracted by any setbacks placed before you. Ignite in me the flame of your steadfast spirit so that I may follow you to the end.

- Lord, when I am rejected, I can be consumed with feelings of anger or revenge. Do not let me give in to these feelings. Instead let me turn away and move on as you do.

Wednesday 28 September
Luke 9:57–62

As they were going along the road, someone said to him, 'I will follow you wherever you go.' And Jesus said to him, 'Foxes have holes, and birds of the air have nests; but the Son of Man has nowhere to lay his head.' To another he said, 'Follow me.' But he said, 'Lord, first let me go and bury my father.' But Jesus said to him, 'Let the dead bury their own dead; but as for you, go and proclaim the kingdom of God.' Another said, 'I will follow you, Lord; but let me first say farewell to those at my home.' Jesus said to him, 'No one who puts a hand to the plough and looks back is fit for the kingdom of God.'

- Enthusiasm and good desires are important, but not enough. Decision and implementation must follow. Am I someone who starts well, but drops off if the going gets rough? Is my following of Jesus conditional on things going smoothly? Jesus says that this will not do.

- I rightly say, 'Lord, I will follow you wherever you go'. This is a beautiful and loving promise. But left to myself I do not have the inner strength to keep it. I must ask Jesus for his strength day by day, and I start now.

Thursday 29 September
Saints Michael, Gabriel and Raphael, Archangels
John 1:47–51

When Jesus saw Nathanael coming towards him, he said of him, 'Here is truly an Israelite in whom there is no deceit!' Nathanael asked him, 'Where did you come to know me?' Jesus answered, 'I saw you under the fig tree before Philip called you.' Nathanael replied, 'Rabbi, you are the Son of God! You are the King of Israel!' Jesus answered, 'Do you believe because I told you that I saw you under the fig tree? You will see greater things than these.' And he said to him, 'Very truly, I tell you, you will see heaven opened and the angels of God ascending and descending upon the Son of Man.'

- Let us reflect on the roles of the three archangels. Michael, our protector against the snares of the devil, prompts us to ask if we are aware of the work of the devil in our lives. Recalling the temptation of Christ, we can be assured that if Satan went after Jesus, he will go after us. Gabriel, the messenger to Zechariah and Mary, suggests that we ask ourselves how we react to the call of God in the changing movements of our lives. Raphael recalls our guardian angels, our personal protectors. Do our guardian angels feel unemployed because we give them so little attention?

Friday 30 September
Luke 10:13–16

'Woe to you, Chorazin! Woe to you, Bethsaida! For if the deeds of power done in you had been done in Tyre and Sidon, they would have repented long ago, sitting in sackcloth and ashes. But at the judgement it will be more tolerable for Tyre and Sidon than for you. And you, Capernaum, will you be exalted to heaven? No, you will be brought down to Hades.

'Whoever listens to you listens to me, and whoever rejects you rejects me, and whoever rejects me rejects the one who sent me.'

- It is striking that Jesus' ministry took place outside of the big cities of the region, in the villages and small towns of Galilee. He had decided that the cities – except for Jerusalem – were not the places where he was to preach. He moved instead among communities of subsistence farmers and day labourers, praying for one day's sustenance at a time. Yet it is among them that God works his 'deeds of power'.

- And what about me? Do I look for this power in places of prestige? Or can I walk with Jesus among the vulnerable?

Saturday 1 October
Luke 10:17–24

The seventy returned with joy, saying, 'Lord, in your name even the demons submit to us!' He said to them, 'I watched Satan fall from heaven like a flash of lightning. See, I have given you authority to tread on snakes and scorpions, and over all the power of the enemy; and nothing will hurt you. Nevertheless, do not rejoice at this, that the spirits submit to you, but rejoice that your names are written in heaven.'

At that same hour Jesus rejoiced in the Holy Spirit and said, 'I thank you, Father, Lord of heaven and earth, because you have hidden these things from the wise and the intelligent and have revealed them to infants; yes, Father, for such was your gracious will. All things have been handed over to me by my Father; and no one knows who the Son is except the Father, or who the Father is except the Son and anyone to whom the Son chooses to reveal him.'

Then turning to the disciples, Jesus said to them privately, 'Blessed are the eyes that see what you see! For I tell you that many prophets and kings desired to see what you see, but did not see it, and to hear what you hear, but did not hear it.'

- We remember that Jesus sent out the seventy to prepare the way for him. He is to follow in their footsteps, he will build on their preparatory work. You can feel that Jesus is excited at this prospect of the next stage of the mission.

- Does it help me to think of my own mission as a Christian in these terms? That through my words and deeds of witness I am preparing the way for Jesus, so that those who have yet to encounter him effectively will do so?

The Twenty-seventh Week in Ordinary Time
2–8 October 2022

Something to think and pray about each day this week:

We are watching out for sightings of God all around us, and we try to find the divine life at the heart of reality. Ignatius left no detailed rule about how much prayer his followers should undertake. Instead he asked that we should *keep God always before our eyes*. This is contemplation in action. It is a tall order, yet we know what it is like to be doing something, whether pleasant or distasteful, with someone else in our mind. I came across migrants working in the diamond mines of South Africa. They endured long hours in the depths of the earth in order to send money home to their families.

Contemplation has been described as 'a long loving look at the real'. This is how God looks at our world. Then God 'gets going' and intervenes on our behalf. In this sense, God is THE 'contemplative in action'. So, of course, is Jesus. He prays, he works, he suffers, but always in the presence of his Father. He has a discerning heart, which is why he can say, 'I always do what is pleasing to him' (John 8:29). As his companions we try to imitate him. It is no accident that the first Jesuits wanted to be known as 'companions of Jesus'.

Brian Grogan SJ,
Finding God in All Things

The Presence of God

Dear Lord, as I come to you today, fill my heart, my whole being, with the wonder of your presence. Help me remain receptive to you as I put aside the cares of this world. Fill my mind with your peace.

Freedom

Lord, grant me the grace to be free from the excesses of this life. Let me not get caught up with the desire for wealth. Keep my heart and mind free to love and serve you.

Consciousness

I exist in a web of relationships: links to nature, people, God.
I trace out these links, giving thanks for the life that flows through them.
Some links are twisted or broken; I may feel regret, anger, disappointment.
I pray for the gift of acceptance and forgiveness.

The Word

God speaks to each of us individually. I listen attentively to hear what he is saying to me. Read the text a few times, then listen.
(Please turn to the Scripture on the following pages. Inspiration points are there, should you need them. When you are ready, return here to continue.)

Conversation

Jesus, you speak to me through the words of the Gospels. May I respond to your call today. Teach me to recognise your hand at work in my daily living.

Conclusion

I thank God for these moments we have spent together and for any insights I have been given concerning the text.

Sunday 2 October
Twenty-seventh Sunday in Ordinary Time
Luke 17:5–10

The apostles said to the Lord, 'Increase our faith!' The Lord replied, 'If you had faith the size of a mustard seed, you could say to this mulberry tree, "Be uprooted and planted in the sea", and it would obey you.

'Who among you would say to your slave who has just come in from ploughing or tending sheep in the field, "Come here at once and take your place at the table"? Would you not rather say to him, "Prepare supper for me, put on your apron and serve me while I eat and drink; later you may eat and drink"? Do you thank the slave for doing what was commanded? So you also, when you have done all that you were ordered to do, say, "We are worthless slaves; we have done only what we ought to have done!"'

- I join the apostles and pray insistently, 'Increase my faith'. I listen with the same openness and wonder to Jesus' encouraging reply as I look at the quality of my faith: it's enough for my faith to be as small as a mustard seed!

- While it seems obvious that the servant eats only after the master has been served, at the Last Supper Jesus did just the opposite: he insisted on washing the feet of his disciples. Then he called them his friends. I ask for the grace to have the freedom to see myself as the worthless servant trying not to be superior to his master.

Monday 3 October
Luke 10:25–37

Just then a lawyer stood up to test Jesus. 'Teacher,' he said, 'what must I do to inherit eternal life?' He said to him, 'What is written in the law? What do you read there?' He answered, 'You shall love the Lord your God with all your heart, and with all your soul, and with all your strength, and with all your mind; and your neighbour as yourself.' And he said to him, 'You have given the right answer; do this, and you will live.'

But wanting to justify himself, he asked Jesus, 'And who is my neighbour?' Jesus replied, 'A man was going down from Jerusalem to Jericho, and fell into the hands of robbers, who stripped him, beat him, and went away, leaving him half dead. Now by chance a priest was going down that road; and when he saw him, he passed by on the other side. So likewise a Levite, when he came to the place and saw him, passed by on the other side. But a Samaritan while travelling came near him; and when he saw him, he was moved with pity. He went to him and bandaged his wounds, having poured oil and wine on them. Then he put him on his own animal, brought him to an inn, and took care of him. The next day he took out two denarii, gave them to the innkeeper, and said, "Take care of him; and when I come back, I will repay you whatever more you spend." Which of these three, do you think, was a neighbour to the man who fell into the hands of the robbers?' He said, 'The one who showed him mercy.' Jesus said to him, 'Go and do likewise.'

- Lord, as I make my way through this and every day, give me eyes to see my marginalised and suffering brothers and sisters. Give me a heart that will love you as you are present in the faces of others. Give me hands that help as well as lips that pray.

Tuesday 4 October
Luke 10:38–42

Now as they went on their way, he entered a certain village, where a woman named Martha welcomed him into her home. She had a sister named Mary, who sat at the Lord's feet and listened to what he was saying. But Martha was distracted by her many tasks; so she came to him and asked, 'Lord, do you not care that my sister has left me to do all the work by myself? Tell her then to help me.' But the Lord answered her, 'Martha, Martha, you are worried and distracted by many things; there is need of only one thing. Mary has chosen the better part, which will not be taken away from her.'

- Jesus may seem to be preferring contemplation to action, praising Mary and criticising Martha. Yet he cannot be telling us to be content with sitting down to listen to his word, for he always insists that true listening to his word means putting it into practice. His objection to Martha is that she is too worried and distracted by many things to be able to really listen to him. Do I merit the same reproach? I ask for a pure heart, really focused on what will not be taken away.

Wednesday 5 October

Luke 11:1–4

He was praying in a certain place, and after he had finished, one of his disciples said to him, 'Lord, teach us to pray, as John taught his disciples.' He said to them,

> 'When you pray, say:
> Father, hallowed be your name.
> Your kingdom come.
> Give us each day our daily bread.
> And forgive us our sins,
> for we ourselves forgive everyone indebted to us.
> And do not bring us to the time of trial.'

- It is clear that prayer was essential for Jesus – for his identity and his mission. Prayer expressed Jesus' relationship with his Father. He taught his followers how to pray, and he made time for it himself, no matter what needs and demands pressed on him. Do I do likewise?

Thursday 6 October

Luke 11:5–13

And he said to them, 'Suppose one of you has a friend, and you go to him at midnight and say to him, "Friend, lend me three loaves of bread; for a friend of mine has arrived, and I have nothing to set before him." And he answers from within, "Do not bother me; the door has already been locked, and my children are with me in bed; I cannot get up and give you anything." I tell you, even though he will not get up and give him anything because he is his friend, at least because of his persistence he will get up and give him whatever he needs.

'So I say to you, ask, and it will be given to you; search, and you will find; knock, and the door will be opened for you. For everyone who asks receives, and everyone who searches finds, and for everyone who knocks, the door will be opened. Is there anyone among you who, if your child asks for a fish, will give a snake instead of a fish? Or if the child asks for an egg, will give a scorpion? If you then, who are evil, know how to give good gifts to your children, how much more will the heavenly Father give the Holy Spirit to those who ask him!'

- I look back to times when I asked and was given, sought and found, knocked and it was opened to me. I also bring to mind when I was not given, when I did not find, and when the door stayed shut. In all simplicity I ask the Lord for faith and trust, for freedom at looking at my relationship with him.

Friday 7 October
Luke 11:15–26

But some of them said, 'He casts out demons by Beelzebul, the ruler of the demons.' Others, to test him, kept demanding from him a sign from heaven. But he knew what they were thinking and said to them, 'Every kingdom divided against itself becomes a desert, and house falls on house. If Satan also is divided against himself, how will his kingdom stand? – for you say that I cast out the demons by Beelzebul. Now if I cast out the demons by Beelzebul, by whom do your exorcists cast them out? Therefore they will be your judges. But if it is by the finger of God that I cast out the demons, then the kingdom of God has come to you. When a strong man, fully armed, guards his castle, his property is safe. But when one stronger than he attacks him and overpowers him, he takes away his armour in which he trusted and divides his plunder. Whoever is not with me is against me, and whoever does not gather with me scatters.

'When the unclean spirit has gone out of a person, it wanders through waterless regions looking for a resting-place, but not finding any, it says, "I will return to my house from which I came." When it comes, it finds it swept and put in order. Then it goes and brings seven other spirits more evil than itself, and they enter and live there; and the last state of that person is worse than the first.'

- Pope Francis called on us to reflect on whether we guard our hearts, feelings, graces and presence of the Holy Spirit, or 'do I let go, feeling secure, believing that all is going well? If you do not guard yourself, he who is stronger than you will come.'

- 'Three criteria!' said the pope. 'Do not confuse the truth. Jesus fights the devil: first criterion. Second criterion: he who is not with Jesus is against Jesus. There are no attitudes in the middle. Third criterion: vigilance over our hearts because the devil is astute. He is never cast out for ever. It will only be so on the last day.'

Saturday 8 October

Luke 11:27–28

While he was saying this, a woman in the crowd raised her voice and said to him, 'Blessed is the womb that bore you and the breasts that nursed you!' But he said, 'Blessed rather are those who hear the word of God and obey it!'

- I spend time rejoicing with Mary, the mother of Jesus, the one who was closest to him, and the greatest influence on his life.

- I ask her to help me grow in trust and freedom of heart, so that I too, like her, can hear the Word of God and keep it.

9–15 October 2022

Something to think and pray about each day this week:

Faith gives an answer to questions like: Why do we exist? What is the meaning of life? Why is there something instead of nothing? Nuclear physics, chemistry or mathematics can't answer those questions. That is not their domain. The question the scientist wants to answer is *how* our world works. For centuries people thought and believed that they could find the answer to that question in the Bible. It has only been a few centuries since Christians started to disassemble these questions, an unravelling that is still going on.

Many people say that they believed as a child, but that they lost their faith when they discovered science. One of the reasons for this is that many people's knowledge of faith has been limited to the knowledge they had of it when they were children. It is not surprising that such a belief is undermined by the confrontation with scientific thinking. For others, it is precisely the practice of science that is the starting point of a path of faith: who or what is at the origin of this incredibly beautiful cosmos?

Nikolaas Sintobin,
Did Jesus Really Exist? And 51 Other Questions

The Presence of God

Dear Jesus, I come to you today longing for your presence. I desire to love you as you love me. May nothing ever separate me from you.

Freedom

Lord, grant me the grace to have freedom of the spirit. Cleanse my heart and soul so that I may live joyously in your love.

Consciousness

Where am I with God? With others?

Do I have something to be grateful for? Then I give thanks.

Is there something I am sorry for? Then I ask forgiveness.

The Word

The word of God comes down to us through the Scriptures. May the Holy Spirit enlighten my mind and my heart to respond to the Gospel teachings.

(Please turn to the Scripture on the following pages. Inspiration points are there, should you need them. When you are ready, return here to continue.)

Conversation

How has God's word moved me? Has it left me cold?

Has it consoled me or moved me to act in a new way?

I imagine Jesus standing or sitting beside me;

I turn and share my feelings with him.

Conclusion

I thank God for these moments we have spent together and for any insights I have been given concerning the text.

Sunday 9 October
Twenty-eighth Sunday in Ordinary Time
Luke 17:11–19

On the way to Jerusalem Jesus was going through the region between Samaria and Galilee. As he entered a village, ten lepers approached him. Keeping their distance, they called out, saying, 'Jesus, Master, have mercy on us!' When he saw them, he said to them, 'Go and show yourselves to the priests.' And as they went, they were made clean. Then one of them, when he saw that he was healed, turned back, praising God with a loud voice. He prostrated himself at Jesus' feet and thanked him. And he was a Samaritan. Then Jesus asked, 'Were not ten made clean? But the other nine, where are they? Was none of them found to return and give praise to God except this foreigner?' Then he said to him, 'Get up and go on your way; your faith has made you well.'

- The healed man finds it in his heart to praise God. His first words had been words of trustful petition: petition and thanks are fundamental movements of prayer. We engage one or the other, sometimes both. Asking for what we want, giving praise for what we are grateful for – these are the essentials of prayer.

Monday 10 October
Luke 11:29–32

When the crowds were increasing, he began to say, 'This generation is an evil generation; it asks for a sign, but no sign will be given to it except the sign of Jonah. For just as Jonah became a sign to the people of Nineveh, so the Son of Man will be to this generation. The queen of the South will rise at the judgement with the people of this generation and condemn them, because she came from the ends of the earth to listen to the wisdom of Solomon, and see, something greater than Solomon is here! The people of Nineveh will rise up at the judgement with this generation and condemn it, because they repented at the proclamation of Jonah, and see, something greater than Jonah is here!'

- Like Jonah, we can be called upon to be a conduit through which God's will is accomplished. Sometimes it doesn't matter if our hearts are not in what we do – the fact that we do it can be enough for God to achieve astonishing results through us.

Tuesday 11 October
Luke 11:37–41

While he was speaking, a Pharisee invited him to dine with him; so he went in and took his place at the table. The Pharisee was amazed to see that he did not first wash before dinner. Then the Lord said to him, 'Now you Pharisees clean the outside of the cup and of the dish, but inside you are full of greed and wickedness. You fools! Did not the one who made the outside make the inside also? So give for alms those things that are within; and see, everything will be clean for you.'

- The Pharisees seem to have been the only group of people who really upset Jesus. They were good people, keen to observe the law as perfectly as possible, but this often made them blind to more important things. Can I see a Pharisee in my heart, big or small? I pray for light and for integrity in all that I do. And I ask pardon for being so inconsistent.

- Give alms from what you have and then indeed everything will be clean for you. I spend some time with these clear words of Jesus, and look at my almsgiving and its quality.

Wednesday 12 October
Luke 11:42–46

'But woe to you Pharisees! For you tithe mint and rue and herbs of all kinds, and neglect justice and the love of God; it is these you ought to have practised, without neglecting the others. Woe to you Pharisees! For you love to have the seat of honour in the synagogues and to be greeted with respect in the market-places. Woe to you! For you are like unmarked graves, and people walk over them without realising it.'

One of the lawyers answered him, 'Teacher, when you say these things, you insult us too.' And he said, 'Woe also to you lawyers! For you load people with burdens hard to bear, and you yourselves do not lift a finger to ease them.'

- How easy it can be to observe the minute requirements of the law and forget its spirit! Jesus insists that the highest obligation we all have is love, and we all know that observing the rules with a spirit of love makes a big difference. I ask for the vision and the openness to observe the whole law, letter and spirit.

- We feel very angry when our lawgivers, civil or religious, impose burdens on us which they then avoid. Do I do that too, in my small world, in my family or at work? I might find myself supporting measures that place burdens that I know are unbearable. Alas for you, Jesus says.

Thursday 13 October
Luke 11:47–54

Woe to you! For you build the tombs of the prophets whom your ancestors killed. So you are witnesses and approve of the deeds of your ancestors; for they killed them, and you build their tombs. Therefore also the Wisdom of God said, "I will send them prophets and apostles, some of whom they will kill and persecute", so that this generation may be charged with the blood of all the prophets shed since the foundation of the world, from the blood of Abel to the blood of Zechariah, who perished between the altar and the sanctuary. Yes, I tell you, it will be charged against this generation. Woe to you lawyers! For you have taken away the key of knowledge; you did not enter yourselves, and you hindered those who were entering.'

When he went outside, the scribes and the Pharisees began to be very hostile towards him and to cross-examine him about many things, lying in wait for him, to catch him in something he might say.

- One of the things we find so difficult to understand is the powerful presence of evil in our midst. Yet it is most certainly there. The chosen people had killed God's prophets, and the contemporaries of Jesus ratify this by attacking him furiously, and finally kill him too. Our generation too commits unspeakable acts of cruelty and oppression against innocent persons and peoples. I pray for help to see this great battle between good and evil around me, and in my own heart too. I pray to be able to choose to be always on the side of good, truth and justice.

Friday 14 October
Luke 12:1–7

Meanwhile, when the crowd gathered in thousands, so that they trampled on one another, he began to speak first to his disciples, 'Beware of the yeast of the Pharisees, that is, their hypocrisy. Nothing is covered up that will not be uncovered, and nothing secret that will not become known. Therefore whatever you have said in the dark will be heard in the light, and what you have whispered behind closed doors will be proclaimed from the housetops.

'I tell you, my friends, do not fear those who kill the body, and after that can do nothing more. But I will warn you whom to fear: fear him who, after he has killed, has authority to cast into hell. Yes, I tell you, fear him! Are not five sparrows sold for two pennies? Yet not one of them is forgotten in God's sight. But even the hairs of your head are all counted. Do not be afraid; you are of more value than many sparrows.'

- People who are suffering or are on the fringes of society may not know that they are 'of more value than many sparrows'. Trusting that the millions of people who suffer terrible trials of injustice here on earth will find consolation in the life after death is a huge leap of faith. Even the most ordinary life has its trials and needs the leap of faith that hopes for life after death. The message is, do not fear. Every little bird is cared for by God. Even the hairs of our heads are counted.

Saturday 15 October
Luke 12:8–12

'And I tell you, everyone who acknowledges me before others, the Son of Man also will acknowledge before the angels of God; but whoever denies me before others will be denied before the angels of God. And everyone who speaks a word against the Son of Man will be forgiven; but whoever blasphemes against the Holy Spirit will not be forgiven. When they bring you before the synagogues, the rulers, and the authorities, do not worry about how you are to defend yourselves or what you are to say; for the Holy Spirit will teach you at that very hour what you ought to say.'

- Everyone who says a word against the Son of Man will be forgiven, but he who blasphemes against the Holy Spirit will not be forgiven. Jesus means that if we continually resist the promptings of the Holy Spirit we will end up hardening our hearts to an extent that we are closed even to receive forgiveness. I pray insistently for the grace to keep an open heart, ready to listen and trust.

The Twenty-ninth Week in Ordinary Time
16–22 October 2022

Something to think and pray about each day this week:

Many of us believe we cannot be happy if we lose a loved one or good health or our job or the country in which we live. However, long before she ascended Calvary, Mary had already given up her own dreams of happiness to entrust herself to what God had in store for her: 'let it be done unto me according to your word'. This unconditional availability had become sewn into the very fabric of her being. If we limit our openness to God, we're also opening the door to sadness. For instance, if we keep telling ourselves that we cannot find joy unless we hold on to a particular someone or something in our lives, we're setting ourselves up to sink into serious misery in the future. Mary, on the other hand, was always effectively saying to herself something like this:

'Because I trust in God's goodness, I'll be able to find joy whatever loss hits me, even if I don't know how I'll adjust to it when it actually occurs.'

Thomas Casey SJ,
Smile of Joy: Mary of Nazareth

The Presence of God

As I sit here, the beating of my heart,
the ebb and flow of my breathing, the movements of my mind
are all signs of God's ongoing creation of me.
I pause for a moment and become aware
of this presence of God within me.

Freedom

I will ask God's help
to be free from my own preoccupations,
to be open to God in this time of prayer,
to come to know, love and serve God more.

Consciousness

At this moment, Lord, I turn my thoughts to you.
I will leave aside my chores and preoccupations.
I will take rest and refreshment in your presence.

The Word

Now I turn to the Scripture set out for me this day. I read slowly over the
words and see if any sentence or sentiment appeals to me.
*(Please turn to the Scripture on the following pages. Inspiration points are there,
should you need them. When you are ready, return here to continue.)*

Conversation

Begin to talk to Jesus about the Scripture you have just read. What part
of it strikes a chord in you? Perhaps the words of a friend – or some story
you have heard recently – will slowly rise to the surface of your consciousness. If so, does the story throw light on what the Scripture passage may
be saying to you?

Conclusion

Glory be to the Father, and to the Son, and to the Holy Spirit,
As it was in the beginning, is now and ever shall be,
World without end. Amen.

Sunday 16 October
Twenty-ninth Sunday in Ordinary Time
Luke 18:1–8

Then Jesus told them a parable about their need to pray always and not to lose heart. He said, 'In a certain city there was a judge who neither feared God nor had respect for people. In that city there was a widow who kept coming to him and saying, "Grant me justice against my opponent." For a while he refused; but later he said to himself, "Though I have no fear of God and no respect for anyone, yet because this widow keeps bothering me, I will grant her justice, so that she may not wear me out by continually coming."' And the Lord said, 'Listen to what the unjust judge says. And will not God grant justice to his chosen ones who cry to him day and night? Will he delay long in helping them? I tell you, he will quickly grant justice to them. And yet, when the Son of Man comes, will he find faith on earth?'

- Jesus is not comparing God to an unjust judge. The parable should be read in the context of an earlier comment by Jesus: 'If you then, who are evil, know how to give good gifts to your children, how much more will the heavenly Father give the Holy Spirit to those who ask him!' (Luke 11:13). So, if even the most unjust of judges will finally concede to the ceaseless petitions of a defenceless widow, then how much more will God answer our prayers!

- The parable offers hope to those among us who are perhaps reluctant to address God with our petitions. It is both an invitation and an encouragement to pray without ceasing, confident of God's desire to respond.

Monday 17 October
Luke 12:13–21

Someone in the crowd said to him, 'Teacher, tell my brother to divide the family inheritance with me.' But he said to him, 'Friend, who set me to be a judge or arbitrator over you?' And he said to them, 'Take care! Be on your guard against all kinds of greed; for one's life does not consist in the abundance of possessions.' Then he told them a parable: 'The land of a rich man produced abundantly. And he thought to himself, "What should I do, for I have no place to store my crops?" Then he said, "I will do this: I will pull down my barns and build larger ones, and there I will store all my grain and my goods. And I will say to my soul, Soul, you have ample goods laid up for many years; relax, eat, drink, be merry." But God said to him, "You fool! This very night your life is being demanded of you. And the things you have prepared, whose will they be?" So it is with those who store up treasures for themselves but are not rich towards God.'

- It is good to remember that Jesus' contemporaries lived lives of immense hardship, under very harsh social and political conditions. Famine or land appropriation were a constant threat for subsistence farmers suffering under excruciating taxation practices.

- In this situation, the landowner who stored his surplus crop, instead of helping to feed and support poorer farmers, would not have won the sympathy of Jesus' listeners. They will have enjoyed this simple reminder that even unscrupulous people like this landowner will die, and his grand plans will look very foolish.

- The parable is told as a warning against greed, but Luke is offering a deeper theological meaning. What are the ways in which I am 'rich towards God'?

Tuesday 18 October
Saint Luke, Evangelist
Luke 10:1–9

After this the Lord appointed seventy others and sent them on ahead of him in pairs to every town and place where he himself intended to go. He said to them, 'The harvest is plentiful, but the labourers are few; therefore ask the Lord of the harvest to send out labourers into his harvest. Go on your way. See, I am sending you out like lambs into the midst of wolves. Carry no purse, no bag, no sandals; and greet no one on the road. Whatever house you enter, first say, "Peace to this house!" And if anyone is there who shares in peace, your peace will rest on that person; but if not, it will return to you. Remain in the same house, eating and drinking whatever they provide, for the labourer deserves to be paid. Do not move about from house to house. Whenever you enter a town and its people welcome you, eat what is set before you; cure the sick who are there, and say to them, "The kingdom of God has come near to you." '

- Lord, sometimes I wonder if I have the ability to recognise you at all in the midst of all my clutter. Am I carrying too many purses, bags and sandals? Make me content with less, which is enough. I pray now in this Sacred Space to be happily aware that the kingdom of God is very near.

Wednesday 19 October
Luke 12:39–48

'But know this: if the owner of the house had known at what hour the thief was coming, he would not have let his house be broken into. You also must be ready, for the Son of Man is coming at an unexpected hour.'

Peter said, 'Lord, are you telling this parable for us or for everyone?' And the Lord said, 'Who then is the faithful and prudent manager whom his master will put in charge of his slaves, to give them their allowance of food at the proper time? Blessed is that slave whom his master will find at work when he arrives. Truly I tell you, he will put that one in charge of all his possessions. But if that slave says to himself, "My master is delayed in coming", and if he begins to beat the other slaves, men and women, and to eat and drink and get drunk, the master of that slave will come on a day when he does not expect him and at an hour that he does not know, and will cut him in pieces, and put him with the unfaithful. That slave who knew what his master wanted, but did not prepare himself or do what was wanted, will receive a severe beating. But one who did not know and did what deserved a beating will receive a light beating. From everyone to whom much has been given, much will be required; and from one to whom much has been entrusted, even more will be demanded.'

- The central point in this text is the need to be attentive and alert. The passage is a call to responsibility. If we know what is expected of us, but we fall short, then we will be held to greater account, especially if our actions are cruel or unjust. This is nevertheless a disturbing, un-comfortable reading.

Thursday 20 October
Luke 12:49–53

'I came to bring fire to the earth, and how I wish it were already kin-dled! I have a baptism with which to be baptised, and what stress I am under until it is completed! Do you think that I have come to bring peace to the earth? No, I tell you, but rather division! From now on, five in one household will be divided, three against two and two against three; they will be divided:

father against son
and son against father,
mother against daughter
and daughter against mother,
mother-in-law against her daughter-in-law
and daughter-in-law against mother-in-law.'

- Jesus cannot wait for the final reality of his mission to come alive – the fire of justice and right living. He is under stress in awaiting his own suffering and crucifixion. And though his message is peace, it is such a hard-won peace that it is more like division because he is fighting off the corruption of the world. He knows that the radical purity of his message will cause people to waver and doubt and oppose his message. He is like the prophet Micah, whom Luke quotes here, who, while seeing the divisions in families, puts his trust in God alone (Micah 7:6).

Friday 21 October
Luke 12:54–59

He also said to the crowds, 'When you see a cloud rising in the west, you immediately say, "It is going to rain"; and so it happens. And when you see the south wind blowing, you say, "There will be scorching heat"; and it happens. You hypocrites! You know how to interpret the appearance of earth and sky, but why do you not know how to interpret the present time?

'And why do you not judge for yourselves what is right? Thus, when you go with your accuser before a magistrate, on the way make an effort to settle the case, or you may be dragged before the judge, and the judge hand you over to the officer, and the officer throw you in prison. I tell you, you will never get out until you have paid the very last penny.'

- In all times, in ours as in Jesus', it is more attractive to live comfortable lives without trying to understand what is going on. Jesus uses harsh words to condemn our laziness and distraction. What are the signs of our times? How can we understand them? Where is God in what is going on around us? How are we called to respond as followers of Jesus?

What would he do if he were living now? It is very easy to condemn the world around us and feel nostalgic about the past: Jesus is calling us to discernment and action in the world we live in now.

Saturday 22 October
Luke 13:1–9

At that very time there were some present who told him about the Galileans whose blood Pilate had mingled with their sacrifices. He asked them, 'Do you think that because these Galileans suffered in this way they were worse sinners than all other Galileans? No, I tell you; but unless you repent, you will all perish as they did. Or those eighteen who were killed when the tower of Siloam fell on them – do you think that they were worse offenders than all the others living in Jerusalem? No, I tell you; but unless you repent, you will all perish just as they did.'

Then he told this parable: 'A man had a fig tree planted in his vineyard; and he came looking for fruit on it and found none. So he said to the gardener, "See here! For three years I have come looking for fruit on this fig tree, and still I find none. Cut it down! Why should it be wasting the soil?" He replied, "Sir, let it alone for one more year, until I dig round it and put manure on it. If it bears fruit next year, well and good; but if not, you can cut it down."'

• The gardener is confident that if he makes another effort the fig tree can bear fruit, in spite of appearances. I too can be involved in what looks like an impossible situation, with someone close to me, in my own family or in the workplace. I pray to be merciful like the Father.

The Thirtieth Week in Ordinary Time
23–28 October 2022

Something to think and pray about each day this week:

Just as we are never conscious of air, because God's presence is always around us, we never notice it. The journey of faith is a gift of a loving God who takes the first step and waits patiently, silently, almost shyly for the human response.

Life is a vocation, a call to seek this shy God.

This shy God did not come into the world with bells and thunder. When I was a young boy I sought God by looking up – trying to see if I could find God through some break in the sky. Today when I look for God I look down, not up, because I find God in small things. As Pope Francis has said, we find the extraordinary in the ordinary.

The greatest joy comes from good relationships – the greatest sorrow and suffering come not from loss of job or property but from broken and betrayed relationships. All relationships of love are rooted in the love this shy God has for all of us.

John Scally,
Waiting in Joy

The Presence of God

'Be still, and know that I am God!' Lord, your words lead us to the calmness and greatness of your presence.

Freedom

God is not foreign to my freedom. The Spirit breathes life into my most intimate desires, gently nudging me towards all that is good. I ask for the grace to let myself be enfolded by the Spirit.

Consciousness

Where do I sense hope, encouragement and growth in my life? By looking back over the past few months, I may be able to see which activities and occasions have produced rich fruit. If I do notice such areas, I will determine to give those areas both time and space in the future.

The Word

The word of God comes down to us through the Scriptures. May the Holy Spirit enlighten my mind and my heart to respond to the Gospel teachings.

(Please turn to the Scripture on the following pages. Inspiration points are there, should you need them. When you are ready, return here to continue.)

Conversation

What is stirring in me as I pray? Am I consoled, troubled, left cold? I imagine Jesus standing or sitting at my side, and I share my feelings with him.

Conclusion

Glory be to the Father, and to the Son and to the Holy Spirit,
As it was in the beginning, is now and ever shall be,
World without end. Amen.

Sunday 23 October
Thirtieth Sunday in Ordinary Time
Luke 18:9–14

He also told this parable to some who trusted in themselves that they were righteous and regarded others with contempt: 'Two men went up to the temple to pray, one a Pharisee and the other a tax-collector. The Pharisee, standing by himself, was praying thus, "God, I thank you that I am not like other people: thieves, rogues, adulterers, or even like this tax-collector. I fast twice a week; I give a tenth of all my income." But the tax-collector, standing far off, would not even look up to heaven, but was beating his breast and saying, "God, be merciful to me, a sinner!" I tell you, this man went down to his home justified rather than the other; for all who exalt themselves will be humbled, but all who humble themselves will be exalted.'

- Am I shocked and scandalised by this parable, or do I discover a Pharisee and a tax-collector in my heart too? Sometimes I cannot avoid feeling morally superior and holier than others, or even a particular person, however much I try not to. I feel I tick all the boxes, unlike others. I humbly ask for light to see and feel the deep roots pride has in my heart, and for the grace of real humility.

- I spend some time just repeating, perhaps with the rhythm of my breathing, the tax-collector's prayer that earned him peace with God: 'God, be merciful to me, a sinner'.

Monday 24 October
Luke 13:10–17

Now he was teaching in one of the synagogues on the sabbath. And just then there appeared a woman with a spirit that had crippled her for eighteen years. She was bent over and was quite unable to stand up straight. When Jesus saw her, he called her over and said, 'Woman, you are set free from your ailment.' When he laid his hands on her, immediately she stood up straight and began praising God. But the leader of the synagogue, indignant because Jesus had cured on the sabbath, kept saying to the crowd, 'There are six days on which work ought to be done; come on those days and be cured, and not on the sabbath day.' But the Lord answered him and said, 'You hypocrites! Does not each of you on the sabbath untie his ox or his donkey from the manger, and lead it away to give it water? And ought not this woman, a daughter of Abraham whom Satan bound for eighteen long years, be set free from this bondage on the sabbath day?' When he said this, all his opponents were put to shame; and the entire crowd was rejoicing at all the wonderful things that he was doing.

- Notice the joy of the woman in the Gospel who for the first time in eighteen years could stand up straight. As a person of faith she praised God who had healed her and given her freedom again.

- I could reflect on the questions: Can I care for and heal through the listening skills that I offer to others? Am I also prone to the tendency of being hypocritical in some of my ways of living?

Tuesday 25 October
Luke 13:18–21

He said therefore, 'What is the kingdom of God like? And to what should I compare it? It is like a mustard seed that someone took and sowed in the garden; it grew and became a tree, and the birds of the air made nests in its branches.'

And again he said, 'To what should I compare the kingdom of God? It is like yeast that a woman took and mixed in with three measures of flour until all of it was leavened.'

- Jesus always compares the Kingdom to something small, which then grows into something big and life-giving, slowly but surely. This pattern often disappoints us, who would prefer something big and noticeable from the very beginning. Those who believe in the kind of Kingdom Jesus preached are people of hope, people who see God's strong presence active in the world, even contrary to what looks to be the case. I pray to be such a hopeful person.

Wednesday 26 October
Luke 13:22–30

Jesus went through one town and village after another, teaching as he made his way to Jerusalem. Someone asked him, 'Lord, will only a few be saved?' He said to them, 'Strive to enter through the narrow door; for many, I tell you, will try to enter and will not be able. When once the owner of the house has got up and shut the door, and you begin to stand outside and to knock at the door, saying, "Lord, open to us", then in reply he will say to you, "I do not know where you come from." Then you will begin to say, "We ate and drank with you, and you taught in our streets." But he will say, "I do not know where you come from; go away from me, all you evildoers!" There will be weeping and gnashing of teeth when you see Abraham and Isaac and Jacob and all the prophets in the kingdom of God, and you yourselves thrown out. Then people will come from east and west, from north and south, and will eat in the kingdom of God. Indeed, some are last who will be first, and some are first who will be last.'

- 'Will only a few be saved?' This looks like an eminently reasonable question, but Jesus does not even find it worth an answer. He prefers to talk of more relevant issues, like the need to choose well, even if this is difficult. How much energy is lost in the Church arguing about irrelevant or marginal questions, while we neglect what is really central and important? I pray for the Church to keep its attention on its central mission of bringing the Good News to all, and avoid all temptations to indulge in empty discussions.

Thursday 27 October
Luke 13:31–35

At that very hour some Pharisees came and said to him, 'Get away from here, for Herod wants to kill you.' He said to them, 'Go and tell that fox for me, "Listen, I am casting out demons and performing cures today and tomorrow, and on the third day I finish my work. Yet today, tomorrow, and the next day I must be on my way, because it is impossible for a prophet to be killed away from Jerusalem." Jerusalem, Jerusalem, the city that kills the prophets and stones those who are sent to it! How often have I desired to gather your children together as a hen gathers her brood under her wings, and you were not willing! See, your house is left to you. And I tell you, you will not see me until the time comes when you say, "Blessed is the one who comes in the name of the Lord."'

- Jesus does not seem overawed by the threat posed by Herod. He does not run away, and even calls him a fox. His integrity was his strength against those who relied on their ability to be violent. As he told Pilate,

'My kingdom is not of this world'. We still live in a world seemingly dominated by the violent, so I pray for integrity, for me and for all others of good will, that we might not be afraid and hold firm to what we believe to be true and right.

Friday 28 October
Saints Simon and Jude, Apostles
Luke 6:12–16

Now during those days he went out to the mountain to pray; and he spent the night in prayer to God. And when day came, he called his disciples and chose twelve of them, whom he also named apostles: Simon, whom he named Peter, and his brother Andrew, and James, and John, and Philip, and Bartholomew, and Matthew, and Thomas, and James son of Alphaeus, and Simon, who was called the Zealot, and Judas son of James, and Judas Iscariot, who became a traitor.

- It seems that Jesus and his father spent the whole night in conversation about the choosing of the twelve apostles. Can I imagine how the conversation went?

- Do I ever consult God about the decisions that I have to make in life, especially those that would have a long-term effect? It is worth the trouble to look for his advice – even if it takes all night.

Saturday 29 October
Luke 14:1.7–11

On one occasion when Jesus was going to the house of a leader of the Pharisees to eat a meal on the sabbath, they were watching him closely. . . .

When he noticed how the guests chose the places of honour, he told them a parable. 'When you are invited by someone to a wedding banquet, do not sit down at the place of honour, in case someone more distinguished than you has been invited by your host; and the host who invited both of you may come and say to you, "Give this person your place", and then in disgrace you would start to take the lowest place. But when you are invited, go and sit down at the lowest place, so that when your host comes, he may say to you, "Friend, move up higher"; then you will be honoured in the presence of all who sit at the table with you. For all who exalt themselves will be humbled, and those who humble themselves will be exalted.'

- Is Jesus being petty, or is he reminding us that we would do well to look at how we behave even in small everyday things to discover what really lies in our hearts? I ask him to give me light and freedom in my everyday dealings with others, especially in my competitive world.

The Thirty-first Week in Ordinary Time
30 October–5 November 2022

Something to think and pray about each day this week:

It seems to be the case that the more gratitude a person experiences the more content they are. It is worth remembering that gratitude also needs to be prayed for so that we may get a glimpse of what God is doing in our lives, as difficult as that may be in adverse circumstances. If we look carefully, we'll be surprised by how blessed our lives are. William Wordsworth highlights this when he writes: 'That best portion of a good man's life; His little, nameless, unremembered acts of kindness and of love.' However, we don't always welcome God's blessings with an open heart. At the time a blessing may feel more like a thorn in the side. It's only afterwards that we come to appreciate it. It's a bit like having minor surgery. It's inconvenient and unwelcome at the time. But when we have recovered, we appreciate what we've been through.

The narrative of Adam and Eve in the first book of the Bible is an extraordinarily perceptive take on how humans tick. They weren't happy with what they had already been given, the purpose of which was to support relationships. 'We want' was their mantra. They were like two-year-olds who had discovered the words, 'No' and 'Mine!', or like the spoilsports in the school playground. Their rejection of their fundamental identity, persons-in-relationship, has continued throughout the centuries. The spoilsports in the playground mess things up for everybody else, because all the actions of a person-in-relationship have consequences for the rest of us. The response to the COVID-19 virus serves to illustrate this global connectedness. If the same energy, galvanised by this virus, were also to be channelled into poverty, hunger, lack of drinking water and other global issues, what a different planet we would inhabit.

Jim Maher SJ,
Pathways to a Decision with Ignatius of Loyola

The Presence of God
'Come to me, all you who are weary and are carrying heavy burdens, and I will give you rest.' Here I am, Lord. I come to seek your presence. I long for your healing power.

Freedom
By God's grace I was born to live in freedom. Free to enjoy the pleasures he created for me. Dear Lord, grant that I may live as you intended, with complete confidence in your loving care.

Consciousness
Knowing that God loves me unconditionally, I look honestly over the past day, its events and my feelings. Do I have something to be grateful for? Then I give thanks. Is there something I am sorry for? Then I ask forgiveness.

The Word
God speaks to each of us individually. I listen attentively to hear what he is saying to me. Read the text a few times, then listen.
(Please turn to the Scripture on the following pages. Inspiration points are there, should you need them. When you are ready, return here to continue.)

Conversation
I know with certainty that there were times when you carried me, Lord. There were times when it was through your strength that I got through the dark times in my life.

Conclusion
Glory be to the Father, and to the Son and to the Holy Spirit,
As it was in the beginning, is now and ever shall be,
World without end. Amen.

Sunday 30 October
Thirty-first Sunday in Ordinary Time
Luke 19:1–10

He entered Jericho and was passing through it. A man was there named Zacchaeus; he was a chief tax-collector and was rich. He was trying to see who Jesus was, but on account of the crowd he could not, because he was short in stature. So he ran ahead and climbed a sycamore tree to see him, because he was going to pass that way. When Jesus came to the place, he looked up and said to him, 'Zacchaeus, hurry and come down; for I must stay at your house today.' So he hurried down and was happy to welcome him. All who saw it began to grumble and said, 'He has gone to be the guest of one who is a sinner.' Zacchaeus stood there and said to the Lord, 'Look, half of my possessions, Lord, I will give to the poor; and if I have defrauded anyone of anything, I will pay back four times as much.' Then Jesus said to him, 'Today salvation has come to this house, because he too is a son of Abraham. For the Son of Man came to seek out and to save the lost.'

- We all like Zacchaeus, the shy man who did not want to attract any attention, yet ended up getting far beyond his expectations. Jesus could see what he really desired in the depths of his heart, and invited himself to Zacchaeus' house. All who saw this began to grumble, but Jesus faced this criticism by proclaiming that salvation had come to Zacchaeus' house. I try to imagine myself present in this scene: would I be like the diffident Zacchaeus, like the complaining crowd or like the merciful and strong Jesus?

Monday 31 October
Luke 14:12–14

He said also to the one who had invited him, 'When you give a luncheon or a dinner, do not invite your friends or your brothers or your relatives or rich neighbours, in case they may invite you in return, and you would be repaid. But when you give a banquet, invite the poor, the crippled, the lame, and the blind. And you will be blessed, because they cannot repay you, for you will be repaid at the resurrection of the righteous.'

- Jesus knows our heart, and poses a radical challenge to the many ways it invents self-seeking. He invites us to have a free and open heart, that does not seek any recompense for being generous: that is its own reward.

- 'You received without payment; give without payment,' Jesus once said (Matthew 10:8). This is what lies at the basis of this seemingly irrational demand of Jesus: we are the poor, the crippled, the lame, the blind whom God has invited to his banquet. Let us try to do the same with others.

Tuesday 1 November
The Solemnity of All Saints
Matthew 5:1–12

When Jesus saw the crowds, he went up the mountain; and after he sat down, his disciples came to him. Then he began to speak, and taught them, saying:

> 'Blessed are the poor in spirit, for theirs is the kingdom of heaven.
> 'Blessed are those who mourn, for they will be comforted.
> 'Blessed are the meek, for they will inherit the earth.
> 'Blessed are those who hunger and thirst for righteousness, for they will be filled.
> 'Blessed are the merciful, for they will receive mercy.
> 'Blessed are the pure in heart, for they will see God.
> 'Blessed are the peacemakers, for they will be called children of God.
> 'Blessed are those who are persecuted for righteousness' sake, for theirs is the kingdom of heaven.
> 'Blessed are you when people revile you and persecute you and utter all kinds of evil against you falsely on my account. Rejoice and be glad, for your reward is great in heaven, for in the same way they persecuted the prophets who were before you.'

- Jesus lived every one of the 'blesseds'. As you list them, notice how he might have lived them himself. He was merciful, pure in heart (single-minded), a peacemaker. All the others find space in his life. Note them as you read the Gospel and in your prayer. Jesus knew each of the Beatitudes from the inside out. He knew just where the blessing and presence of God may be found.

Wednesday 2 November
The Commemoration of all the Faithful Departed (All Souls)
John 6:37–40

'Everything that the Father gives me will come to me, and anyone who comes to me I will never drive away; for I have come down from heaven, not to do my own will, but the will of him who sent me. And this is the will of him who sent me, that I should lose nothing of all that he has given me, but raise it up on the last day. This is indeed the will of my Father, that all who see the Son and believe in him may have eternal life; and I will raise them up on the last day.'

- On this day I may choose to bring before the Lord some person or persons who have already passed away, and pray for them, in gratitude for all I have received from them, or ask for pardon for my mistakes in dealing with them, or ask for God's mercy on them. I find special consolation in Jesus' words in today's Gospel: 'Anyone who comes to me I will never drive away'.

Thursday 3 November
Luke 15:1–10

Now all the tax-collectors and sinners were coming near to listen to him. And the Pharisees and the scribes were grumbling and saying, 'This fellow welcomes sinners and eats with them.'

So he told them this parable: 'Which one of you, having a hundred sheep and losing one of them, does not leave the ninety-nine in the wilderness and go after the one that is lost until he finds it? When he has found it, he lays it on his shoulders and rejoices. And when he comes home, he calls together his friends and neighbours, saying to them, "Rejoice with me, for I have found my sheep that was lost." Just so, I tell you, there will be more joy in heaven over one sinner who repents than over ninety-nine righteous people who need no repentance.

'Or what woman having ten silver coins, if she loses one of them, does not light a lamp, sweep the house, and search carefully until she finds it? When she has found it, she calls together her friends and neighbours, saying, "Rejoice with me, for I have found the coin that I had lost." Just so, I tell you, there is joy in the presence of the angels of God over one sinner who repents.'

- The Pharisees and scribes were grumbling because Jesus was too friendly with sinners. It is the eternal temptation of those who consider themselves good, and one of the major challenges of the Gospel: God, in Jesus, shows himself close to those who make mistakes, even big ones! In fact Jesus does not defend himself or say the Pharisees were exaggerating; on the contrary he shows how right they were by telling the three parables of mercy. O Sacred Heart of Jesus, make my heart like yours!

Friday 4 November
Luke 16:1–8

Then Jesus said to the disciples, 'There was a rich man who had a manager, and charges were brought to him that this man was squandering his property. So he summoned him and said to him, "What is this that I hear about you? Give me an account of your management, because you cannot be my manager any longer." Then the manager said to himself, "What will I do, now that my master is taking the position away from me? I am not strong enough to dig, and I am ashamed to beg. I have decided what to do so that, when I am dismissed as manager, people may welcome me into their homes." So, summoning his master's debtors one by one, he asked the first, "How much do you owe my master?" He answered, "A hundred jugs of olive oil." He said to him, "Take your bill, sit down quickly, and make it fifty." Then he asked another, "And how much do you owe?" He replied, "A hundred containers of wheat." He said to him, "Take your bill and make it eighty." And his master commended the dishonest manager because he had acted shrewdly; for the children of this age are more shrewd in dealing with their own generation than are the children of light.'

- Lord, you are telling me to be shrewd by using wisely whatever wealth I have. Having money is a responsibility. I can use it selfishly, or with a sensitivity to others' needs. God gave us temporal things to use. My wealth consists not in what I keep but in what I give away. You will judge me by how I use the things of which I am only a steward. The only riches we take from this world are those we have given away.

Saturday 5 November

Luke 16:9–15

'And I tell you, make friends for yourselves by means of dishonest wealth so that when it is gone, they may welcome you into the eternal homes.

'Whoever is faithful in a very little is faithful also in much; and whoever is dishonest in a very little is dishonest also in much. If then you have not been faithful with the dishonest wealth, who will entrust to you the true riches? And if you have not been faithful with what belongs to another, who will give you what is your own? No slave can serve two masters; for a slave will either hate the one and love the other, or be devoted to the one and despise the other. You cannot serve God and wealth.'

The Pharisees, who were lovers of money, heard all this, and they ridiculed him. So he said to them, 'You are those who justify yourselves in the sight of others; but God knows your hearts; for what is prized by human beings is an abomination in the sight of God.'

- What is my relationship with money? How much of my time and energy does it take up? Has it become my master? What do I think Jesus is inviting me to do in relation to my possessions? I talk to him honestly about it.

The Thirty-second Week in Ordinary Time
6–12 November 2022

Something to think and pray about each day this week:

Joy in believing might seem an 'extra' in today's challenging climate for faith. Many of us struggle simply to hold on to faith, not to mention being exuberant about it all. And yet, of course, there is deep happiness in faith. First of all, everything around us is a gift and behind all the gifts stands the giver. Secondly, love is at the heart of it all and, in the faith, nothing is ever 'lost' or 'wasted'. Faith, hope and love endure and the greatest of these is love. Finally, why not 'permit' ourselves true joy in all that God has done for us and still does for us in Jesus and in the Holy Spirit?

Kieran J. O'Mahony OSA,
Hearers of the Word: Advent & Christmas, Year A

The Presence of God

'Be still, and know that I am God!' Lord, your words lead us to the calmness and greatness of your presence.

Freedom

Leave me here freely all alone. / In cell where never sunlight shone. / Should no one ever speak to me. / This golden silence makes me free!
—Part of a poem by Bl. Titus Brandsma, written while he was a prisoner at Dachau concentration camp

Consciousness

Knowing that God loves me unconditionally, I can afford to be honest about how I am.
How has the day been, and how do I feel now? I share my feelings openly with the Lord.

The Word

I take my time to read the word of God slowly, a few times, allowing myself to dwell on anything that strikes me.
(Please turn to the Scripture on the following pages. Inspiration points are there, should you need them. When you are ready, return here to continue.)

Conversation

Sometimes I wonder what I might say if I were to meet you in person, Lord. I think I might say, 'Thank you', because you are always there for me.

Conclusion

I thank God for these moments we have spent together and for any insights I have been given concerning the text.

Sunday 6 November
Thirty-second Sunday in Ordinary Time
Luke 20:27–38

Some Sadducees, those who say there is no resurrection, came to him and asked him a question, 'Teacher, Moses wrote for us that if a man's brother dies, leaving a wife but no children, the man shall marry the widow and raise up children for his brother. Now there were seven brothers; the first married, and died childless; then the second and the third married her, and so in the same way all seven died childless. Finally the woman also died. In the resurrection, therefore, whose wife will the woman be? For the seven had married her.'

Jesus said to them, 'Those who belong to this age marry and are given in marriage; but those who are considered worthy of a place in that age and in the resurrection from the dead neither marry nor are given in marriage. Indeed they cannot die any more, because they are like angels and are children of God, being children of the resurrection. And the fact that the dead are raised Moses himself showed, in the story about the bush, where he speaks of the Lord as the God of Abraham, the God of Isaac, and the God of Jacob. Now he is God not of the dead, but of the living; for to him all of them are alive.'

- To believe in your own personal resurrection is a wonderful gift in this life. It gives meaning to all that makes up your life. It is expressed also in our prayers that we offer for the repose of the souls of all those who have gone before us, which gets great emphasis during this month of November.

Monday 7 November
Luke 17:1–6

Jesus said to his disciples, 'Occasions for stumbling are bound to come, but woe to anyone by whom they come! It would be better for you if a millstone were hung around your neck and you were thrown into the sea than for you to cause one of these little ones to stumble. Be on your guard! If another disciple sins, you must rebuke the offender, and if there is repentance, you must forgive. And if the same person sins against you seven times a day, and turns back to you seven times and says, "I repent", you must forgive.'

The apostles said to the Lord, 'Increase our faith!' The Lord replied, 'If you had faith the size of a mustard seed, you could say to this mulberry tree, "Be uprooted and planted in the sea", and it would obey you.'

- The fact that we have failed ourselves and failed others does not excuse us from a continual effort to forgive and love. We must never forget that that process starts with ourselves.

- Lord grant that, at the end of my days, I will be able to say with Paul, 'I have fought the good fight, I have finished the race, I have kept the faith.'

Tuesday 8 November
Luke 17:7–10

'Who among you would say to your slave who has just come in from ploughing or tending sheep in the field, "Come here at once and take your place at the table"? Would you not rather say to him, "Prepare supper for me, put on your apron and serve me while I eat and drink; later you may eat and drink"? Do you thank the slave for doing what was commanded? So you also, when you have done all that you were ordered to do, say, "We are worthless slaves; we have done only what we ought to have done!"'

- Pope Francis, commenting on this reading, said, 'Jesus taught us that "the leader becomes as one who serves", and that "if anyone would be first, he must be servant of all". Thus, Jesus overturns the values of worldliness. It is no coincidence that when we serve the Lord freely, we feel an ever more profound peace. It is like hearing once again the Lord say: "Come, come, good and faithful servant!"'

- Today, let me realise that, in the words of the Prophet Micah, all that is necessary is 'to act justly, love tenderly and walk humbly before my God'.

Wednesday 9 November
The Dedication of the Lateran Basilica
John 2:13–22

The Passover of the Jews was near, and Jesus went up to Jerusalem. In the temple he found people selling cattle, sheep, and doves, and the money-changers seated at their tables. Making a whip of cords, he drove all of them out of the temple, both the sheep and the cattle. He also poured out the coins of the money-changers and overturned their tables. He told those who were selling the doves, 'Take these things out of here! Stop making my Father's house a market-place!' His disciples remembered that it was written, 'Zeal for your house will consume me.' The Jews then said to him, 'What sign can you show us for doing this?' Jesus answered them, 'Destroy this temple, and in three days I will raise it up.' The Jews then said, 'This temple has been under construction for forty-six years, and will you raise it up in three days?' But he was speaking of the temple of his body. After he was raised from the dead, his disciples remembered that he had said this; and they believed the scripture and the word that Jesus had spoken.

- 'We are the temple of God in the world', wrote Saint Paul. Have I really grasped this colossal reality that I am a living temple, in which the word of God is eternally spoken?

Thursday 10 November
Luke 17:20–25

Once Jesus was asked by the Pharisees when the kingdom of God was coming, and he answered, 'The kingdom of God is not coming with things that can be observed; nor will they say, "Look, here it is!" or "There it is!" For, in fact, the kingdom of God is among you.'

Then he said to the disciples, 'The days are coming when you will long to see one of the days of the Son of Man, and you will not see it. They will say to you, "Look there!" or "Look here!" Do not go, do not set off in pursuit. For as the lightning flashes and lights up the sky from one side to the other, so will the Son of Man be in his day. But first he must endure much suffering and be rejected by this generation.'

- The kingdom of God is within reach; only God can inspire me and enable me to reach a little further to allow the reign of God to come a little more into effect.

- The kingdom of God is beyond the sight of many; I ask God to bless me that I may see how God's Spirit is already at work in the world around me. I might look again at where I feel most challenged, in the hope of seeing how God might be working for good.

Friday 11 November
Luke 17:26–37

'Just as it was in the days of Noah, so too it will be in the days of the Son of Man. They were eating and drinking, and marrying and being given in marriage, until the day Noah entered the ark, and the flood came and destroyed all of them. Likewise, just as it was in the days of Lot: they were eating and drinking, buying and selling, planting and building, but on the day that Lot left Sodom, it rained fire and sulphur from heaven and destroyed all of them – it will be like that on the day that the Son of Man is revealed. On that day, anyone on the housetop who has belongings in the house must not come down to take them away; and likewise anyone in the field must not turn back. Remember Lot's wife. Those who try to make their life secure will lose it, but those who lose their life will keep it. I tell you, on that night there will be two in one bed; one will be taken and the other left. There will be two women grinding meal together; one will be taken and the other left.' Then they asked him, 'Where, Lord?' He said to them, 'Where the corpse is, there the vultures will gather.'

• The only way to be prepared is to live a good life, one based on love. Then the coming of the Son of Man will not be a disaster but our final liberation.

Saturday 12 November
Luke 18:1–8

Then Jesus told them a parable about their need to pray always and not to lose heart. He said, 'In a certain city there was a judge who neither feared God nor had respect for people. In that city there was a widow who kept coming to him and saying, "Grant me justice against my opponent." For a while he refused; but later he said to himself, "Though I have no fear of God and no respect for anyone, yet because this widow keeps bothering me, I will grant her justice, so that she may not wear me out by continually coming."' And the Lord said, 'Listen to what the unjust judge says. And will not God grant justice to his chosen ones who cry to him day and night? Will he delay long in helping them? I tell you, he will quickly grant justice to them. And yet, when the Son of Man comes, will he find faith on earth?'

- Jesus gently reminds us of the need to pray and not lose heart. He knows we need to hear these words from time to time as we ask ourselves whether prayer does make a difference at all. I ask for the grace to hear Jesus encouraging me in my efforts to pray always, helping me not to lose heart.

The Thirty-third Week in Ordinary Time
13–19 November 2022

Something to think and pray about each day this week:

This journey of life is filled with such beauty at times. We could all do with slowing down and appreciating that beauty more often. Too often, we allow it to pass us by without recognition. We do sometimes catch it, though. Sometimes, we realise we are in the presence of beauty and we allow ourselves to freeze time – to stay in that presence. In those moments, we are conscious enough to really experience beauty. While these moments may not come very often, when they do, they are often very emotional. They connect us to a central truth that no matter what suffering there is in the world (and there is suffering in this world) and in our lives (there is and will be suffering in our lives), there is also beauty. We cannot explain why it is so, we can only accept that it is so.

This acceptance thing is hard to do. However, in accepting suffering, we are also free to accept, and savour all the more, the beauty we see and experience in the world.

Try praying for others: hold close to your heart in prayer all those who are suffering at this time; hold close to your heart in prayer all those who are sick; hold close to your heart in prayer all those who do not or cannot see beauty in their lives at this moment.

Jim Deeds & Brendan McManus SJ,
Finding God in the Mess

The Presence of God

'Come to me, all you who are weary and are carrying heavy burdens, and I will give you rest.' Here I am, Lord. I come to seek your presence. I long for your healing power.

Freedom

By God's grace I was born to live in freedom. Free to enjoy the pleasures he created for me. Dear Lord, grant that I may live as you intended, with complete confidence in your loving care.

Consciousness

Knowing that God loves me unconditionally, I look honestly over the past day, its events, and my feelings. Do I have something to be grateful for? Then I give thanks. Is there something I am sorry for? Then I ask forgiveness.

The Word

God speaks to each of us individually. I listen attentively to hear what he is saying to me. Read the text a few times, then listen.

(Please turn to the Scripture on the following pages. Inspiration points are there, should you need them. When you are ready, return here to continue.)

Conversation

I know with certainty that there were times when you carried me, Lord. There were times when it was through your strength that I got through the dark times in my life.

Conclusion

Glory be to the Father, and to the Son and to the Holy Spirit,
As it was in the beginning, is now and ever shall be,
World without end. Amen.

Sunday 13 November
Thirty-third Sunday in Ordinary Time
Luke 21:5–19

When some were speaking about the temple, how it was adorned with beautiful stones and gifts dedicated to God, he said, 'As for these things that you see, the days will come when not one stone will be left upon another; all will be thrown down.'

They asked him, 'Teacher, when will this be, and what will be the sign that this is about to take place?' And he said, 'Beware that you are not led astray; for many will come in my name and say, "I am he!" and, "The time is near!" Do not go after them.

'When you hear of wars and insurrections, do not be terrified; for these things must take place first, but the end will not follow immediately.' Then he said to them, 'Nation will rise against nation, and kingdom against kingdom; there will be great earthquakes, and in various places famines and plagues; and there will be dreadful portents and great signs from heaven.

'But before all this occurs, they will arrest you and persecute you; they will hand you over to synagogues and prisons, and you will be brought before kings and governors because of my name. This will give you an opportunity to testify. So make up your minds not to prepare your defence in advance; for I will give you words and a wisdom that none of your opponents will be able to withstand or contradict. You will be betrayed even by parents and brothers, by relatives and friends; and they will put some of you to death. You will be hated by all because of my name. But not a hair of your head will perish. By your endurance you will gain your souls.'

- Pope Francis has highlighted the need for compassion in our dealings with one another. This intervention by Pope Francis may be seen as coming from Jesus, when he said in the text above, 'I will give you words and wisdom that none of your opponents can withstand or contradict'.

Monday 14 November
Luke 18:35–43

As he approached Jericho, a blind man was sitting by the roadside begging. When he heard a crowd going by, he asked what was happening. They told him, 'Jesus of Nazareth is passing by.' Then he shouted,

'Jesus, Son of David, have mercy on me!' Those who were in front sternly ordered him to be quiet; but he shouted even more loudly, 'Son of David, have mercy on me!' Jesus stood still and ordered the man to be brought to him; and when he came near, he asked him, 'What do you want me to do for you?' He said, 'Lord, let me see again.' Jesus said to him, 'Receive your sight; your faith has saved you.' Immediately he regained his sight and followed him, glorifying God; and all the people, when they saw it, praised God.

- Jesus does not cure unbidden. He waits to be asked. What may seem from the outside as a desperate need (i.e. for sight) could for the sight-less be such an habitual state that they could not imagine themselves otherwise. So Jesus checks: What do you want me to do for you? Lord, there is a sort of sight I ask from you: to use my eyes fully, to relish every nuance of colour that surrounds me, to pick up the life and feeling in others' faces and bodies, to appreciate and be open to the glorious world of vision that I would miss if I was like this blind man.

Tuesday 15 November
Luke 19:1–10

He entered Jericho and was passing through it. A man was there named Zacchaeus; he was a chief tax-collector and was rich. He was trying to see who Jesus was, but on account of the crowd he could not, because he was short in stature. So he ran ahead and climbed a sycamore tree to see him, because he was going to pass that way. When Jesus came to the place, he looked up and said to him, 'Zacchaeus, hurry and come down; for I must stay at your house today.' So he hurried down and was happy to welcome him. All who saw it began to grumble and said, 'He has gone to be the guest of one who is a sinner.' Zacchaeus stood there and said to the Lord, 'Look, half of my possessions, Lord, I will give to the poor; and if I have defrauded anyone of anything, I will pay back four times as much.' Then Jesus said to him, 'Today salvation has come to this house, because he too is a son of Abraham. For the Son of Man came to seek out and to save the lost.'

- In my prayer, Lord, I am often like Zacchaeus, making huge efforts to catch a glimpse of you, only to find that you are waiting for me, calling me by name, inviting yourself into my heart. Once I am with you, I find happiness in putting things right, ordering my life, finding the springs of generosity and justice that have been stifled by old habits. Jesus, as I sit at the computer, you look at me as you looked at Zacchaeus. You call me by name, and invite me to join you. You do not make demands, but in your company I want to change something in myself, and to offer it to you.

Wednesday 16 November
Luke 19:11–28

As they were listening to this, he went on to tell a parable, because he was near Jerusalem, and because they supposed that the kingdom of God was to appear immediately. So he said, 'A nobleman went to a distant country to get royal power for himself and then return. He summoned ten of his slaves, and gave them ten pounds, and said to them, "Do business with these until I come back." But the citizens of his country hated him and sent a delegation after him, saying, "We do not want this man to rule over us." When he returned, having received royal power, he ordered these slaves, to whom he had given the money, to be summoned so that he might find out what they had gained by trading. The first came forward and said, "Lord, your pound has made ten more pounds." He said to him, "Well done, good slave! Because you have been trustworthy in a very small thing, take charge of ten cities." Then the second came, saying, "Lord, your pound has made five pounds." He said to him, "And you, rule over five cities." Then the other came, saying, "Lord, here is your pound. I wrapped it up in a piece of cloth, for I was afraid of you, because you are a harsh man; you take what you did not deposit, and reap what you did not sow." He said to him, "I will judge you by your own words, you wicked slave! You knew, did you, that I was a harsh man, taking what I did not deposit and reaping what I did not sow? Why then did you not put my money into the bank? Then when I returned, I could have collected it with interest." He said to the bystanders, "Take the pound from him and give it to the one who has ten pounds." (And they said to him, "Lord, he has ten pounds!") "I tell you, to all those who have, more will be given; but from those who have nothing, even what they have will be taken away. But as for these enemies of mine who did not want me to be king over them – bring them here and slaughter them in my presence."'

- In this Gospel, Jesus talks about the talents. We have all been given gifts. If we use these gifts wisely for our own benefit and the benefit of others, we grow and blossom. If on the other hand we fail to use them, we remain stuck and stagnant. It is in the order of things to grow and develop, and as we do so, we open our minds and hearts to all the goodness that God wants to give us.

Thursday 17 November
Luke 19:41–44

As he came near and saw the city, he wept over it, saying, 'If you, even you, had only recognised on this day the things that make for peace! But now they are hidden from your eyes. Indeed, the days will come upon you, when your enemies will set up ramparts around you and surround you, and hem you in on every side. They will crush you to the ground, you and your children within you, and they will not leave within you one stone upon another; because you did not recognise the time of your visitation from God.'

- Where, or with whom we are gathered is not the important thing. It is the closeness to Christ and to each other that matters and not the place. As I pray with Sacred Space I am reminded of the many thousands around the world who gather and unite in this prayer each day.

Friday 18 November
Matthew 14:22–33

Immediately he made the disciples get into the boat and go on ahead to the other side, while he dismissed the crowds. And after he had dismissed the crowds, he went up the mountain by himself to pray. When evening came, he was there alone, but by this time the boat, battered by the waves, was far from the land, for the wind was against them. And early in the morning he came walking towards them on the lake. But when the disciples saw him walking on the lake, they were terrified, saying, 'It is a ghost!' And they cried out in fear. But immediately Jesus spoke to them and said, 'Take heart, it is I; do not be afraid.'

Peter answered him, 'Lord, if it is you, command me to come to you on the water.' He said, 'Come.' So Peter got out of the boat, started walking on the water, and came towards Jesus. But when he noticed the strong wind, he became frightened, and beginning to sink, he cried out, 'Lord, save me!' Jesus immediately reached out his hand and caught him, saying to him, 'You of little faith, why did you doubt?' When they got into the boat, the wind ceased. And those in the boat worshipped him, saying, 'Truly you are the Son of God.'

- Jesus took some time apart to be at prayer. His time with God did not close him to the world, but inspired him to go to the help of the troubled disciples. The time that I spend at prayer builds me up in my relationship with God and strengthens me to act in God's name.

- Peter had courage when his eyes were on Jesus, but foundered when he focused on himself and his situation. I ask God to help me to keep Jesus before me.

Saturday 19 November
Luke 20:27–40

Some Sadducees, those who say there is no resurrection, came to him and asked him a question, 'Teacher, Moses wrote for us that if a man's brother dies, leaving a wife but no children, the man shall marry the widow and raise up children for his brother. Now there were seven brothers; the first married, and died childless; then the second and the third married her, and so in the same way all seven died childless. Finally the woman also died. In the resurrection, therefore, whose wife will the woman be? For the seven had married her.'

Jesus said to them, 'Those who belong to this age marry and are given in marriage; but those who are considered worthy of a place in that age and in the resurrection from the dead neither marry nor are given in marriage. Indeed they cannot die any more, because they are like angels and are children of God, being children of the resurrection. And the fact that the dead are raised Moses himself showed, in the story about the bush, where he speaks of the Lord as the God of Abraham, the God of Isaac, and the God of Jacob. Now he is God not of the dead, but of the living; for to him all of them are alive.' Then some of the scribes answered, 'Teacher, you have spoken well.' For they no longer dared to ask him another question.

- How easy it is for religious people to waste time and energy in spurious debates that neither advance the cause of the Gospel nor shed any light on real-life issues. Yet they can become a distraction from our real tasks as Christians. Like the Sadducees in today's Gospel reading we can easily find ourselves caught up in endless discussions on minor points of the liturgy or of Church law, without realising we are wasting precious time and perhaps creating needless division.

The Thirty-fourth Week in Ordinary Time
20–26 November 2022

Something to think and pray about each day this week:

We humans, though late arrivals on Planet Earth, are destroying it. We must undergo a painful conversion and learn to live in harmony and communion with all the species that preceded us and made our world so beautiful. Through us the universe can celebrate itself in a unique mode of conscious self-awareness. Our story is numinous, sacred and revelatory. It is both our personal and our community story because it took nothing less than the collaboration of the universe to bring humans into being!

Carl Sagan, an astrophysicist with a gift for communication, humorously reminds us that to make an apple pie from scratch, you'd need a whole universe! Is this true? Well, think of your kitchen, its cement and wood, its lighting, its gadgets, especially the cooker – already you have involved the vast world of technology. Then consider the apples, flour, sugar and water – behind them is the history of agriculture, which in turn involves clay, metals, water, heat and atmosphere. Add in electricity and energy for the cooking. And of course you need Earth to work on, not to mention yourself as cook, for you are not self-made but owe your origin to stardust. Everything is indeed interconnected: the making of an apple pie is a collaborative and global event! Creation is a seamless weave of which our lives are meant to be a part. We are to be in tune with the symphony of things, singers in the chorus rather than hecklers and disrupters.

Brian Grogan SJ,
Creation Walk: The Amazing Story of a Small Blue Planet

The Presence of God

'I am standing at the door, knocking', says the Lord. What a wonderful privilege that the Lord of all creation desires to come to me. I welcome his presence.

Freedom

Everything has the potential to draw forth from me a fuller love and life. Yet my desires are often fixed, caught, on illusions of fulfilment. I ask that God, through my freedom, may orchestrate my desires in a vibrant loving melody rich in harmony.

Consciousness

To be conscious about something is to be aware of it.
Dear Lord, help me to remember that you gave me life.
Thank you for the gift of life.
Teach me to slow down, to be still and enjoy the pleasures created for me. To be aware of the beauty that surrounds me: the marvel of mountains, the calmness of lakes, the fragility of a flower petal. I need to remember that all these things come from you.

The Word

I read the word of God slowly, a few times over, and I listen to what God is saying to me.
(Please turn to the Scripture on the following pages. Inspiration points are there, should you need them. When you are ready, return here to continue.)

Conversation

What feelings are rising in me as I pray and reflect on God's word? I imagine Jesus himself sitting or standing near me, and I open my heart to him.

Conclusion

I thank God for these moments we have spent together and for any insights I have been given concerning the text.

Sunday 20 November
Our Lord Jesus Christ, King of the Universe
Luke 23:35–43

And the people stood by, watching; but the leaders scoffed at him, saying, 'He saved others; let him save himself if he is the Messiah of God, his chosen one!' The soldiers also mocked him, coming up and offering him sour wine, and saying, 'If you are the King of the Jews, save yourself!' There was also an inscription over him, 'This is the King of the Jews.'

One of the criminals who were hanged there kept deriding him and saying, 'Are you not the Messiah? Save yourself and us!' But the other rebuked him, saying, 'Do you not fear God, since you are under the same sentence of condemnation? And we indeed have been condemned justly, for we are getting what we deserve for our deeds, but this man has done nothing wrong.' Then he said, 'Jesus, remember me when you come into your kingdom.' He replied, 'Truly I tell you, today you will be with me in Paradise.'

- Glamour and splendour mark the presence of earthly royalty. Jesus is not recognisable as king to those expecting power or glory. We need to train ourselves to look for signs of Jesus' reign. His real identity can be seen only by the humble.

- The 'good thief' saw things as they were: he knew his own sinfulness; he recognised Jesus' character; he asked for little yet was rewarded for his honesty. Humility brings a true perspective and is the ground for meeting God. I pray for humility.

Monday 21 November
Luke 21:1–4

He looked up and saw rich people putting their gifts into the treasury; he also saw a poor widow put in two small copper coins. He said, 'Truly I tell you, this poor widow has put in more than all of them; for all of them have contributed out of their abundance, but she out of her poverty has put in all she had to live on.'

- With whom do you identify in this story? Those who casually give money that they will not miss in the slightest? Or those who give from the little they have? This can also include not just money, but giving of our time, energy and abilities to others even when we are tired or very busy. There is a difference between 'giving alms' and sharing ourselves, our goods and good fortune with those who have less, a lot less, than us. Are you being asked to give of yourself today?

Tuesday 22 November
Luke 21:5–11

When some were speaking about the temple, how it was adorned with beautiful stones and gifts dedicated to God, he said, 'As for these things that you see, the days will come when not one stone will be left upon another; all will be thrown down.'

They asked him, 'Teacher, when will this be, and what will be the sign that this is about to take place?' And he said, 'Beware that you are not led astray; for many will come in my name and say, "I am he!" and, "The time is near!" Do not go after them.

'When you hear of wars and insurrections, do not be terrified; for these things must take place first, but the end will not follow immediately.' Then he said to them, 'Nation will rise against nation, and kingdom against kingdom; there will be great earthquakes, and in various places famines and plagues; and there will be dreadful portents and great signs from heaven.'

- I may lose what is most precious to me: a relationship, health, family, security, work, possessions. What sustains me through these times? In my difficulties do I set my heart on God, so that I grow stronger as a result?

- In our times, the destruction of the environment brings us suffering. Does this give birth only to desolation, or to compassion and a practical response? And do we believe that nature can be remade by the God who first created it?

Wednesday 23 November
Luke 21:12–19

'But before all this occurs, they will arrest you and persecute you; they will hand you over to synagogues and prisons, and you will be brought before kings and governors because of my name. This will give you an opportunity to testify. So make up your minds not to prepare your defence in advance; for I will give you words and a wisdom that none of your opponents will be able to withstand or contradict. You will be betrayed even by parents and brothers, by relatives and friends; and they will put some of you to death. You will be hated by all because of my name. But not a hair of your head will perish. By your endurance you will gain your souls.'

- Endurance is a quality that is valued from the time of Genesis. Jacob wrestled with God for an entire night, and found he had resources he didn't know he had. He displayed endurance, courage and tenacity and was rewarded with becoming the patriarch of a great nation.

- There comes a time in one's spiritual life where one can choose either to despair or to endure. Saint Paul, writing to the Romans, extols this virtue: 'Endurance produces character, and character produces hope, and hope does not disappoint us, because God's love has been poured into our hearts through the Holy Spirit which has been given to us.'

Thursday 24 November
Luke 21:20–28

'When you see Jerusalem surrounded by armies, then know that its desolation has come near. Then those in Judea must flee to the mountains, and those inside the city must leave it, and those out in the country must not enter it; for these are days of vengeance, as a fulfilment of all that is written. Woe to those who are pregnant and to those who are nursing infants in those days! For there will be great distress on the earth and wrath against this people; they will fall by the edge of the sword and be taken away as captives among all nations; and Jerusalem will be trampled on by the Gentiles, until the times of the Gentiles are fulfilled.

'There will be signs in the sun, the moon, and the stars, and on the earth distress among nations confused by the roaring of the sea and the waves. People will faint from fear and foreboding of what is coming upon the world, for the powers of the heavens will be shaken. Then they will see "the Son of Man coming in a cloud" with power and great glory. Now when these things begin to take place, stand up and raise your heads, because your redemption is drawing near.'

- I pray: 'Jesus, when the evil and suffering of the world tempt me to lose faith, let the words of Saint Thomas Aquinas calm me. He writes that

God is so powerful and good that he would allow no evil in any of his works unless he could bring good out of it.'

Friday 25 November
Luke 21:29–33

Then he told them a parable: 'Look at the fig tree and all the trees; as soon as they sprout leaves you can see for yourselves and know that summer is already near. So also, when you see these things taking place, you know that the kingdom of God is near. Truly I tell you, this generation will not pass away until all things have taken place. Heaven and earth will pass away, but my words will not pass away.'

- We are told that the world in which we live will one day disappear, but the words of Jesus, words of truth and life, will be forever valid. These words represent a vision of life and those timeless values that we understand as emanating from God.

- As we come to the end of the Church year it is a time for us to consider whether we want to belong to the kingdom that Jesus is inaugurating and not only to belong but also to make it our life's work. Then, no matter when he comes to call us, we are ready.

Saturday 26 November
Luke 21:34–36

'Be on guard so that your hearts are not weighed down with dissipation and drunkenness and the worries of this life, and that day does not catch you unexpectedly, like a trap. For it will come upon all who live on the face of the whole earth. Be alert at all times, praying that you may have the strength to escape all these things that will take place, and to stand before the Son of Man.'

- The end of the world may not come in my lifetime, but my death will bring the end of my engagement with it. So I need to be ready when Jesus comes for me.

LOYOLA PRESS.
A JESUIT MINISTRY

Join a Worldwide Community of Prayer

Make a "Sacred Space" in your day with the worldwide prayer community at **www.SacredSpace.ie**. Inspired by the spirituality of St. Ignatius of Loyola, the daily updates help you pray anywhere, anytime.

Sacred Space is brought to you by the Irish Jesuits.

Sacred Space
YOUR DAILY PRAYER ONLINE